# The Bible speaks today

*Series Editors*: J. A. Motyer (OT)
John R. W. Stott (NT)

# The Message of Philippians

## Jesus our Joy

# Titles in this series

# The Message of Philippians

## Jesus our Joy

**J. A. Motyer**
*formerly Principal of Trinity College, Bristol*

**Inter-Varsity Press**
Leicester, England
Downers Grove, Illinois, U.S.A.

Inter-Varsity Press
38 De Montfort Street, Leicester LE1 7GP, England
P.O. Box 1400, Downers Grove, Illinois, USA

*First published* 1984

*Reprinted* 1985, 1988, 1991

**British Library Cataloguing in Publication Data**
Motyer, J. Alec
    The Message of Philippians: Jesus our joy
    —(The Bible speaks today)
    1. Bible N.T. Philippians—Commentaries
    I. Title    II. Series
    227.'660        BS2705.3
    ISBN 0–85110–710–9

**Library of Congress Cataloging in Publication Data**
Motyer, J. Alec
    The Message of Philippians
    (The Bible speaks today)
    1. Bible. N.T. Philippians—Commentaries.  I. Bible.
    N.T. Philippians.  English.  Revised Standard.  1984.
    II. Title.    III. Series
    BS2705.3.M577  1984        227'.6077        83–22684
    ISBN 0–87784–310–4

Set in 11 on 12pt Garamond by Parker Typesetting Service, Leicester
Printed and bound in Great Britain by
Biddles Ltd, Guildford and King's Lynn

*Inter-Varsity Press is the book-publishing division of the Universities and Colleges Christian Fellowship (formerly the Inter-Varsity Fellowship), a student movement linking Christian Unions in universities and colleges throughout the United Kingdom and the Republic of Ireland, and a member movement of the International Fellowship of Evangelical Students. For information about local and national activities write to UCCF, 38 De Montfort Street, Leicester LE1 7GP.*

*InterVarsity Press, USA, is the book-publishing division of InterVarsity Christian Fellowship, a student movement active on campus at hundreds of universities, colleges and schools of nursing in the United States of America, and a member movement of the International Fellowship of Evangelical Students. For information about local and regional activities, write Public Relations Dept., InterVarsity Christian Fellowship, 6400 Schroeder Rd., P.O. Box 7895, Madison, WI 53707–7895.*

21  20  19  18  17  16  15  14  13  12  11  10  9  8

12  11  10  09  08  07  06  05  04  03  02  01

# General preface

*The Bible speaks today* describes a series of both Old Testament and New Testament expositions, which are characterized by a threefold ideal: to expound the biblical text with accuracy, to relate it to contemporary life, and to be readable.

These books are, therefore, not 'commentaries', for the commentary seeks rather to elucidate the text than to apply it, and tends to be a work rather of reference than of literature. Nor, on the other hand, do they contain the kind of 'sermons' which attempt to be contemporary and readable, without taking Scripture seriously enough.

The contributors to this series are all united in their convictions that God still speaks through what he has spoken, and that nothing is more necessary for the life, health and growth of Christians than that they should hear what the Spirit is saying to them through his ancient – yet ever modern – Word.

J. A. MOTYER
J. R. W. STOTT
*Series Editors*

To
Jessie Ball & Mary Carpenter

It was my wish to give joy to two dear friends by dedicating this book to them, but the Lord, who ever has greater joys in mind than we can bestow, took Jessie Ball to be with himself on 28 May 1983.

# Contents

# Author's preface

In 1966 the Inter-Varsity Fellowship published my book, *The Richness of Christ, Studies in the Letter to the Philippians.* Fifteen years later the Inter-Varsity Press and the New Testament Editor of the series *The Bible Speaks Today* gave me one of life's rare second chances. The present book is the result.

Little remains of the 1966 edition: everything has been revised, most has been re-written and much new material has been added. In all this I cannot be too grateful to Mr Stott for his ever-helpful criticisms and his promptings to explore the text in directions I would not otherwise have noticed; to Miss Jo Bramwell of the Inter-Varsity Press whose careful and detailed work gives to the book such qualities of clarity and readability as it possesses; and to the Revd. Frank Entwistle, Publishing Director of the Press, whose characteristic blend of patience and pressure has been just what I needed. These have been true friends to me and have made me aware how good is the fellowship of those who love our Lord.

If this is the result of working at the nuts and bolts of producing a book on *Philippians*, how much more ought it to be the result of studying it! I have been learning over again at how many points *Philippians* addresses today's church. I can say without exaggeration that I long for its teaching about the unity of the church and about the ministry of the church to be heard and heeded. In these areas we have, for far too long, been asking wrong questions and following misleading trails: we need *Philippians* to challenge, correct and guide. Yet these things (and others which could be mentioned) are only by-products: calls to unity, teaching about ministry – what are these unless we get back to knowing him, our Lord Jesus, understanding who and what he is, and making him all our joy?

ALEC MOTYER

# Chief abbreviations

AV
: The Authorized (King James') Version of the Bible (1611).

Calvin
: John Calvin, *Commentaries on the Epistles to the Philippians, Colossians and Thessalonians*, 1548; translated by J. Pringle, 1851 (Eerdmans, 1957).

Collange
: J.–F. Collange, *The Epistle of Saint Paul to the Philippians*, 1973; translated by A. W. Heathcote (Epworth Press, 1979).

GNB
: The Good News Bible (Today's English Version) (The Bible Societies and Collins, NT 1966, ⁴1976; OT 1976).

Grayston
: K. Grayston, *The Epistles to the Galatians and to the Philippians* (*Epworth Preacher's Commentaries*, Epworth Press, 1957).

Kent
: H. A. Kent, *Expositor's Bible*, ed. F. A. Gaebelin, vol. 11 (Pickering and Inglis, 1978).

Lightfoot
: J. B. Lightfoot, *St. Paul's Epistle to the Philippians* (Macmillan, 1878; reissued Oliphants, 1953).

LXX
: The Old Testament in Greek according to the Septuagint, 3rd century BC.

Martin
: R. P. Martin, *The Epistle of Paul to the Philippians* (*Tyndale New Testament Commentaries*, IVP, 1959).

Moule
: H. C. G. Moule, *Philippian Studies* (Hodder and Stoughton, 1902; reissued Pickering and Inglis, 1956).

9

| | |
|---|---|
| NASB | The New American Standard Bible (1963). |
| NEB | The New English Bible (NT 1961, [2]1970; OT 1970). |
| NIV | The New International Version of the Bible (Hodder and Stoughton, NT 1974, OT 1979). |
| RSV | The Revised Standard Version of the Bible (NT 1946, [2]1971; OT 1952). |
| RV | The Revised Version of the Bible (1885). |
| *TWNT* | G. Kittel and G. Friedrich (eds.), *Theologisches Worterbuch zum Neuen Testament* (1932–74; E. T. *Theological Dictionary of the New Testament*, ed. G. W. Bromiley, 1964–76). |
| Vaughan | C. J. Vaughan, *Lectures on St. Paul's Epistle to the Philippians* (Macmillan, 1864). |
| Vincent | M. R. Vincent, *The Epistles to the Philippians and Philemon* (*International Critical Commentaries*, Clark, 1897). |

# Introduction:
# Paul and Philippi

Philippians is a joyful letter, but its undercurrent is a sober
realization that time is running out. Paul himself was facing a
possible death sentence; the church was tensed up, ready for
the assault of a menacing world and for the insidious encroach-
ment of false doctrine. Above all, God's clock was turning
relentlessly to the hour which would be both End and Climax.

If these things were so when Paul wrote, not only has the
passage of the years brought the end measurably closer, but the
distinctive facts and pressures of the late twentieth century
bring home the message of Philippians in a very pointed way.
The brevity of human life, the sad spectacle of a church in
massive retreat before the world and crumbling in its denominational castles – these things combine to prompt questions in
us. What objectives should control the rest of my life? What is
the real nature of the church? What is the faith of the church
and how can we maintain it steadfastly and untarnished in a day
of threat and of doctrinal confusion? And what does our Lord
promise to us? What will we find him to be in the hour of need?
How can we enjoy his benefits, and will we find them sufficient? This most gracious and unassuming of Paul's letters is a
tract for our times.

### Full of the knowledge of his will

Everything worked to bring Paul to Philippi with a clear sense
that he was right at the centre of God's will.

His second missionary journey got off to a very unpromising

start, and eventually seemed to run out of steam.[1] These are the facts, and it would be risky to venture far towards filling in what the Bible leaves unsaid. Nevertheless there is a marked contrast between, on the one hand, the Holy Spirit's direction and the church's unanimity out of which the first journey was born,[2] and, on the other hand, the later absence of reference to the guidance of God, the heart-breaking dislocation of the great partnership of Paul and Barnabas, and the somehow cool-sounding commendation of the brethren.[3]

Paul was later to write to the Philippians about how necessary it is to take a united stand in the truth and work of the gospel.[4] Was he thinking ruefully of what might have been accomplished if only he and Barnabas had waited? Had it come to him belatedly that the Lord of time cannot be glorified by the impetuosity of his servants? In the inception of the second journey was the work of God done but the will of God missed?

At all events Paul and his company struck north from Syrian Antioch, taking the great main road through the Cilician Gates into Paul's own homeland. The indefatigable evangelism of the apostolic church reveals itself in that there are churches to be strengthened[5] where no record has been preserved of how they were founded or who founded them. The vigour of the churches Paul himself founded at Antioch, Lystra and Derbe[6] is seen in that now he must travel 'from town to town' to pass on the decisions of the Council of Jerusalem.[7] What volumes it speaks for Paul himself that apparently without hesitation he returns yet again[8] to Lystra, the scene of his own cruel sufferings![9]

But now Paul's company enters the doldrums. Acts 16:6-8 is unique in the New Testament, and would indeed be a classic within any literature, in conveying the sense of running one's head into a stone wall:

And they went through the region of Phrygia and Galatia, having been forbidden by the Holy Spirit to speak the word in Asia. And when they had come opposite Mysia, they

---

[1]Acts 15:36–40; 16:6–8.   [2]Acts 13:1–3.   [3]Acts 15:36–40.
[4]Phil. 1:27 – 2:3; 3:17 – 4:3.   [5]Acts 15:41.   [6]Acts 13 – 14.
[7]Acts 16:4; cf. 15:22–29.   [8]Cf. Acts 14:21.   [9]Acts 14:19–20.

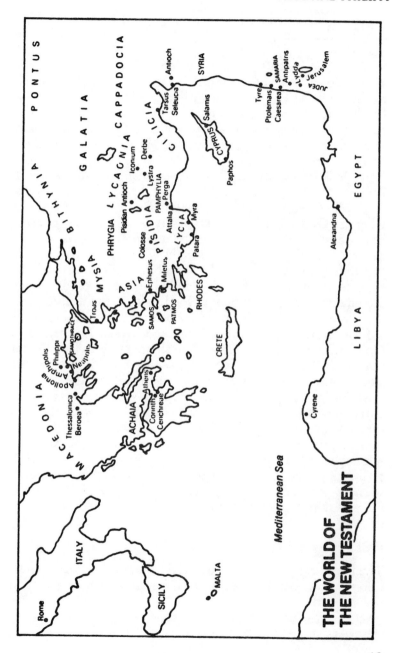

THE WORLD OF
THE NEW TESTAMENT

attempted to go into Bithynia, but the Spirit of Jesus did not allow them; so, passing by Mysia, they went down to Troas.

Galatia occupied the central area of what we now know as Turkey; the district of Phrygia lay to the west of Galatia, Mysia to the north of Phrygia, and Bithynia, along the coast of the Black Sea, completed the square within which every road seemed blocked by an incessant 'No' from heaven until finally they turn west, stopping nowhere in Mysia till they reach the coast at Troas on the north-west Mediterranean tip of Turkey.

There is so much in all this that we wish we had been told. But this passage that is so full of the reality of the guidance of God (albeit negative guidance) tells us nothing of the means whereby God made his will so plain. We only know that the impasse was resolved at Troas.[10] Paul received a vision. His cautious reaction contrasts strongly with his assertiveness at the outset of the journey:[11] he submits the vision to the consideration of the fellowship and takes no action until they are unanimous. The vision was Paul's alone; the decision and the consequent preaching ministry belonged to them all.[12]

From now on everything is marked by the prospering of God and the patience of man. The shipping-lanes from Troas ran north, hugging the coast, bypassing the entrance to the Bosphorus, slipping between the mainland and the offshore island of Samothrace.[13] Thus, after two days at sea, the apostolic party arrived at the Macedonian seaport of Neapolis, but (presumably with a sense of divine permission to do so) pressed on to the more important Philippi. The assault of the gospel of Christ upon the power, culture and corruption of Greek civilization had begun in earnest. Yet it began without a sounding of trumpets. The party 'stayed several days', making no move until the sabbath had come.

## Philippi

The honour of being the provincial capital belonged to Thessalonica, but Philippi had its own importance both past and

[10]Acts 16:9–10.   [11]Acts 15:38.   [12]Acts 16:10.
[13]Acts 16:11.

present. It took its name from the father of Alexander the Great, Philip of Macedon, who captured the city from the Thracians in 360 BC. More recently it had been the scene of the decisive battle in which armies loyal to the murdered Julius Caesar, fighting under the joint command of Octavian (later the emperor Augustus) and Mark Antony, defeated the rebel forces of Brutus and Cassius. It was to honour this event that the dignity of being a 'colony' was conferred on the now-enlarged city.[14]

As a 'colony' Philippi was in fact 'Rome in miniature'.[15] In conferring the *ius Italicum* Augustus gave Philippi a privilege 'by which the whole legal position of the colonists in respect of ownership, transfer of land, payment of taxes, local administration and law, became the same as if they were on Italian soil'.[16] As Roman citizens they enjoyed freedom from scourging and arrest and the right of appeal to Caesar.[17] The coins of Philippi bore Latin inscriptions.

## Paul's first European church

Thus a city with a famous past and a privileged and proud present was about to hear the good news of a status conferred not by man but by God,[18] proclaimed by a man who had come to see all human and inherited dignities as so much rubbish in contrast with the surpassing worth of knowing the Lord Jesus Christ.[19]

The founding of the church at Philippi offers a paradigm for every such exercise. The key factors on *the human side* were prayer, preaching, concern for the individual and sacrificial commitment to the work of God. The church was quite literally born in the place of prayer,[20] which, following the initial visit, apparently became the daily focal point of the mission. The message preached was the unchanging apostolic

---

[14]See below, on 1:27.
[15]W. Hendriksen, *The Epistle to the Philippians* (Banner of Truth, 1963), p.7.
[16]K. Lake and H. J. Cadbury, *The Beginnings of Christianity*, 4, ed. F. J. Foakes Jackson and K. Lake (Macmillan, 1933), p.190.
[17]*Cf.* Acts 16:37–38; 25:11. See further on 1:27; 3:20.
[18]Phil. 3:9.    [19]Phil. 3:8.    [20]Acts 16:13, 16, 18.

theme of salvation through faith in the Lord Jesus Christ.[21] The words of the demon-possessed girl who followed Paul, 'These men are servants of the Most High God, who proclaim to you the way of salvation', indicate that the theme was prominent beyond dispute. In the light of this, we must understand the jailor's question to mean not 'How can I be saved from being called in question for what has happeneded in the jail tonight?' but, 'How can I come to enjoy that salvation which has been your theme since you arrived?'

As well as the jailor and Lydia, there were others who came to know Jesus as Saviour at this time, for Acts 16:40 can speak of 'the brethren'. But these two particular people illustrate the apostolic objective to found the church by bringing individuals to personal commitment to Christ as Saviour. Paul and Silas were to begin in a small way with a few women gathering at a prayer-place outside the town. But it would seem that in such work the Lord who is proclaimed rarely fails to test his agents to see whether they themselves are wholly committed. Paul and Silas, with their bodies cramped in the stocks, and lying, doubtless, on their lacerated backs, gave the jailor a glorious reply in their midnight worship.[22]

Church-founding, however, is also *the work of God*. We see that at Philippi God gave spiritual illumination,[23] confirmed the gospel in works of power,[24] and so ordered circumstances that, along avenues which human logic cannot trace, he brings his servants to where someone is waiting to hear the saving word.[25] Thus he shows himself to be sovereign over the human heart. How beautifully Luke describes Lydia's experience![26] Did he observe the dawning comprehension in Lydia's face, as if, mysteriously and wonderfully, an inner lamp had suddenly been switched on?

But the Lord is sovereign also in spiritual warfare. Why was Paul 'troubled' by the demon-possessed girl's cry?[27] Maybe it was simply because publicity from such a quarter was no advantage to the gospel. More likely, it was because she spoke

---

[21]Acts 16:17, 30–31.    [22]Acts 16:25.    [23]Acts 16:14.
[24]Acts 16:18.    [25]Acts 16:19–31.    [26]Acts 16:14.
[27]The only other place where the verb *diaponeomai* occurs, Acts 4:2, is instructive.

of the apostle's message as (literally) 'a way of salvation'. The uniqueness and exclusiveness of the message of Christ was compromised. Paul's decisive action shows that it was incompatible with his understanding of Christ to think of him as one Saviour among many candidates. The majestic ease with which the sovereign God triumphed over the demon reveals a heavenly agreement regarding the exclusive claims of Jesus.

As so often, however, the sovereignty of God takes its most seemingly mysterious paths in the ordering of circumstances. We would see it as reasonable that a saving God should use his power to save, and that the only God will use his power to show that there is no other; but, granting that he has determined to bring the jailor to himself, why does he accomplish this by introducing his servants into prison under arrest and under the lash? To this no answer is given: he is the Lord; he does what seems best to him.

At all events, it was in this way that the gospel of God came to Philippi and created a church. It is surely no wonder that people in whom Paul saw all the supernatural powers of grace at work, and for whom he had himself given so much, should be as dear to him as his letter reveals.

## The letter to the Philippians

Bible study not infrequently faces us with problems which need almost more of the skill of a detective than the expertise of a scholar. One such problem is that of the place from which Paul wrote his letter to Philippi. Only one thing is certain: he wrote from prison (1:13). Of the four known imprisonments which the apostle suffered, that which happened in Philippi itself can, of course, be ruled out; and his Jerusalem imprisonment[28] was too short to allow for the range of activities implied in Philippians. This leaves the Caesarean[29] and Roman[30] imprisonments as possible points of origin for the letter, and to these many New Testament specialists add the possibility of an imprisonment at Ephesus which, though not recorded in Acts, obviously could have taken place during the period covered by Acts 19.

[28]Acts 21:27 – 23:31.     [29]Acts 23:31 – 26:32.     [30]Acts 28:30–31.

17

There are some points in the detailed study of Philippians where our understanding of what Paul is saying would be affected by knowing where he was when he wrote. For example, the range of experiences covered by 'what has happened to me' (1:12) would be significantly wider if Paul were writing from Rome, simply because a longer time would have elapsed and the events of his earlier imprisonments and those of his actual journey to Rome would be included. Or, again, the location exercises its influence on our understanding of the choices Paul mentions in 1:22, for if he were in Caesarea or Ephesus, then, as a Roman citizen, he could at least prolong his earthly life by an appeal to Caesar, and to this extent the choice between life and death would lie in his own hands. Nevertheless, for the purposes of the present studies, and without claiming any ultimate certainty in the matter, Rome will be assumed to be the place of imprisonment referred to in 1:13.[31]

Wherever it originated, the letter itself is very personal in tone, full of the warmth of a relationship as precious to the Philippians as to the apostle. It is plainly a product of the heart,[32] but it is also a product of the head. Thanks to the arrival of Epaphroditus, Paul is up-to-date with news about the church and can address himself to specific needs as they have been made known to him.

## Unity in the church

Apart from Epaphroditus, Paul mentions only two other Philippians by name – the quarrelling women, Euodia and Syntyche.[33] What a serious thing it was – and even risky – for Paul to call public attention to them! No more serious, he would doubtless reply, than the need they exemplified and the danger to the church if it went unremedied.

Unity within the fellowship is one of the three major themes which Paul weaves into this lovely letter. As with all his letters, Philippians begins with an opening benediction. He then, as so often, alludes to his own ministry of prayer,

---

[31]Those who would like to follow up some of the lines of evidence regarding the place of Paul's imprisonment should see the Appendix to the present volume.
[32]E.g. 1:7–8.    [33]Phil. 4:2.

indicative of both the love and the hopes he has for them.[34] Just as he has heard of them from Epaphroditus, he desires that they should know how things stand with him;[35] but having disposed of the news-sharing for the moment, he abruptly plunges into a fresh topic: 'Only this! Worthily of the gospel of Christ exercise your citizenship . . . stand firm in one Spirit, with one mind . . .'.[36] There is no gradual introduction, no leading up to the theme; but rather an outburst. And it is to this topic that he returns before rounding off the letter with further personal allusions.[37] Euodia and Syntyche are not an isolated phenomenon; they are a symptom of a malaise which could prove fatal for the church.

## Under attack

The word 'fatal' is in no way too strong. Paul, as he unmistakably implies, sees in disunity a sin threatening the heart of the church, a weapon destroying the church's effectiveness, and a weakness rendering it impotent against a hostile world.

On the two major occasions when Paul calls the Philippian church to unity (2:2; 4:2) he prefaces his command by recalling certain facts or truths about the church. In 2:1[38] he reminds them that they are 'in Christ', that the Father's 'love' has been poured on them and that, by the Spirit, they have been given the gift of fellowship. It is this trinitarian work which has made them what they are. To live in disunity rather than in blended harmony is to sin against the work and person of God. In 4:1, it is surely no accident that Paul twice addresses the Philippians as his 'beloved' and once as 'brethren'. Before he calls the disagreeing parties to resolve their differences he reminds them of their status: they belong to the same family ('brethren') in which the animating spirit is the truest of love ('beloved . . . beloved'). In the light of this, disunity is a deeply abhorrent offence.

[34]Phil. 1:1–11.     [35]Phil. 1:12–26.
[36]Phil. 1:27, my translation.
[37]The expression '(be) of the same mind' is common to 2:2 and 4:2, but in the latter the RSV sadly varies the translation to 'agree', obscuring the link between these two parts of the letter. See RV.
[38]For this interpretation, see on 2:1 below.

**19**

Turn now to look through Paul's prison window at the Roman scene as he watches it. On the one hand his coming and his behaviour under duress have had an invigorating effect on the church.[39] Confidence in the Lord is abounding and many more than previously are being drawn into the work of evangelism. But, on the other hand, divisions have begun to show themselves: there are two parties among the 'brethren'.[40] Over all alike Paul extends this beautiful, 'family' word; but it serves only to expose – not to conceal – the disunity which ought not to be. What a sad concomitant to their new-found energy in gospel preaching!

Paul does not share all the details with us and therefore it is safer to raise questions than to make assertions. The single fact is that new life and new divisions appear side by side in the Roman church. Can we be wide of the mark in asking if Paul is not here giving an illustration in order to teach a principle? We look back to Paul's Rome; we look around today's church: do we not see over and over again that, when renewal comes, disunity comes? We could think of the founding of the Brethren movement of the last century, with all its genuine recovery of New Testament structures and practices in church life, all its bright hopes of a great movement of God – and then a heart-breaking tale of divisions and parties, whereby much that could have been an upward road ran into the sand. We could think of many churches touched today by spiritual renewal only to be at once devitalized by splits, parties and secessions. Can there be doubt that disunity is a primary weapon against the effectiveness of the church?

Returning, however, to the two main passages in which the apostle calls the church to unity (2:2; 4:2), something else is found in each preceding context: the church under attack from earthly foes. In 1:28 Paul speaks of 'opponents' and of the possibility of the church being 'frightened' – literally 'stampeded'. It is in the light of this that he writes his 'So . . .' (literally, 'therefore') in 2:1. There is an effective reply to a hostile world – a united church.

It is impressive to find the same train of thought in 4:1, where the word 'Therefore' (literally, 'so then') links the threat

---

[39]Phil. 1:12–14.    [40]Phil. 1:15–17.

against the church and the resource whereby the church can meet the threat. This time the threat arises from those whom Paul calls 'enemies of the cross of Christ'.[41] Interestingly and importantly their enmity to the cross is not doctrinal but ethical. For all we know, their mental grasp of what the Lord achieved by his cross was scripturally exact and their doctrine of the atonement impeccable, but they lived as enemies of the cross – in their behaviour deifying their appetites, honouring shameful values, concentrating on this world. To Paul this denies the saving efficacy of Christ, the very thing the church exists to proclaim and the very Person[42] whom the church expectantly awaits. And once more the call for unity sounds out – to 'stand firm thus', i.e. in solid unanimity regarding the meaning of the cross and the sort of life that conforms to the full salvation which the Lord Jesus accomplished.

## The coming great day

In bringing before his readers the foregoing two main themes – the unity of the church and the reality of the attack upon the church – Paul has allowed a galaxy of Christian truths to come together. By statement or by implication he speaks of the spiritual warfare in which the unseen foe brings the deadly weapon of disunity to bear on the church, the personal and corporate battle for moral righteousness of life, the evangelistic task of the church, the work of God (Father, Son and Holy Spirit) in bringing the church into being, and the central place of Christ as Saviour. All these are brought together in the third major theme in Philippians, the expected return of our Lord Jesus Christ.

With six references to the Lord's coming 'day', universal exaltation and near personal return,[43] Philippians is in line with the emphasis of the whole New Testament on the importance of this delightful expectation. It is *a day towards which the Father is working*, for nothing else is consonant with his glory than that every creature without exception shall own Jesus to be Lord.[44] To this end the Father is constantly engaged in the

---

[41]Phil. 3:17.    [42]Phil. 3:20.
[43]Phil. 1:6, 10; 2:16; 2:9–11; 3:20–21; 4:5.    [44]Phil. 2:9–11.

21

task of making Christian believers ready for the great day.[45]

It is also *a day towards which Christians must work*. Since the Lord is at hand, the present duty of each Christian is to live in his likeness, to make urgent progress in holiness so as to have a harvest of righteousness ready for him, and to long to bring others to faith so that they may be glad together before his throne.[46] And it is *a day on which the Lord Jesus himself will work*. When he manifests his glory, every foe will submit.[47] By his totally effective power he will rid us of the shackles and debilitations of our humiliating sinfulness and transform us into his own glorious image.[48] All will reach its intended consummation.

## The Lord Jesus Christ

Three themes, then, intertwine to make up the letter to the Philippians. But the uniting factor is not any one of them, nor even all of them – neither a present situation nor a coming event – but the Person of our Lord Jesus Christ.

He is the fully divine Lord, of one being and equal glory with God, rightful possessor of the divine name, together with the Father the source of grace and peace and heavenly riches.[49] The Holy Spirit is the Spirit of Jesus.[50] To his people he is the coming One, the Lord of the future;[51] but he is also the Jesus of the past – of the cross, of the experience of personal faith reposed in him by the sovereign gift and call of God, and of that gift of righteousness which satisfies God's requirements.[52] Likewise, he is the present Lord Jesus Christ: he will come as the Transformer, but he is even now transforming, for he is the source of the present fruit of righteousness which Christians would bring forth to his glory.[53] He is their joy.[54] In all circumstances he gives confidence and security, for he is Lord of circumstances, and when proved is found sufficient.[55] They regard him as worthy of all devotion, and will serve him to the

[45]Phil. 1:6.    [46]Phil. 4:5; 1:10–11; 2:16–17.
[47]Phil. 2:9–11.    [48]Phil. 3:20–21.    [49]Phil. 2:6, 9–11; 1:2; 4:19.
[50]Phil. 1:20.    [51]Phil. 1:6, 10; 2:9–11, 16; 3:20–21; 4:5.
[52]Phil. 2:8; 3:18; 1:29; 3:14; 3:9.
[53]Phil. 3:21; 1:11.    [54]Phil. 1:18; 3:1, 3; 4:4, 10.
[55]Phil. 1:14; 4:7; 1:13, 26, 29; 2:19, 23; 4:19.

end.[56] Their objective is that he should be seen in them.[57] It is in him they find their present oneness, which they seek to implement by loving each other as he has loved them and by conforming their emotions to his.[58] He is their message to the world, and their chief prize when this passing world is done.[59]

This is the richness of Christ; this is the Jesus who is his people's joy.

[56]Phil. 3:7–8; 2:21, 30.    [57]Phil. 1:20; 2:5; 3:10–14.
[58]Phil. 4:21; 2:1–4; 1:8.
[59]Phil. 1:15, 17–18, 27, 20–23.

# 1:1–2
# 1. The Christian defined

*Paul and Timothy, servants of Christ Jesus,*
*To all the saints in Christ Jesus who are at Philippi, with the*
*bishops and deacons:*
*²Grace to you and peace from God our Father and the Lord*
*Jesus Christ.*

It sounds strange to us that Paul should address his letter not 'to
the Philippians' but to *the saints*. The strangeness, of course,
arises from the fact that modern usage would lead us to expect
'*Saint* Paul . . . to the Christians at Philippi', not '*Slave* Paul
. . . *to the saints* . . . *at Philippi*'. Right through the New
Testament, however, '*saints*' (occurring over sixty times) is the
customary word for 'Christians'.[1] Many references[2] show that
'saints' is used to describe those who believe in the Lord Jesus
Christ in the same way as we today use the word 'Christians'.
    An example will help us to come close to the biblical
meaning. In 1 Corinthians 1:2 'the church of God which is at
Corinth' is described as consisting of 'those sanctified in Christ
Jesus, called to be saints'. That is to say, the church belongs to
God ('the church of God'), it is to be found in a given place ('at
Corinth', or Philippi, or wherever there are believers) and its
members are in the church because they are 'in Christ' and are
therefore 'saints by calling' (as we might translate the final

[1]'Christian' occurs only three times: Acts 11:26; 26:28; 1 Pet. 4:16.
[2]Typical are Acts 9:13, 32, 41.

24

words of the quotation). As a title, 'saints' points in one direction to what Christ has done for them,[3] and in the other direction to the obligation which now falls upon us to live out the new position God has given to us.[4]

Now the present verses in Philippians are no less definite. On the surface Paul is opening his letter with a conventional greeting. But when we penetrate beneath the surface and ask what he is teaching, nothing will better satisfy the verses than to say that he is defining what a Christian is, and that at the heart of the definition lies this familiar word *saints*.

## 1. The Christian's title

What is meant by calling the Christian a saint? Behind the Greek word, *hagios* (which does duty both as the noun 'saint' and as the adjective 'holy') – and indeed behind its Hebrew counterpart, *qodeš* – there is the idea of being 'separate' or 'apart'. This immediately makes us ask, 'Separate from what?' But the idea the words express is rather that of 'belonging to a different order of things' or 'living in a different sphere'. 'Holy' is therefore the Bible's special word for describing God. Indeed the noun 'holiness' is the most intimate Bible word for the divine nature. God's 'name' – the summary description of all that he has shown himself to be – is described in the Bible as 'his *holy* name' more often than all other descriptions ('his great name', *etc.*) put together. In Luke 1:35, the power of the Most High is the *Holy* Spirit and Son of God is the *holy* child.

Central to the whole Bible is Isaiah 6:3, 'Holy, holy, holy is the LORD of hosts.' According to the Hebrew use of repetition, the repeated word 'holy' indicated that this describes the total divine nature and that the holiness of God is itself superlative of its kind.[5] When Isaiah heard this heavenly cry in praise of God's

---

[3] *Cf.* Rom. 1:7; Col. 1:12–13.    [4] *Cf.* Col. 3:12.
[5] *E.g.* in Gn. 14:10, 'full of ... pits' translates 'pits, pits', *i.e.* 'covered with pits all over'. In Dt. 16:20, 'Justice, and only justice' translates 'righteousness, righteousness', *i.e.* 'perfect righteousness/justice'. Is. 6:3 is the only place in the Old Testament where the idiom of repetition is extended to use the word a third time: thus it emphasizes that 'holiness' expresses the whole of the divine nature and that God's holiness is uniquely superlative.

holiness he fell immediately under deep conviction of sin.[6] In this way, using the experience of one man, the Bible underlines for us that the holiness of the Lord is not only something true of his whole nature and something unique in its kind, but also that it is a moral holiness: it is the moral perfection of his whole being.

And this is the word (and the idea) which is being used to describe the Christian.

It would have been easy for Paul to address his letter to the 'Philippians' (as in 4:15), but this would not suit his purpose. He is not here concerned with what they are by nature and in this world, but with what they are by grace and in the sight of God. Politically they are Philippians, and no small honour attached to this. But grace has made them partakers of the divine nature – conferring on them the honour of honours, that the holy God should give them his title and his character and call them *saints*.

## 2. The Christian's Lord

Paul does not, however, address the Philippians simply as *saints*, but as *saints in Christ Jesus*. By itself 'saint' might suggest self-effort resulting in self-improvement, costly effort reaching loftier heights of living. It might, in fact, suggest the unbiblical meaning given to the word in ecclesiastical and popular use. But in reality the Christian's position as a 'saint' involves a reorientation away from self and towards Christ.

The exclusive place which the Lord Jesus Christ occupies in relation to the Christian has three aspects, which Paul indicates here by the words *in, of* and *from*: a saint *in Christ Jesus*, a servant *of Christ Jesus*, and grace and peace *from . . . the Lord Jesus Christ*. We shall take these phrases in turn.

### a. The relationship in which the Christian lives

Throughout his letters, Paul uses 'in Christ' as a comprehensive description of every Christian. The phrase touches every aspect

[6]Time taken here to look up Is. 6 and to read verses 1–7 would be time well spent.

of what God has done for us, of what we now enjoy and of the prospect opening before us in time and eternity.[7] We are not surprised therefore to find Philippians rich in what it reveals about being 'in Christ'.

It is 'in Christ' that salvation comes to us. We read in 3:14 of 'the call of God in Christ Jesus'. God's call, as we shall see when we study 3:14, is not an invitation awaiting our response but an authoritative summons – his royal edict of conscription – bringing us into a living relationship with the Lord Jesus. The means by which he makes his call effective is by giving us the gift of faith (1:29), thus enabling us to possess something which we are privileged to call 'our own salvation'.[8] But the call itself is issued in Christ Jesus, because all God's saving purposes are centred in Christ and worked out by him.

In Christ we are secure and have everything we need[9] with the peace of God as a garrison patrolling our hearts and his glorious riches laid open to meet our needs. In Christ we become new people with new feelings,[10] a new mind or way of looking at things,[11] new encouragements or incentives to live as Christians should,[12] and new abilities to bring those incentives to fruition.[13] In Christ we have a whole new way of looking at life, seeing his hand and his sovereign will in all things. Paul says his imprisonment is 'in Christ'[14] and testifies that it was when he helped the Roman believers to see this that they came to new confidence in the Lord.

To be in Christ, then, is to possess what is often spoken of as full salvation: everything necessary to our past, present, future and eternal welfare has been secured for us by the action of God in Christ and is stored up in Christ for us to share and enjoy. But it is not only benefits and blessings that are in Christ; we are in him ourselves.[15] Full salvation belongs

---

[7]For a fuller treatment, see J. R. W. Stott, *Focus on Christ* (Collins, Fount Paperbacks, 1979), pp.51–68.

[8]2:12.    [9]4:7, 19.

[10]1:8. The RSV obscures the 'in Christ' aspect of this verse. More literally, 'I long after you all in the tender mercies of Christ Jesus' (RV), *i.e.* as a Christian I actually partake in the emotional responses of Christ.

[11]2:5.    [12]2:1.    [13]4:13.    [14]1:13, literally.    [15]1:1; 4:21.

to us as a matter of objective fact, but it is through union with our living Saviour that we experience its warmth and personal reality.

*b. The Lord whom the Christian serves*

The phrase 'called to be saints' parallels another in Romans 1:6–7, 'called to belong to Jesus Christ'.[16] It is *in Christ* that a person becomes a saint. At once an element of loyalty or of ownership is involved. The saint is possessed by Christ and rejoices in this fact. In Philippians Paul declares as much when he describes himself and Timothy as *servants of Christ Jesus.*

He actually says something stronger: 'slaves of Christ Jesus'.[17] The slave, 'bought with a price',[18] is completely at the disposal of the purchaser, to do his bidding. A self-willed, idle or disobedient slave is a contradiction in terms. There is, of course, nothing servile about a saint. On the contrary, we are now for the first time free, free from the penalty, bondage and degradation of sin. We are now truly human, for Christ is true Man, and those who are in him possess a human nature matching their Creator's intention.[19] But the saint is obedient. Great though our privileges are, they are not to be equated with dressing-gown and slippers; they are staff and shoes for pilgrimage, armour for battle and a plough for the field. Responsive obedience characterizes us, for the 'saint in Christ Jesus' is necessarily also a 'servant of Christ Jesus'.

No Christian can evade this responsibility. In this even Paul the apostle is no different from any other believer. What is true of him is true also of his special assistant, Timothy; and what is true of them is true of the Philippians, of whom verse 7 says 'you are all partakers with me of grace'. The Lord Jesus makes different appointments in his church – some to be apostles as Paul was, some to be special assistants and envoys as Timothy was, some to be elders, some to be deacons – but it is only by

---

[16]The words 'to be' suggest making an effort to become something we are not. The Greek, however, would be better served by a translation like 'by calling, saints … by calling, Jesus Christ's'. Our efforts are required not so that we may become what we are *not*, but so that we may display in our behaviour what we *are* in Christ.

[17]See RSV margin.  [18]1 Cor. 6:20.  [19]*E.g.* Eph. 4:24.

grace that they are in the church at all. None can partake of grace and fight shy of service. The *in Christ* of gracious salvation, if it is real, issues in the *of Christ* of responsive, obedient service.

### c. The Giver from whom the Christian receives

It is plainly no easy task to live as an obedient, serving saint. Where does such ability come from? Paul answers by pointing to a giver and a gift: *Grace . . . and peace from God our Father and the Lord Jesus Christ.*

Think of what Paul writes in these opening verses about our Lord Jesus Christ. In the Old Testament Moses and the prophets had a title of great honour: they were 'servants of the Lord'.[20] When we hear Paul describe himself and Timothy as *servants of Christ Jesus* we can hardly help hearing an echo from the past. Here as 'everywhere in the Epistles . . . the attitude of Paul toward Christ is not merely the attitude of man to man, or scholar to master; it is the attitude of man toward God'.[21] Turning now to verse 2 we find that Paul is being practical when he acknowledges the deity of the Lord Jesus. In the phrase *from God our Father and the Lord Jesus Christ*, the single preposition *from* governs both names, and has the effect of hyphenating them together into one single source of blessing. All the divine greatness of *God* and *the Lord*, all the divine love and saving efficacy of *the Father* and *Jesus Christ* come together in divine unanimity to pour out upon the saints whatever they need for their days on earth.

And all that they need is summed up in the gift which is specified as *grace and peace. Grace* is God being gracious, adopting an attitude of all-sufficient favour towards helpless and meritless sinners, and acting in line with that; God coming to them in free, unprovoked love, to give them the opposite of their deservings. The beginning and foundation of our lives as Christians, our 'redemption through his blood', was an experience of 'the riches of his grace'.[22] The same 'grace of our Lord

[20]*E.g.* Nu. 12:7; Dt. 34:5; Zc. 1:6; *etc.*
[21]J. G. Machen, *The Origin of Paul's Religion* (Eerdmans, Grand Rapids, 1925), p.198, quoted by Martin, p.56.
[22]Eph. 1:7.

Jesus Christ' brought him down to us with the very purpose that we 'might become rich'.[23] The firstfruits of grace is *peace*, specifically peace with God. This is beautifully illustrated in the Easter evening scene where the Lord Jesus first pronounces the benediction 'Peace be with you' and then – as if to trace peace to its source – displays the marks of his cross.[24]

But *peace* means more than 'peace with God'. In the Old Testament, peace (*šalôm*) combines 'harmony' (outward peace with God and man) with completeness or fulfilment (inward peace in those who are made whole). Similarly, in the New Testament, peace is Godward[25] and inward.[26] But it is also that harmony in Christian relationships which we possess[27] and pursue.[28] Furthermore, peace is both our experience and our strength in hard times.[29] It sums up in one word the all-sufficient blessings which God gives to his saints and which his presence enables them to experience.[30] Kent aptly defines *peace* here in Philippians as 'the inner assurance and tranquillity that God ministers to the hearts of believers and that keeps them spiritually confident and content even in the midst of turmoil'.[31]

When Paul wishes these blessings on Christians, he is not desiring their salvation all over again, though the blessings are those of salvation. He is, first, assuring them of the unchanged attitude of God. The God who planned and accomplished and freely gave salvation is the same God who, by his unchanged grace, gives his people everything they need. Furthermore, just as it was the grace of God that first brought peace to sinners, so grace always precedes peace, for God is always taking the initiative to act on behalf of his people and to keep them in possession of those blessings which he purchased for them with the blood of his Son. Grace is, in fact, God being gracious. The saint is never left to walk the path of obedience alone: the saving God remains

---

[23]2 Cor. 8:9.    [24]Jn. 20:19–20.    [25]Rom. 5:1; Col. 1:20.
[26]Mk. 5:34; Rom. 8:6; Gal. 5:22; Col. 3:15.
[27]Eph. 4:3.    [28]2 Tim. 2:22; Heb. 12:14; Jas. 3:18.
[29]Phil. 4:7; 2 Thes. 3:16.
[30]2 Cor. 1:2; 13:11; Phil. 4:9; 1 Thes. 5:23; Heb. 13:20f.
[31]Kent, p.104.

the same; the provision of salvation is always available; grace and peace will prove to be enough.

## 3. The Christian's setting

*All the saints* are *in Christ*, and therefore all without exception receive the divine provision of *grace and peace*. Equally they are *at* (Gk. 'in') *Philippi*, and therefore all without exception face the often hard graft of living for Christ in the midst of the realities of this world.

Being a 'saint' means, as we noted, belonging to a different order of things. It is the positive separation brought about by passing into divine ownership, coming under the Lordship of Christ. True (biblical) separation is, then, to imitate God, whose central command to us in this respect runs right through the Bible: 'Be holy, for I am holy.'[32] It is unfortunately easy for us to distort the scriptural ideal of separation by developing a life-style which simply sets out to contradict whatever is current in society around us. This approach used to reign undisputed – and still does, in not a few quarters, as young Christians are drilled in what not to do – on the ground that such behaviour is 'worldly'.

It amuses us to poke fun at the well-intentioned efforts of older Christians, then and now, to keep our feet out of life's pitfalls. Indeed, much of what passed for 'separation' would make entertaining reading. At the same time we should think twice before doing so for, in our generation, we have made the potentially far more serious error of forgetting that there is such a thing as separation. Our elders forbade us to go to the cinema to see what we now recognize as totally harmless films. Have we improved on that situation by permitting into our living-rooms films and other television programmes with a plainly immoral and anti-Christian content?

But the heart of the matter is this: the saint's separation is not a reaction against but a response to; not a mere determination to be different from the world but a whole-hearted determination to be like God by obeying his word. This is the positive difference which demonstrates to the onlooker that the saint

[32] Lv. 11:44; *cf.* Lv. 11:45; 19:2; 20:26; Mt. 5:48; 1 Pet. 1:15; *etc.*

31

belongs to another order, sphere and scheme of things.

One of the richest features of this new order of things is that the individual seeks to live out the separated life in the fellowship of *all the saints*. Here again we see that separation arises through belonging, for the Lord who joins us to himself also joins us, at the same time, to the whole company of his people. For us today, this theme of the fellowship of all the saints has its wider and its narrower aspects. The narrower aspect (and the one with which Paul chiefly concerns himself in Philippians) is the unity of the fellowship in the local church; the wider aspect, very much our problem today, is the divisions which hold one group of believers aloof from another.

We are far too unconcerned in both areas. To Paul, Christian unity was highly prized and belonged not on the edge of Christian truth but near to its very centre. This should be our attitude too. Where Scripture is plain in its meaning, ought we not to love all those who consent to that meaning, and ought we not to express our love by leaping over all barriers so as to worship together, to partake in the Lord's ordinances together and work for the gospel together? And where Scripture is unclear, or where Christians who revere Scripture reach different conclusions, is it right to unchurch those who have been saved by the same blood and seek to order their lives by the same God-inspired book? Dare we be so sure of our own wisdom, so confident in our own understanding, that we desert the authority of the Bible in favour of the authority of our own interpretation of it?

And while we are asking questions, let us ask this practical one also. Why should the world heed our evangelism if it does not see in the church that Christ has solved the problems of isolation, alienation and division which curse and blight its own life? This is what the world is waiting for today, as did Philippi in Paul's day. It waits for the sight of a people who have solved its problems through the reality of being in Christ and whose life-style sets forth the old God-given morality with fresh loveliness as the holy likeness of Jesus is seen in them.

# 1:1–2
## 2. Leaders alongside

*Paul and Timothy, servants of Christ Jesus,*
   *To all the saints in Christ Jesus who are at Philippi, with the bishops and deacons:*
   *²Grace to you and peace from God our Father and the Lord Jesus Christ.*

If we are to be faithful to what we find in the opening verses of Philippians, and at the same time allow them to speak to us today, we must stay with them a while longer. For in the rich company at Philippi Paul saw not only *all the saints* but also *the bishops and deacons.* Within the local church there was fellowship (*all the saints*) and leadership (*the bishops and deacons*). The leadership, however, was not an imposition upon the fellowship but an extension of it. For the saints are not 'under' but *with* ('in company with') the bishops. When we add to this fact that in the same verse we find Paul the apostle and Timothy the apostle's legate, we have a remarkably full summary of the constitution of a New Testament church: the body of believers, the companionate leadership of local church officers, the overarching apostolic work of Paul and the occasional ministry of a person like Timothy coming into the local situation from outside.

### Under the old covenant
One of the great, uniting themes of the Bible is that of the

church, the people of God. The Ne    estament speaks of the church of Jesus in Old Testament phraseology: the 'Israel' of God and God's 'temple' and the 'bride'.[1] Throughout the Bible the church was equipped with leaders. I 1 the Old Testament, the Lord decreed a ministry,[2] and Paul draws on Old Testament scriptures as well as a command of the Lord Jesus in urging support for apostles and elders.[3]

Exodus 19:6 expresses the Lord's ideal for the church: 'You shall be to me a kingdom of priests and a holy nation.' But the people of Israel as a whole proved unworthy to be this kingdom of priests and was directed to delegate its priestly functions to one of its tribes (see, *e.g.*, Nu. 8). Thus, in the Old Testament, ministry arose out of the state and needs of the church. This remains a biblical principle: the doctrine of the church dictates the doctrine of the ministry.

### The kingdom of priests: the priesthood of all believers

In the New Testament, because the Lord Jesus Christ is our Mediator, 'we have confidence to enter the sanctuary by the blood of Jesus'.[4] We have right of access through the torn veil into the Holy of Holies,[5] and Christians are therefore a company of high priests in full possession of high-priestly privileges. Again, the New Testament says that believers are 'built into a spiritual house, to be a holy priesthood, to offer spiritual sacrifices',[6] and that 'you who believe' are 'a royal priesthood, a holy nation'.[7] God's intention to have a kingdom of priests has been fulfilled in the Israel of God.

The priesthood of all believers is thus an essential part of the biblical idea of the church. In this sense 'church' and 'ministry' are identical. As Christians we not only exercise the priestly function of entering God's holy presence in cleansed purity, but we are also to hold fast to our confession and help one another to grow in godliness – activities which compare well

---

[1]Gal. 6:16; 1 Cor. 3:16–17; Eph. 5:23ff.; Rev. 19:7; *cf.* Je. 2:1–3; Is. 62:5; *etc.*
[2]*E.g.*Lv. 7:6, 8–10; Nu. 8; Dt. 12:18f.; 14:22–27.
[3]*E.g.* 1 Cor. 9:9–14; 1 Tim. 5:17f.
[4]Heb. 10:19.    [5]Heb. 10:20.    [6]1 Pet. 2:5.    [7]1 Pet. 2:7, 9.

with priestly duties in the Old Testament.[8] Paul, indeed, sees the saints as agents in the work of ministry by which the church grows.[9] In the New Testament there is no such thing as 'clergy' and 'laity':we are all ministers and all receive ministry. What we need today is not a so-called 'theology of the laity' but a return to the biblical doctrine of the church.

## Organization and order

Within the church the Lord raises up special ministries. Their task is to enable the church to exercise its God-intended functions. They are part of the church's equipment, not part of its essence.[10] As is always the case in the Bible, the existence and activity of such ministries arise out of the needs of the church, and they can be exercised only in ways that are suited to what the church is. Thus, for example, the New Testament never speaks of any ministry as mediating between God and the church. The Old Testament required a mediating priesthood. But when the New Testament uses the word 'priest(s)' (*hiereus*), it always refers either to Jesus or to *all* believers.[11] It never refers to an individual Christian or Christian minister. For if it is true that we all have priestly access to God because of the finished work of Christ, then a priestly tribe is unnecessary and impossible; it is ruled out by the doctrine of the church.

## The apostles

Among the leaders of the New Testament church, pride of place in every sense goes to the apostles.

The word 'apostle' (*apostolos*) means 'one sent', and this permits the New Testament writers to apply the term to people outside 'the twelve'.[12] Nevertheless in its strict sense it belongs to the twelve and to no others, whether contemporary or

[8]Heb. 10:19ff.; Mal. 2:5–7.
[9]Eph. 4:12; *cf.* NIV, 'to prepare God's people for works of service'.
[10]*E.g.* 1 Cor. 12:28; Eph. 4:7, 11f.
[11]*E.g.* of the Lord Jesus, Heb. 10:21; of all believers, Rev. 1:6. The word does, of course, remain in use in the New Testament referring to the Old Testament priest, *e.g.*Mt. 8:4.
[12]*E.g.* Acts 14:4, 14.

subsequent.[13] Three things marked out the apostles in the special or strict sense of the word.[14] First, they had seen the Lord. Secondly (for many in New Testament times had seen the Lord, in his earthly days), they had received a specific, personal call from God. Paul can insist that his apostleship came 'not from men nor through man, but through Jesus Christ and God the Father'. Thirdly, the apostles were foundation-layers. Pictorially, the New Testament underlines the uniqueness and the unrepeatable nature of apostleship when it speaks of the foundations of 'the holy city Jerusalem' as twelve in number and bearing on them 'the twelve names of the twelve apostles of the Lamb'.[15]

Because the New Testament accords such high dignity to the apostles and regards them as irreplaceable, today's church should be cautious about giving any Christian minister the title 'apostle'. We should suspect any modern claim to apostolic status. To claim to possess an apostolic *function* is one thing – and, indeed, anyone who prays or preaches can credibly register such a claim.[16] But to claim apostolic *status* is quite a different matter,[17] tantamount to tearing down the city of God and adding to its foundations.

The foundation which the apostles laid was not organizational but doctrinal. Their teaching was intended to be authoritative and was accepted as such.[18] It is continuance in apostolic *doctrine* that constitutes apostolic succession.

[13]*Cf.* J. N. Geldenhuys, *Supreme Authority* (Marshall, Morgan and Scott, 1953), pp. 46–97.

[14]*E.g.* Acts 1:21f.; 1 Cor. 9:1; Gal. 1:1; Eph. 2:20.       [15]Rev. 21:14.

[16]Acts 6:4.

[17]*The Final Report* of the Anglican-Roman Catholic International Commission, for example, speaks of 'bishops in their function of apostolic leadership' (p.63) which, like so much else in the report, could mean anything or nothing. It comes more plainly near what the Church of Rome certainly believes and what some Anglicans appear to believe when it speaks of 'sacraments assured...by a pastoral ministry of apostolic order' (p. 85). It is doubtful if the title 'apostolic' can ever be given to a function of ministry (leadership, church-planting, teaching, *etc.*) without initiating a movement, steady and sure, towards seeing that minister as possessing apostolic status or inheritance or some unique speciality inherent in his position.

[18]1 Cor. 2:12f.; Gal. 1:6–12; 1 Thes. 2:13f.; 2 Thes. 2:15; 3:6; 2 Pet. 3:15–18; *etc.*

This is seen at its clearest in 2 Timothy where Paul, knowing his death to be imminent, does not regard Timothy as his successor in the office of apostle. Nor, indeed, does he lead Timothy to expect that in the new and menacing situations ahead he will receive fresh revelation from God to enable him to steer a straight course for the church. On the contrary, the only unequivocal reference to the Holy Spirit in 2 Timothy describes him as guarding truth already given, and it is by this body of truth which Timothy already possessed that he is to live, minister, lead and evangelize.[19]

> After the death of the apostles, the apostolic office retains its value in one way only: as providing the norm of the fundamental tradition now committed to writing . . . the fundamental testimony, that of the New Testament . . . The scripture is the norm of all dogma, because it crystallized the primary shape of the tradition, and hence becomes regulative for the teaching of the church.[20]

## Elders/overseers and deacons

The impression we receive in the New Testament is of local churches loosely federated under apostolic authority, with each church managing its own affairs under the leadership of overseers (who are also called elders) and deacons.

Deacons were obviously a distinct office, but we are told nothing about the functions a deacon was meant to fulfil. There is insufficient evidence to enable us to identify the deacons of 1 Timothy 3:8ff. with the 'seven' appointed in Acts 6 to 'serve tables',[21] even though the identification is not in itself unreasonable. The word 'deacon' (*diakonos*) and its related verb (*diakoneō*) are used too widely – of ministering the gospel as well as of ministering to bodily or social needs – for us to say what the deacons (and deaconesses, *cf.* Rom. 16:1) may or may

[19]See 2 Tim. 1:13f.; 2:15; 3:10–17; 4:2.
[20]E. Brunner, *The Misunderstanding of the Church* (Lutterworth, 1952), pp. 33f.
[21]The strengths and weaknesses of this identification can be assessed in L. Berkhof, *Systematic Theology* (Banner of Truth Trust, 1959), p. 587.

not have done in the enviably flexible arrangements of ministry in a New Testament church.

The word 'flexibility' seems equally to apply to those church leaders who are described as 'elders' and 'overseers' ('bishops' in older translations). It is clear, however, that the two titles describe the same person. Possibly such an official could also be called 'pastor' or 'teacher'.[22] The title 'elder' expresses seniority and experience; 'overseer', 'pastor' and 'teacher' refer to the functions of leadership, care and instruction. Indeed 'teaching' is the only specific function required of elders: apart from this the lists devote their attention to personal qualities rather than job-descriptions.[23]

One thing, however, is plain: there were 'elders' (plural) in every church. From the first reference to apostolic practice in Acts 14:23 onwards through the uniform testimony of the New Testament,[24] and even earlier according to the testimony of Acts 11:30, local leadership was committed not to an individual but to a group. And if we ask why their respective functions are not more closely defined, then surely the answer is this: ministry arises from the nature and needs of the church, not *vice versa*. The elders shared the qualities which fitted them for office. They probably shared also that one thing without which a church cannot exist: the ministry of God's Word. But otherwise they wrapped their ministry round the needs of the local church in which they served.

In this respect the appointment of the 'seven' in Acts 6 may provide a model. A need arose in the church (verses 1–2) which exposed a gap in the ranks of the leadership; the assumption was made that, if this was a true need of the church, then God would have his gifted servants at hand (verse 3) ready to be recognized, authorized (verses 5–6) and to step into the breach. Was it so throughout the churches? The clearly recognized and

[22]The titles 'elder' and 'overseer/bishop' are synonymous in Acts 20:17, 28 and Tit. 1:5, 7. 'Overseer' and 'elder' are associated with 'pastor' in Acts 20:28; 1 Pet. 5:1-4; *etc.* 1 Tim. 5:17 suggests that 'teacher' is another word for the same people.

[23]1 Tim. 3:1ff.; Tit. 1:5ff. In 1 Tim. 5:17 the reference may be to a distinct group of 'teaching elders' (*cf.* RV, RSV, NIV), but the relevant words could be translated 'especially since they labour . . .', indicating that the elder as such was always involved in the ministry of the Word.

[24]*E.g.* Acts 20:17; Tit. 1:5; Jas. 5:14; 1 Pet. 5:1.

authoritative office of 'elder', rescued from the menace of individual authoritarianism by being vested in a group, provided the church with a flexible tool of ministry, adaptable to any need in any part of the world.[25]

## The place, the area and the world

The scattered churches were not isolated. Their great link with each other was the person of the apostle; they also shared apostolic letters with each other; and in addition there is evidence in the New Testament of a variety of travelling ministers, dependent on the hospitality and support of the churches to which they came.[26]

From time to time and from place to place there were also those who exercised area-authority. The 'elder' of 2 John 1 and 3 John 1 saw himself as in some sense overseeing the churches to which he wrote, and both Timothy and Titus were charged with maintaining purity of doctrine and due order in church life, and with appointing elders in a whole group of churches within their care.[27]

Nevertheless, there is so much that we simply do not know. Did the apostles keep their fingers on the appointment of local leaders, as some verses suggest?[28] The paucity of apostles, the rapid spread of churches, the problems of travel and the pervasive impression of local freedom in the churches make it unlikely that there was a rule in this matter. Like so much else, it is left open. There is no set number of elders, provided that there is more than one. The New Testament does not require

[25]Was there such a person as 'the ruling elder'? James seems to have occupied a position of recognized prominence in the church at Jerusalem (cf. Acts 21:18; Gal. 2:9, 12). The evidence in Acts 15:13ff. can easily be overstretched: James plainly said the last word in the debate, but this does not mean that he 'had the last word'. Diotrephes (3 Jn. 9) was obviously a 'ruling elder', but he offers an example no church would wish to perpetuate. It may 'stand to reason' that a group of leaders will function best if they acknowledge a chairman, but to trace the post-New Testament office of 'bishop' back to a supposed practice of 'ruling elders' – or even to apostolic rule – is to run where there is no evidence in the Bible.

[26]Col. 4:16; Acts 11:27; 18:24–28; 21:10; 3 Jn. 7; etc.

[27]1Tim. 1:3f.; 2:8–15; 3:14; 5:1–25; Tit. 1:5; 2:1; 3:1.

[28]E.g. Acts 6:3; 14:23; Tit. 1:5.

that there should be an area oversight. Timothy and Titus exemplify what may be, not what must be. If the needs of a group of churches are best met in this way, then so be it. The use of the title 'bishop' in this connection, while it cannot claim New Testament authorization, is no more objectionable than giving a deacon the task of caring for the finance and fabric. But all ministries, local or area-wide, must be judged by the test of utility, the extent to which they arise from and meet the needs of the church. As such needs are met and pass away, and as churches face new situations and even new threats, the composition of the eldership may change, increasing or decreasing in size. So also the need for an area pastor may arise or disappear. Such was the liberty of life in the apostolic churches, and such should be the flexibility enjoyed today under the authority of the Scriptures as the continuing form and norm of apostolic authority.

## Leaders alongside

Philippians 1:1 has provided a springboard into the New Testament church, but its own contribution to the total picture, though made unobtrusively, is deeply important.

How is leadership to be exercised? What is the relationship between leaders and led? The one word *with* provides the answer: '. . . the saints', writes Paul, '. . . *with* the bishops and deacons.' The strong natural leader chooses the easy path of being out front, taking it for granted that all will follow; the low-profile leader 'plays it cool', submerges his own identity and takes the risk that the tail will soon wag the dog. The more demanding exercise, the sterner discipline and the more rewarding way are found in companionate leadership, the saints *with* the overseers and deacons.

This kind of leadership has many facets. It involves realizing that leader and led share the same Christian experience: both are sinners saved by the same precious blood, always and without distinction wholly dependent on the same patient mercy of God.[29] It involves putting first whatever creates and maintains the unity of the Spirit in the bond of peace.[30] It means

[29]Phil. 3:4–14; 1 Tim. 1:12–16.     [30]Phil. 4:2.

that leaders see themselves first as members of the body, and only then as ministers. In this way they face every situation from within the local body of Christ and not as people dropped in from outside (or even from above!). [31] It involves patiently waiting for the Holy Spirit to grant unanimity to the church in making and executing plans.[32] It involves open relationships in which the leaders do not scheme to get their own way or play off one against another, but act with transparent integrity.[33] It involves willingness to be overruled, to jettison role-playing and status-seeking, to be ready to cast a single vote with everyone else.[34] It involves putting the welfare of the body of Christ before all personal advantage, success or reputation[35] and it involves co-equal sacrifice for the Lord and his gospel.[36] It is the leadership of those who are content to stand among the saints as those who serve.[37]

[31]This is the truth behind the prohibition of 'novices' (1 Tim. 3:6), and behind the gentle courtesy of 1 Pet. 5:1.
[32]Acts 16:9f. See p. 14 above.    [33]Tit. 2:7.    [34]1 Cor. 16:12.
[35]1 Cor. 9:1-23.    [36]1 Cor. 9:24-27; 2 Cor. 11:23-33; Gal. 6:17.
[37]Lk. 22:27.

# 1:3–7
## 3. Assurance

*I thank my God in all my remembrance of you, <sup>4</sup>always in every prayer of mine for you all making my prayer with joy, <sup>5</sup>thankful for your partnership in the gospel from the first day until now. <sup>6</sup>And I am sure that he who began a good work in you will bring it to completion at the day of Jesus Christ. <sup>7</sup>It is right for me to feel thus about you all, because I hold you in my heart, for you are all partakers with me of grace, both in my imprisonment and in the defence and confirmation of the gospel.*

As we now move forward with Paul into his letter, we find him thanking God for the fellowship of the saints in Philippi. They have been one with him in gospel work and witness and he gratefully sees this as a gracious act of God. Yet, while he is engaged in thanksgiving, his thoughts are really focusing on one great truth, Christian assurance.

The content of verses 3–7 runs like this. Paul's memory of the Philippians yields the double fruit of thanksgiving to God (3) and joyful intercession for them (4). The particular matter for thanksgiving (5) is their fellowship in furthering the gospel. But all the while, whether taken up with thanksgiving or supplication, he has one unchanging conviction (6): God will never let them go, but will make them fully perfect. This conviction, Paul holds, is securely based (7), for it arises from his love for them, and, loving them as he does, he cannot but feel assured that they will remain in Christ. Love, however, could be no more than wishful thinking. So Paul moves on to find an objective ground for his conviction about the Philippians: their commitment to the defence and proclamation of the gospel is clear proof that they really partake of divine grace.

Verse 6 is thus the pivot on which the whole passage turns. The thanksgiving and supplication of verses 3–5 arise out of the conviction of verse 6; the conviction of verse 6 rests on the evidence of verse 7. We must therefore begin our study by examining this key verse.

## 1. The divine basis of assurance

What God has done and is doing is the great theme of verses 3–7, and nowhere is this more evident than in verse 6. No other agent is at work but he alone, and what he does covers the beginning, the continuation and the completion of Christian experience.

In the first place, *he . . . began a good work in you*. There is a great solemnity about the verb used (*enarchomai*), both here and in Galatians 3:3 (its only other appearance in the New Testament). It means 'to inaugurate', and the tense employed points to a decisive and deliberate act; both the impulsive and the imperfect are ruled out. Here was something planned and executed to perfection.

The Philippian woman, Lydia, exactly illustrates this 'inauguration of the good work'. Paul's message at Philippi focused on salvation, and we may be sure that what he said to the jailor he had previously said to Lydia and the other women gathered at the place of prayer: 'Believe in the Lord Jesus, and you will be saved – you and your household.'[1] No doubt Lydia could remember the date of her conversion and tell the story of how she had put her trust in Jesus. But when that same story is told in Acts it is cast not in terms of the faith she exercised. Rather, 'the Lord opened her heart to give heed to what was said by Paul'.[2] It was he who began the good work. This is the true, inner story of every conversion: it is a work of God originating before the foundation of the world when he chose us in Christ.[3]

Salvation would be a wretchedly unsure thing if it had no

[1]Acts 16:31. See above, p.16.    [2]Acts 16:14.    [3]Eph. 1:4.

other foundation than my having chosen Christ. The human will blows hot and cold, is firm and unstable by fits and starts; it offers no security of tenure. But it is the will of God that is the ground of salvation. No-one would be saved had not the Lord been moved by his own spontaneous and unexplained love[4] to choose his people before the world was, and, at the decisive moment, to open our hearts to hear, understand and accept 'the word of truth, the gospel of your salvation'.[5] This, then, is assurance: God has willed my salvation.

Secondly, he who has inaugurated Christian experience undertakes to continue it: *He . . . will bring it to completion*; or, since the verb is intensive in form and can here express a continuous sense, 'will evermore put his finishing touches to it'.[6]

God never gives up. There is no more dramatic elaboration of this truth in the whole Scripture than Ezekiel 20. The prophet does not spare his people. Their rebellion against the Lord has been real and dreadful and has made their history twisted and tortuous. Three times the bell of condemnation rings (verses 8, 13, 21): 'but they rebelled'. Four times the bell of assurance rings (verses 9, 14, 22, 44): 'I acted for the sake of my name'. He would not let his people go; he was moved by impulses and motives locked within his own nature. It was he who 'chose Israel' (verse 5) and he pledges to be faithful to that choice until the day when 'all the house of Israel, all of them' (verse 40) will serve him on his holy mountain. He will never desert his declared intention to have his people for himself. And as the Israel of God, the true inheritors of Ezekiel's promises, we can say that he will go on perfecting us. The fact that we shall continue in grace is as certain as the fact that God, who cannot lie, will go on working in us.[7]

The assurance God gives us not only guarantees the outcome; it guarantees too every experience of every day, for in all things God is 'putting the finishing touches'. Good news, bad news, difficulty, blessing, unexpected happiness, unexpected trouble – it all has a purpose. Concerning all such situations

---

[4]*Cf.* Dt. 7:7–8.     [5]Eph. 1:13.
[6]The verb is *epiteleō*, and the translation is suggested by Moule, p.27.
[7]Tit. 1:2; *cf.* Nu. 23:19.

faith affirms, 'Without this, I would not be ready for the day of Christ.' This is the immediate, practical and strengthening benefit of the truth of Christian assurance.

Thirdly, the outcome is guaranteed. God is working to a schedule, and *the day of Jesus Christ* is fixed in the Father's diary.[8] It is as if he is under contract to himself and to his Son. The day will come and everything and everyone will be ready in time for it. There will be no last-minute rush, no botching up, nothing that will 'do for now'; strikes will not delay it nor carelessness mar it. The Father has weighed up the merits of his Son and the proper response to his work at Calvary, and nothing will suffice but that he should bring his Son out from the invisible glories of heaven and show him publicly to a wondering and worshipping world. For his own glory, the Father must one day see every knee bowed to Jesus and hear every tongue acknowledge his Lordship. And our salvation is as assured as the coming of that day! For it is we, the saints, the believers, the objects of *the good work*, who must be made ready for his coming 'on that day to be glorified in his saints, and to be marvelled at in all who have believed'.[9]

Here is confidence indeed. Our salvation can no more be forfeited than the Father can break his pledged word to glorify his Son. No wonder, then, that Paul uses the language of a man who has no doubts: *I am sure*. The perseverance of the saints rests on the perseverance of God with the saints.

## 2. The human evidence of assurance

When Paul made such strong and important claims on behalf of the Philippians he was moved by observable facts more than by loving intuitions. He recollected their partnership in the gospel (verse 5) and so moved on to express certainty about their eternal state (verse 6). In the same way (verse 7), though the apostle rightly thinks that the love he feels for them could be aroused only by Christians as genuine as himself, he is moved to confess that he has them in his heart[10] because they are one

[8]Mk. 13:32.    [9]2 Thes. 1:10.
[10]Though the word order of the Greek favours the translation 'I have you in my heart' (*cf.* RV, RSV, NIV, NASB, GNB), the translation 'you have me in your heart' (*cf.* NEB) cannot be ruled out. If this is accepted, it

with him in *the defence and confirmation of the gospel*. In other words, Christian assurance arises from observable facts providing evidence that these people are truly children of God.

We must not, of course, despise inward, personal and spiritual convictions about Christian assurance. It is a wonderful experience to sense the Spirit himself bearing witness with our spirit that we are children of God,[11] or to sense afresh that God's love has been poured into our hearts through the Holy Spirit,[12] just as in human relationships we prize the sense of being loved by those whom we love. Yet, at the same time, if the professed awareness of being a child of God is not matched by the outward evidence of the kind of life a child of God should live, is not the 'awareness' a thin, even an unreal, thing? The truth of Christian assurance plays a large part in John's first letter. It rests in part on our experience of God's Spirit living in us,[13] but, unquestionably, John's emphasis falls on the public testimony of our lives – the evidence of genuine compassion, of keeping his commandments, of living as Jesus lived and of loving the brethren.[14] These are the grounds on which we can know that we are children of God. Consequently, the Bible calls Christians to 'confirm' their 'call and election'[15] by means of the evidence of a life growing in Christian values and habits.

Paul found such evidence in the Philippians. There are six separate strands of evidence, but they all interwine around the common theme of the 'gospel'. We may start therefore by noting that Paul saw among them and himself *unanimity in the truth*: he speaks of their *partnership in the gospel* (verse 5), and of their work in *the defence and confirmation of the gospel* (verse 7). He does not need to define what he means by 'the gospel'. He is able to take for granted that they hold to the same good news as he, which can be summed up in the words 'salvation by faith in Christ', as in the one-sentence sermon preached to the Philippian jailor, 'Believe in the Lord Jesus,

---

means that Paul feels it right to be confident about the Philippians' eternal security in Christ because he discerns in them a true love for himself as evidenced by their identification in the cause and privileges of the gospel.

[11]Rom. 8:16.   [12]Rom. 5:5.   [13]1 Jn. 3:24; 4:13.
[14]1 Jn. 3:14ff.; 2:3; 5:2; 2:6.
[15]2 Pet. 1:10.

and you will be saved.'[16] This unanimity of doctrine and of experience is, throughout the New Testament, the basis of fellowship. Indeed the word 'partnership' means 'joint-ownership', 'participation in a common purpose'. Holding the truth is a mark of the Christian, and a ground of assurance.[17]

Paul moves on to mention, secondly, their *concern for the spread of the gospel*, for verse 5 should be translated as in the Revised Version, 'the furtherance of the gospel'.[18] Those who truly possess the gospel also propagate it. The gospel is not to be hidden away, but worked with.[19] And their evangelistic concern was coupled with the work of *establishing* believers in their faith, described by Paul as the *confirmation of the gospel*. This word 'confirmation' (*bebaiōsis*) is related to the word Peter used, in the quotation already made about confirming one's call and election. It occurs again in Hebrews 6:16 in the expression 'an oath . . . for confirmation', with the idea of giving something a firmer or more enduring basis, or making it more certain in some respect than it was before. In the present case, therefore, it well expresses the work of edification or strengthening which is the necessary complement to evangelism.[20]

The remaining three items may be taken together. Paul saw in the Philippians *perseverance*, in that they had prolonged their fellowship *from the first day until now* (verse 5), and *endurance*, in that they were ready to stand for the gospel even when it could involve *imprisonment* for its adherents. He also saw their *identification* with the gospel whenever it was called in question, as they leapt to its *defence* (verse 7). The leading idea of these three is, of course, perseverance. Their association with the gospel was not transient, nor conditional upon favourable circumstances. Nor was it silent. They kept on in their faith; they held on to their faith in opposition; they spoke up for their faith when challenged. They persevered. They did not expect people to believe their claim to be the children of God simply because they *said* so; they showed

[16]Acts 16:31.    [17]1 Jn. 4:13–14.

[18]Lit., 'your fellowship unto (*eis*) the gospel', *i.e.* 'in active pursuance' of its advancement. *Cf.* NEB, GNB.

[19]*Cf.* Lk. 19:11–27.    [20]*Cf.* Acts 14:22.

that it *was* so. They provided human evidence on which assurance was well based.

## 3. Confidence and carefulness

But though he saw in them evidence for assurance, Paul saw it much more as evidence of grace. When he examined the life of his Philippian friends, and considered their practical devotion to the gospel, he added, *you are all partakers with me of grace.* It was the grace of God at work in them which produced this fruit.

Really, therefore, Paul's confidence for the Philippians arose from the fact that he saw them as a work of God. In verse 3, he thanks *God* when he thinks of them. If there is anything worthy of praise among them, God is its Author. In verse 6, he views them as begun, continued and completed by divine workmanship. In verse 7, their lives bear fruit because they partake of God's grace. God is at work, and where God works he will certainly accomplish the task.

This truth is, of course, axiomatic: God's work is by definition effective. But in the present passage there are two other truths lying alongside, each of which raises its own problem. First, though God is at work and that effectively and completely, the Philippians have also been at work, active for the gospel and sacrificially identified with Paul (verses 5, 7). If God is doing all, why do they need to do anything? Secondly, though Paul is confident that they are externally secure in Christ, he ceaselessly prays for them (verses 3, 4, 9). If they securely possess eternal blessings, why does he pray, as if some doubt still attached to them?

In each of his letters Paul draws on the rich reservoir of truth which lies behind all his letters. We must here remind ourselves of one of the Bible's basic truths, found, for example, in Romans 6:1–11 and Ephesians 2:1–10: to become a Christian is to pass from death to life. It is as pointless to expect or exhort the sinner to work for salvation as to look to a corpse to generate life. To change the metaphor, once a habit is well and truly formed, the freedom to be otherwise than the habit dictates has been lost. In the same way the sin-nature and the sin-habit have 'hooked' the sinner. Our past – both what we have inherited and what we have chosen – cannot be unpicked: the sinner is dead because of his sin. Salvation, if it is to come at all, must be all of God. But the divine work of salvation actually transfers the sinner from death to life. According to Romans 6:1–23, we are united with Christ in his death and resurrection whereby God's free gift of life becomes ours. Or (as in Eph. 2:1–10) we are united with Christ in his resurrection, ascension and heavenly glory, equivalent to a new creative act of God. Now, if the gift of life is real, it will show itself in a new life-style; if the new creation is real, it will show itself in new activities. In the work of salvation God builds into us new abilities – abilities to obey (on which Rom. 6 concentrates), abilities to achieve those good works which he has prepared for us to do (Eph. 2:10). It is not, therefore, that the Philippians' works (verses 5, 7) or ours replace the work of God as though it was not necessary, or supplement it as though it was not sufficient; they are rather the evidence that the work of grace has been done.

We may therefore look at ourselves and at each other as Paul looked at the Philippians, and rejoice when we see these positive evidences that we have been made partakers of salvation with eternal glory. But our relationship has to be a lot more careful and caring than that of a mutual admiration society. All we see of each other is the outward; the inner heart only the Lord can see. It is dreadfully possible to profess spiritual realities, to seem to walk in their goodness, yet to come short of actually participating in them. The outward eye cannot distinguish the Christian who falls back from the unbeliever. What care we should therefore exercise towards each other! This is why the apostle ceaselessly prays that the Philippians will always abundantly experience the reality of Christ (cf. verse 9). In the eyes of God the matter is settled. He knows the full reality. The individual can be equally secure on the matter, in his inner consciousness, because the Holy Spirit testifies that we are sons of God.[21] But among our fellow-Christians, we must bathe in prayer our growing confidence in our relationship with God, supported by the evidence of our lives. This is the main way in which we can show pastoral and spiritual concern for one another.

[21]Rom. 8:16.

The great and true doctrine of Christian assurance is thus no friend to pride. The salvation we are assured of is wholly wrought by God for helpless, hopeless sinners. It does not lead us to be complacent, for our assurance increases as we see hard evidence of our spiritual progress. It does not make us lazy, for a large part of the evidence is the depth of our commitment to the cause of the gospel. Nor does it make us independent of one another, for we need one another's prayers to maintain and further our ongoing walk with God. Thus the apostle, who used very emphatic language to express his confidence about his friends, was equally emphatic about his prayerful concern: *always . . . every prayer . . . for you all.*

Assurance, biblically understood, keeps the saints on their toes.

# 1:8-11
# 4. Growing for glory

*For God is my witness, how I yearn for you all with the affection of Christ Jesus. ⁹And it is my prayer that your love may abound more and more, with knowledge and all discernment, ¹⁰so that you may approve what is excellent, and may be pure and blameless for the day of Christ, ¹¹filled with the fruits of righteousness which come through Jesus Christ, to the glory and praise of God.*

In our preceding chapter we saw Paul at prayer, earnestly concerned for the welfare of his Philippians. We turn now to study the prayer itself.

Like all his recorded prayers, this one is wholly occupied with their spiritual needs. In particular this is a prayer about growth. The keynote is sounded in verse 9, *abound more and more*, and again in verse 11, *fruits of righteousness*.

## 1. Harvest time

Paul gives us an ordered picture of the developing Christian life: there is a growing-point from which the young plant thrusts out its shoots; these, in turn, bear the blossom and yield the fruit. It will aid our study if we start with the harvest time.

Christian growth, says Paul, is for *the day of Christ*, that is, with a view to Christ's coming. He is on his way and we must be prepared for him. The responsibility to be ready is wholly ours. It is our *love* which is to *abound more and more*; it is we

51

who are to advance in *knowledge* and to see to it that we are *pure and blameless* when he comes again. Does this in any way contradict the truth we noted at verse 6, that salvation is all of God, leaving no room for effort or contribution from us? Certainly not! For, as we also saw, the grace which saves also energizes. The free gift of salvation is also a gift of new life. The Christian, saved by grace, demonstrates what has happened by exercising new energies. Consequently – as is implied in Paul's prayer – the word of God to all who have become Christians is always a call to act – to work, run, imitate, to be a soldier, athlete and farmer.[1] There is a whole programme of good works planned out by God for those whom he has re-created in Christ.[2] In other words it is by obedience – active, costly, personal, voluntary, disciplined obedience – that we enter into conscious experience of what our salvation in Christ means. This is why the Bible can say that God gives the Holy Spirit to those who obey him.[3]

The Christian, then, is a person with an objective, a deadline to meet, a Lord to please, or, in Paul's harvest metaphor, someone with *fruits of righteousness* to produce *to the glory and praise of God*. God will never be more glorified than when, at the public manifestation of his Son in that day, there will be no discordant note, for every knee shall bow and every tongue confess that Jesus Christ is Lord, to the glory of God the Father.[4] And even now there is no greater glory to God than when believers are ready for their Lord, showing the same concern as God the Father that the triumph day of the Saviour will be without blemish.

But, to be practical, how can these things happen?

## 2. Growth to harvest

In preparation for the coming Lord, Paul proposes no new, sudden experience to fit Christians for the presence of Christ. On the contrary, there is a programme of growth, starting with a seed (verse 9) and ending with a harvest (verse 11). As we shall now see, he takes this metaphor of growth very seriously.

---

[1]Phil. 2:12; 3:13f.; 4:9; 2 Tim. 2:3–6.    [2]Eph. 2:10.
[3]Acts 5:32.    [4]Phil. 2:10f.

The growing-point for the Christian, as Paul discerns it, is *love*, a seed from which he anticipates vigorous growth as it abounds *more and more*.[5] Its upthrusting shoots are received and held by two stakes, *knowledge and all discernment*,[6] and under their control begin to put forth leaves and blossoms: first the distinctive life-style of the Christian as we *approve what is excellent*[7] and then, at the very heart of this life-style,[8] the fair blossom of holiness in both the inner person (*pure*) and the outer behaviour (*blameless*).[9] Finally there is the perfected fruit, a *righteousness* adequate even for the great Day itself.

To Paul, then, the life of the Christian is a life of programmed growth. His vision is clear as he looks forward to the completion of God's handiwork (verse 6) in a life that is *pure and blameless*, completely filled with the fruit of righteousness. But all this is in the future, an ideal reality to which the believer progressively approximates. If there were any other way, any easier path, any shorter route to perfection, would not the yearning love of the apostle say so? But there is no such thing, no sudden righteousness.

The contrast between what we might wish and what the all-wise providence of God has decreed is perfectly touched off in Psalm 126:4–6. The people of God feel their need for a new and restoring work of the Lord and long that it should happen with all the suddenness and fullness exemplified by the rains

[5]RV's 'yet more and more' accurately reflects the Greek in creating the impression of limitless growth. The verb 'to abound' by itself would convey the same impression (*cf.*, *e.g.*, 1 Cor. 14:12; 15:58; 2 Cor. 8:9), but coupled with the adverbial phrase it describes a growth that is luxuriant indeed.

[6]For the meaning of 'to abound in' (*perisseuein en*), see, *e.g.*, Rom. 15:13 where 'to abound in hope' means to live lives increasingly influenced by the sure hope which the Christian holds. In Phil. 1:9 a love abounding in knowledge, *etc.*, is a love regulated in its operation by knowledge, *etc.* See further below, pp. 56ff.

[7]The phrase 'approve what is excellent' receives comment below, p. 58.

[8]RSV is not especially good at bringing out the connections between the various items in this complex sentence of Paul's. The growth of a knowledgeable and discerning love is 'with a view to your approving . . .'; the 'approving of what is excellent' is 'in order that you may be pure', *etc.*; *i.e.* a consciously held purpose.

[9]On 'pure' and 'blameless', see below, p. 59.

which, at an instant, fill the dried-up river-beds in the Negeb.
But this is not the Lord's way: sowing in tears must precede
reaping with joy; the seed must be carried out before the
sheaves can be carried in. We might well wish it otherwise; we
sometimes hear different programmes proposed by preachers;
we may be offered this experience or that technique as a quick
way to holiness. But of such things Paul knew nothing – not
even for his beloved Philippians.

## 3. The seed

We must turn, then, to examine some details of this programme
of growth. We notice at once that Paul sees love as the
growing-point of the Christian life: it is *your love* which is to
*abound more and more*. He does not mention any object
towards which their love is to be directed; he speaks rather of
that virtue of love which is to pervade their whole being and
character and which will then prompt and mark every attitude
and action.

Paul was a man with a profound knowledge of love in his
own life. Before he lets the Philippians know that he is praying
about the place love should have in their experience (verses
9ff.), he has opened up his own loving heart to them (verse 8).
Consciously or unconsciously he was setting an example of
what love means to the Christian. His love for them was real. It
was not a façade, a good show put on for the benefit of others or
to keep up an apostolic pretence. So real was his love that he
does not hesitate to make God his witness in the matter – God
who knows the heart. His love was also intense; *I yearn for
you*, a verb (*epipotheō*) expressing a clamant longing and need
(used, for example, in 2:26, of homesickness). 'I am homesick
for you,' he says in effect, 'restless till we can be together again.'
But the third feature of his love outruns even these two: it is
love like the love of Christ: *with the affection of Christ Jesus*.
Certainly, this means that he patterns his love for them on that
of Christ. But the expression he uses demands more than
imitation. Paul is saying that he has come to such a depth in his
union with Christ that their hearts are beating as one – even
more, that the greater heart, the heart of Christ, has taken
possession of his servant. The love of Christ has become the

centre of Paul's character.

It would be natural for the Philippians to question whether they could ever love as though the heart of Jesus had taken over. Such an emotional identification with the Lord is so remote from the fickleness and waywardness which we customarily experience as to be beyond belief. Paul, however, does not speak to them as people who lack love and need to ask for it, but as people who possess love (*your love*, verse 9) and need to make it grow. At Philippi, love showed itself to be of the very essence of the new nature given to the believer. No sooner had Lydia become a Christian than she pressed Paul and his company to become her house-guests. No sooner had the jailor become a Christian than, though he had earlier fastened the apostle's feet in the stocks, he began to bathe his wounds.[10] When the hostility of the people made Paul leave Philippi, the church, by contrast, identified with the persecuted apostle (verses 5–7) and sent him help more than once (4:16). Love was their new nature in Christ.

Expressed in varying ways, this remains the constant New Testament claim about the Christian. Indeed, it is a feature unique to Christian experience. When Paul elsewhere says that 'if any one is in Christ, he is a new creation'[11] he is teaching that God has done for us everything that needs to be done; when Peter says that 'his divine power has granted to us all things that pertain to life and godliness', there is the same note of completeness; and he adds the explanation that in this way, by God's promise, we 'become partakers of the divine nature'.[12] Both Paul and Peter speak of this work of God in the past tense: it is our foundation inheritance as believers. The remainder of our earthly life is an outworking of what God has already 'in-worked'. We are called to become what we are.

This is the mighty imperative of Christian ethics. Every other ethical system calls us to the costly effort of becoming what we are *not*. But in the full salvation already bequeathed to us in Christ, the new nature is already ours, waiting for expression, poised for growth, until its potential is triggered by our obedience to the word of God. For the Philippians the special and immediate line of obedience, as Paul discerned it,

[10]Acts 16:15, 24, 33.    [11]2 Cor. 5:17.    [12]2 Pet. 1:3–4.

was love: this was, as we have seen, an area in which the grace of God was already notably at work; it was also an area in which their life as a church was becoming imperilled.[13]

And for us too, as we come to this letter, it is Paul's summons to us. We too easily acquiesce in poor relationships. We assume divisions and arguments to be inevitable in local church life. We tolerate – sometimes even seem to be proud of – a divided visible church. We fly from the hurtful self-exposure and sheer effort of the work of reconciliation. We tremble lest even talking across the denominations somehow puts central gospel truth at risk. And throughout all this we forget that the truth of the love of Christ is the most central thing of all and the most gentle and potent force for renewal.

## 4. True growth

When we ask in what ways this seed of *love* is to *abound more and more*, the answer is that the growth of love is controlled and directed by *knowledge and discernment*.

A concordance will help us to understand the words Paul uses here. The word translated *knowledge* (*epignōsis*) occurs twenty times in the New Testament, always referring to knowledge of the things of God, religious, spiritual, theological knowledge.[14] Often it has the idea of seeing right to the heart of the matter, grasping something as it really is, as when Paul speaks of the law bringing 'knowledge of sin'.[15] It is associated with the teaching work of the Holy Spirit.[16] When it refers to Christian life and growth it has four features. First, this knowledge is the means of salvation: salvation is described as 'knowledge of the truth'.[17] Secondly, knowledge marks out the Christian as such:[18] the Christian is a person 'in the know'. Thirdly, knowledge is one of the evidences of Christian growth:[19] a verse like Colossians 2:2 is especially relevant to the present passage in Philippians. Fourthly, knowledge is the state of the full-grown Christian.[20]

[13]*Cf.* 1:27; 2:1–4; 4:1–3.   [14]*E.g.* Rom. 1:28, RV; Col. 2:2.
[15]Rom. 3:20; *cf.* Rom. 10:2.   [16]Eph. 1:17; *cf.* Col. 1:9.
[17]1 Tim 2:4; 2 Tim. 2:25; 3:7; Heb. 10:26; *cf.* 2 Pet. 1:3; 2:20.
[18]Tit. 1:1; 2 Pet. 1:2.
[19]Col. 1:10; 2:2; 3:1–10; Phm. 6; 2 Pet. 1:8.   [20]Eph. 4:13.

We grow in proportion as we know. Without knowledge of salvation there can be no progress to maturity. If we do not know the Lord, how can we love him? And the more we know him, the more we shall love him. Consequently we can put it this way: when Paul sees Christians growing as their love abounds in knowledge, he sees every Christian as a student. Truth is an essential ingredient in Christian experience. To be a Christian one must come to know the truth. To grow as a Christian is to grow in one's grasp of the truth, in breadth and in depth. Ignorance is a root cause of stunted growth.

'Everyone a Bible student' must be a Christian watchword – and a Christian characteristic. But a problem remains. Is it not true that many people seem to increase in knowledge without growing as Christians, a mental growth unmatched by a growth in character? It is to avoid this danger that Paul goes on to speak of love abounding in all *discernment*. The word (*aisthēsis*) occurs only here in the New Testament, but a first cousin is found in Hebrews 5:14, where it is translated *faculties*. The parent verb (*aisthanomai*) is well established in the meaning 'to perceive', 'to grasp the significance of'.[21] *Aisthēsis* is 'the employment of the faculty which makes a person able to make a moral decision'.[22] By using the word in double harness with *knowledge*, Paul links knowing the truth with applying the truth to life; he joins 'What does the Bible teach?' to 'How does this truth affect daily life?'. And this in fact is what the Bible really means by 'knowing': it is not a mere exercise of the head, for nothing is truly known until it has also passed over into obedience.

Knowing and discernment are thus basic to the whole task of Christian living, but surely especially to the duty of Christian love. The hymn-writer caught the matter perfectly:

> That I may love what Thou dost love,
> And do what Thou wouldst do.[23]

In this respect Christian love is no different from any other sort of love: it can both waste itself upon unworthy objects and also

---

[21] *E.g.* Lk. 9:45.    [22] Martin, p. 65.
[23] E. Hatch, 'Breathe on me, Breath of God'.

bestow itself on proper objects in unworthy ways. In other words it needs divine illuminative *knowledge* in order to know what to love, and *discernment* to know how to love. This is love modelled on the love of Christ, learned from Scripture and applied in obedient living.

## 5. Fruit to perfection

The harvest process continues: the seed of love grows to become something greater than itself. Paul opens up to us a whole life that is different. It is different in the principles which it holds dear (*approve what is excellent*); it is different in its inner character (*pure*) and its outer conduct (*blameless*); and different in its ultimate product, the final *fruits of righteousness* which have been its constant objective.

There is such a thing as a 'higher life' for the Christian. It is described here as *what is excellent* (verse 10), literally 'the differing things'. The verb (*diapherō*, which here appears as a participle) is well established as meaning both what is different and also what is superior in quality. The identical wording used here in Philippians occurs in Romans 2:18, where it shows that the higher life is that which obeys the will of God as expressed in the Word of God. In the light of our discussion of the word *knowledge* above, there can be no doubt that this is the life Paul is here commending to the Philippians.

Experience teaches that there are two dangers besetting any thought of a distinctive or different life for the Christian. One is that we will forget all about it and unthinkingly become children of our age, reflecting and practising the ways of the world – though, of course, putting a Christian gloss on them! The other danger is to value difference for its own sake. What really makes the Christian life distinctive, and places it on a higher level than that of the world, is that it has its source in God. We learn how to live it from his revealed Word, and his Son gives us the definitive example to follow.

We are to approach this 'higher life' thoughtfully, commit ourselves to it, and work it out in practical terms. For this is the meaning of the verb *approve* (*dokimazein*, verse 10.) It includes both the mental side of recognizing worth, and also the practical side of putting it to the test of experience.

Paul does not speak of sudden transformations, traumatic once-for-all decisions, or spiritual 'experiences' and crises. He describes a patient progression as we examine issues in the light of Scripture and steadily follow the will of God.

The objective is that our whole lives should be filled with righteousness (verse 11). The work of approving what is excellent is *in order that you may be pure and blameless . . . (i.e.) filled with the fruits of righteousness . . .*', the practical righteousness of holy living. This is the 'full corn' of a crop ready for harvest: to be *pure and blameless*, ready for the day of Christ (verse 10), a comprehensive holiness of inner and outer life alike. *Pure* is a quality that should pervade the innermost parts of the Christian's mind and heart. Not even the all-seeing eye of God can discern anything offensive in inner life and character. *Blameless*, by contrast, means both 'without stumbling' and 'giving no offence', and calls for purity of the outer life and example, a life against which no charge can be justly laid.[24] Nothing less than this properly expresses the full salvation Jesus has accomplished and given to us; no lower objective will satisfy him who required of his friend Abraham that he should 'walk before me, and be blameless'.[25]

## 6. Power

How can we avoid being overwhelmed by such a demand? When the task appears so hopeless, should we not abandon it? But before we succumb to these temptations, let us ask two other questions. First, are we motivated to succeed? And second, are we aware that what appears a hopeless goal is in reality a guaranteed outcome? For it is these questions that pinpoint the respective emphases of verses 10 and 11.

In the first eleven verses of chapter 1 there are no less than

[24]*Eilikrinēs*, 'pure', is sometimes said to mean literally 'judged of in the sunlight'. There is no plain linguistic evidence for this, but the idea accords with usage; a *transparent* purity, a purity which could stand exposure. The word looks inward and in some examples is linked with the thought of being under divine scrutiny; see 1 Cor. 5:8; 2 Cor. 1:12; 2:17; 2 Pet. 3:1. 'Blameless', *aproskopos*, occurs at Acts 24:16; 1 Cor. 10:32.
[25]Gn. 17:1.

seven distinct references to the Lord Jesus Christ. Of these, two (verses 6, 10) look forward to the day of Christ, and the one before us (verse 10) presents that day as the great objective towards which we, as Christ's men and women, are not only moving but aiming. Our dearest sins, our ingrained habits, our failures in holiness, must surely be challenged, deposed and scorned in the light of the thought that the Lord we love is coming. This is the true and practical sense of the words:

> Turn your eyes upon Jesus;
> Look full in his wonderful face;
> And the things of earth will grow strangely dim
> In the light of his glory and grace.

Such gazing upon Jesus may be mocked only when it is allowed to become a retreat from reality, a pietistic fogging of the world's problems which we are here rather to solve. But the words are priceless when they call and re-call us to the place where our enthusiasms are rekindled and where love for Jesus and longing for his coming motivate us to victory in the hard-won fight.

But there is more to the day of Christ than this. Other factors are at work, in particular the ceaseless work of the Father to have everything ready for the great day of his Son (verse 6). Thus we move from verse 10 into verse 11. We are still facing the demand for a righteousness that fills the whole of life, but now we learn that it is *fruit*, that it comes to its fullness *through Jesus Christ*, and that it is designed *to the glory and praise of God*.

In one of his stories, the Lord Jesus described the tireless attention a gardener gives to his plants.[26] But when the plant is full-grown the gardener has to confess ignorance on how the growth has taken place. His careful tending is not insignificant – nor is it optional, for the untended plant will die – yet something other than man makes it grow. It is the same with the *fruits of righteousness*. Our obedience, discipline and hard graft are not insignificant or optional. On the contrary, they are the God-intended context of growth. But something else ener-

[26]Mk. 4:26–29.

gizes the growth till the fruit is ready for harvets: all is done *through Jesus Christ, to the glory and praise of God* (verse 11). The Father (verse 6) is ceaselessly at work for the glory of the Son; the Son (verse 11) is ceaselessly at work for the glory of the Father.

In this setting the daily task of obedience remains hard, but not fruitless. We are often neglectful, frequently failing, ever inadequate; yet the end is secure, for God is at work.

## 5. Yesterday, today and for ever

*I want you to know, brethren, that what has happened to me has really served to advance the gospel, ¹³so that it has become known throughout the whole praetorian guard and to all the rest that my imprisonment is for Christ; ¹⁴and most of the brethren have been made confident in the Lord because of my imprisonment, and are much more bold to speak the word of God without fear.*

*¹⁵Some indeed preach Christ from envy and rivalry, but others from good will. ¹⁶The latter do it out of love, knowing that I am put here for the defence of the gospel; ¹⁷the former proclaim Christ out of partisanship, not sincerely but thinking to afflict me in my imprisonment. ¹⁸What then? Only that in every way, whether in pretence or in truth, Christ is proclaimed; and in that I rejoice.*

*¹⁹Yes, and I shall rejoice. For I know that through your prayers and the help of the Spirit of Jesus Christ this will turn out for my deliverance, ²⁰as it is my eager expectation and hope that I shall not be at all ashamed, but that with full courage now as always Christ will be honoured in my body, whether by life or by death. ²¹For to me to live is Christ, and to die is gain. ²²If it is to be life in the flesh, that means fruitful labour for me. Yet which I shall choose I cannot tell. ²³I am hard pressed between the two. My desire is to depart and be with Christ, for that is far better. ²⁴But to remain in the flesh is more necessary on your account. ²⁵Convinced of this, I know that I shall remain and continue with you all, for your progress and joy in the faith, ²⁶so that in me you may have ample cause to glory in Christ Jesus, because of my coming to you again.*

We are always interested in the circumstances of our friends, and Paul knew that the Philippians were concerned to know how he was faring. Consequently, having greeted them and thanked God for them, and having expressed his prayerful hopes for them, he turned to tell them about himself.

The verses are no less absorbing to us than they must have been when first read aloud to the church. How much we owe to Paul and how grateful we are for such a window as this, not only into his experiences but also into his mind! And our motive is more than loving curiosity, for Paul belonged to that never-to-be-repeated apostolic band – the men who could say 'Be imitators of me'.[1] The result is that we find here something more than extracts from the diary of a fascinating man: this is an example of true Christian living; this is a statement of principle for the guidance of the saints.

Paul is giving us his testimony. The verses are full of 'I' and 'me'. In verse 12 Paul looks back on the *past*; in verses 13–18 he looks about him at his *present* circumstances; and in verses 19–26 he probes the *future*. But there is one great, over-riding truth which shines throughout these three sections into which the passage falls.

## 1. The past

The topic is announced in the words *what has happened to me* (verse 12). But Paul fills them with a special importance, even solemnity, by using his introductory expression *I want you to know, brethren*, which he elsewhere uses to call attention to something he believes to be of great significance.[2] We can be glad that he did so, for the remainder of the verse is so apparently simple that we might easily have failed to think about it. What happened to him, he says, *really served to advance the gospel.*

---

[1] *E.g.* 1 Cor. 11:1; Phil. 3:17.
[2] Rom. 1:13; 1 Cor. 10:1; 11:3; 1 Thes. 4:13; *etc.*

What had happened to him? The answer depends, of course, on the place from which Paul was writing, but we will continue to assume that he was writing from Rome. In this case, *what . . . happened* began when the apostle reached Jerusalem, forewarned by the Holy Spirit that imprisonment and afflictions were awaiting him there.[3]

Trouble was not long delayed. Though Paul went out of his way to reassure Jewish scruples, an entirely false accusation was levelled at him by his own people. He was nearly lynched by a religious mob and ended up in the Roman prison, having escaped a flogging only by pleading citizenship. His whole case was beset by a mockery of justice, for, though right was on his side, he could not secure a hearing. He was made the subject of unjust and unprovoked insult and shame, malicious misrepresentation and deadly plot. He was kept imprisoned owing to official craving for popularity, or for money, or because of an over-punctilious façade of legalism.[4] The deceit, malpractice and vilification that surrounded him were past belief, yet he looks back and asserts that *what . . . happened to me has really served to advance the gospel!*

Even then his sufferings were not over. There came the prolonged trial of the storm at sea, where his life hung, as it seemed, by a thread, both because of the elements and because of petty officiousness.[5] Eventually, when he reached Rome, it was far from the ambassadorial entry that he had doubtless looked for.[6] He came in the company of the condemned, bound by a chain and destined to drag out at least two years under arrest awaiting the uncertain decision of an earthly king. Nevertheless, still imprisoned, still chained, still unheard, still uncertain, he looks back and declares: *What. . . happened to me has really served to advance the gospel.*

Of course, he had also enjoyed his moments of relief. His story was not one of unbroken sadness. He had seen men faithful to him when it was unpopular and even dangerous to be so: the courageous 'son of Paul's sister', the steadfast Aristarchus, the beloved Luke who self-effacingly conceals his welcome presence under the pronoun 'we'; unexpected allies like

---

[3]Acts 21:17; 20:22f.    [4]Acts 21:7 – 26:32.    [5]Acts 27.
[6]*Cf.* Acts 19:21.

the centurion, Julius; unknown ones who cared for him in his need and faced a stained reputation by walking out to meet his sad procession as it neared Rome.[7] The Lord himself was not forgetful either, but stood by in a consciously realized presence at critical moments.[8] All these Paul remembered when he looked back and said that *what has happened to me has really served to advance the gospel*.

But notice the word *really*. It shows in which direction his memory is leading him. There would be no need to say that a list of encouraging and helpful things had tended 'really' to promote the gospel. He stresses therefore the masses of dark threads that the recent years had woven into the pattern of his life – the animosities and bodily pains, the lies, misrepresentations and deceitfulness, the miscarriage of justice, the chains which forcibly kept him from travelling for the gospel, the mental turmoil of appealing to Caesar against his own people, the nearness of death and the diminution of hope, the triumph of wickedness and the continued suppression of the truth. He invites us to take these things and look them in the face, for it is these which have resulted – contrary to what their surface appearance might have suggested – in the progress of the gospel.

One factor had, in reality, controlled the past. As he looks back he can see it and it is something that is always true. It happens not just for apostles and special people. It is true for every believer, for in each and every case 'he who began a good work in you will bring it to completion at the day of Jesus Christ' (1:6). God rules. The pressures of life are the hands of the Potter who is also our Father;[9] the fires of life are those of the Refiner.[10] He does not abandon the perfecting process to others; nor is he ever, in his sovereign greatness, knocked off course by the malpractice of evil men or by the weakness of good men. 'God is not man, that he should lie, or a son of man, that he should repent. Has he said, and will he not do it? Or has he spoken, and will he not fulfil it?'[11]

---

[7]Acts 23:16; 27:1ff., 43; 28:15.   [8]Acts 23:11; 27:23.
[9]Is. 64:8.   [10]Mal. 3:3.   [11]Nu. 23:19.

## 2. The present

Paul did not leave his problems behind when the door of his house-prison closed behind him. When he reviews his present circumstances for the benefit of the Philippians and us, he reveals a situation of real personal vexation. It is most noticeable how he avoids dwelling on the inconvenience to himself of his bonds – though it takes little imagination to feel the tugging chain whenever he moved, even to reach for a drink of water; or the tiresomeness of never being alone but always under surveillance.

Yet these things are not elaborated. Paul directs the gaze of his readers elsewhere, into the Christian world in which he is placed. There is a group on each side, and he between them. The one is composed of those who are unfeignedly his friends, acting out of goodwill and love for the apostle and his cause; the others are moved by some sort of spleen against him. It is not a situation he can ignore, for he has been thrust into it by those who have made him explicitly the target of their attack. Moreover, he is an apostle in the church and therefore must take some line. What is he to choose? Will he excommunicate these people because of their attitude towards him and the unfavourable atmosphere which they doubtless created, or will he ignore them altogether?

Paul does not make himself neutral in all this, nor does he take a merely negative attitude. He has a positive and clear approach to the problems of the present. He states it in verses 18f.: *What then? Only that in every way, whether in pretence or in truth, Christ is proclaimed; and in that I rejoice. Yes, and I shall rejoice.* 'Christ is proclaimed' – not just 'Christ is unoffended or uninvolved'. How often Christians justify a course of action on the ground of an uninvolved Christ! How often we feel that we may do this or that, engage in this or that, simply because 'it does not hinder me as a Christian' or 'it has no bearing on Christian living one way or the other'! Paul was more positive: is Christ *preached*? Does this clearly give a testimony to him? Does it promote the declaration of Christ, the cause of the gospel?

What is Paul saying here? He is saying that the principle which he sees as governing all history, and which has governed his own immediate past, must also be put to work in making our present decisions. That principle is that God directs his government of his people towards the day of Christ's glory. Paul perceives that God turns events to *advance the gospel*, and he himself makes his daily decisions according to what he sees will best and most *proclaim Christ*. There is no difference in fact, only a different way of saying the same thing: one factor runs through all – Christ and his glory.

## 3. The future

The same governing interest holds good as the apostle considers the future. He faces the same possibilities as we all do: he will either die or live. He may be uncertain, as all must be, of the circumstances surrounding these alternatives. But the experiences themselves are inescapable. What principle, then, guides him into the coming days? His answer is magnificent: *now as always Christ will be honoured in my body, whether by life or by death* (verse 20). Paul is not a 'know-all' as he approaches the future. Even to his eye it remains uncharted. But his mind is made up on one thing: let the future bring what it will, *Christ will be honoured*. He leaves no room for uncertainty on this score. His task, whatever the future turn out to be, is not to carry a snapshot of Christ in his wallet for occasional sharing with chosen people, but to show an enlarged, life-size Christ to all who care to look, a Christ displayed in Paul's every dimension and capacity – a Christ 'magnified in my body' (RV).

The Lord Jesus Christ is thus the central, controlling factor for Paul – and for all who would live in the apostolic mould. Our faith in the Father of the Lord Jesus is such that we know that all things are working towards the day of Christ, whether they seem so or not. Our Lord is the key of all history and of personal history, and he must be made the deciding factor in every Christian choice. Pre-eminence belongs to that which advances the gospel and proclaims the Saviour. He is also the object of the Christian's supreme resolve as we face the future: the glory of Christ must be our great and controlling interest. In the heat of trial, in the thick of life, in the press of circumstances, the Christian is one who 'sees no man, save Jesus only'.

# 1:13–14
# 6. Suffering

*. . . so that it has become known throughout the whole praetorian guard and to all the rest that my imprisonment is for Christ;* [14]*and most of the brethren have been made confident in the Lord because of my imprisonment, and are much more bold to speak the word of God without fear.*

We have now taken a bird's-eye view of this great passage (1:12–26) and we have seen the single principle of the glory of Christ which runs throughout. In the course of his review, however, the apostle displays himself in three typical situations. He is faced by personal suffering (verses 13–14), a divided church (verses 15–18), and an uncertain future (verses 19–26). We must now study his example and teaching under each of these three headings.

The linking thought in verses 13 and 14 is the expression *my imprisonment*, or 'my bonds' (RV). In this undramatic way Paul calls attention to himself as a sufferer. We have already noticed that he does not elaborate his discomforts so as to call attention to himself: that would be inappropriate in a man professing to subdue his body so that Christ may be glorified through him. He does not, therefore, concentrate our gaze on the chained wrist, but, as it were, holding up the chain before our eyes, he makes us look through its links at the effect of these 'bonds' upon the work and the church.

## 1. The fruitfulness of Christian suffering

Refusing the way of self-pity, then, Paul does not describe the effect of the bonds upon himself but their effect upon others. And first, he tells us that his bonds were a testimony to the world. Indeed, it is this which helps him to his great conclusion that the things which happened to him had served to advance the gospel as it became *known throughout the whole praetorian guard and to all the rest that my imprisonment is for Christ*, or RV, 'my bonds became manifest in Christ'.

The *praetorian guard* was a picked division of crack imperial troops. Membership was much sought after, since double pay and different conditions of service were enjoyed, and there were good pension prospects as well as special duties. We gather from the reference here that one duty was to mount guard over prisoners awaiting trial before the Caesar himself, and we can imagine a long line of praetorians who took it in turn to be Paul's warders. No doubt the apostle to the Gentiles was not slow to tell them of the Lord Jesus Christ. In addition to such testimony, they witnessed many sessions between Paul and those who freely visited his house.[1] So the gospel had advanced among the praetorian guard, and also amongst *all the rest*, making a general impact upon the Roman public. But when asked to say how this impact was made he holds up his chains; 'my bonds became manifest' (RV). It was precisely his suffering that was fruitful in making a testimony to the world.

His bonds had a second effect: they were a stimulus to the church. Christians were stirred up to bolder and more effective preaching. This fourteenth verse is very instructive on the subject of Christian testimony. We learn who are the *agents* in witness: *the brethren*. The modern church, sadly, would be more inclined to say that testimony is the work of 'bishops and deacons' (1:1), those set apart for 'full-time' service. They are the mouthpiece of the church to the world. It was not so in the apostolic church. *The brethren* were out on the job telling the world about Christ. Needless to say this teaching prevails through the New Testament, and, indeed, Paul returns to it in Philippians 2:15f. where it is the individual Christian, the man or woman who can speak of personal salvation (2:12), who is to be seen as a 'light in the world, holding forth the word of life'

[1] Acts 28:30f.

(RV). Here, incidental to his example of Christian suffering, is a piece of apostolic teaching on the nature of ministry and service in the church to which we must, for our very life's sake, return in the present day. The example of Paul shows us what can happen when one person is wholly given to the Lord; but we have yet to see what would happen if a whole church were on the march, a people of God on fire for God. Something like this began to happen in Rome during Paul's imprisonment.

Paul tells us also of the *power* which marked their service, and where it came from. They were *confident in the Lord*. Paul does not spell out what was the link between his 'bonds' and their increase of confidence. *For Christ* indicates that Paul very plainly accepted his imprisonment as an opportunity to show his devotion to the Lord. But the Greek is literally 'in Christ' and this expresses a fuller and deeper idea. When Christ linked Paul with himself he linked him also to the divine plan that Paul should go to prison. No doubt the Romans saw Paul's devotion, and such an example could only be a stimulus. But no doubt, also, they saw his unbroken confidence that Jesus is Lord, to be trusted even when everything appears to go wrong, in sovereign control even when his servant seemed to fall into the power of man. Surely it is this trustworthy Christ that they saw afresh and they came to trust him more confidently.

Confidence showed itself in the *manner* of their witness which was *more bold* and *without fear*. There is something remarkable about this. Paul was in prison for the very reason that he was bold and without fear in his stand for Christ, yet suddenly the instinct of self-preservation began to wither in them and a new fearlessness took over.

The *substance* of their witness follows next. Since they found power coming to them from the Lord, what should they speak of but him? What they actually said is described in verse 14 as *the word of God*, which means that their message did not come from themselves but was God's truth. The focal point or substance of their message was that they preached *Christ* (verses 15, 17, 18). The verb 'preach' (*kēryssein*) means 'to do the work of a herald' – *i.e.* to transmit faithfully and clearly what someone else, a higher authority, has commanded to be proclaimed. Here too there is surely a mandate for the present day: to declare with clarity a message coming from

God and centred upon the Lord Jesus Christ.

The church was stimulated to this action of gospel proclamation by Paul's sufferings. His suffering was a positive, fruit-bearing thing.

## 2. The explanation of the fruitfulness

Not every suffering Christian is as fruitful as was the apostle, nor even fruitful in any sense at all. Many a Christian suffers without exercising any influence for good upon the world or the church. In other words, the fruitfulness, though it stemmed from Paul's suffering – his 'imprisonment', his 'bonds' – is not explained by it. There must be some other explanation.

Three truths, all about Paul the sufferer, encircle the fact of his suffering. The first we have already observed, but must now return to it again in its proper place: in his suffering he was *self-effacing.* He did not use the occasion of suffering either to turn his thoughts in upon himself or to make himself the object of other people's attention and interest. These verses (13–14), with their common foundation in the words 'my imprisonment', are as outward-looking as any pair of verses in the New Testament. He makes us look at the bonds, not at the wrists which they chafed and bruised; and he makes us look at the bonds only so that we may better appraise the impact they made upon the world and the church.

Secondly, Paul the sufferer was still *witnessing* to Christ. He writes that *it has become known . . . that my imprisonment is for Christ.* How did it become known? One chained man looks much the same as another. The manacles tell nothing, but the man does. Here was a prisoner whose talk was all of Another. Whether he sat alone with his guard, or whether a visitor called, the talk was always the same; it was all Christ. The suffering was the occasion of testimony to the Lord.

The verbal testimony was rooted in Paul's inner attitude towards his suffering. He saw himself – chain and all! – as a man *under orders.* He writes, 'I am put here for the defence of the gospel' (verse 16; AV, verse 17). The term as used here is military. When the time came that a praetorian's period of guard duty was over, he was relieved by another. The chain was passed from hand to hand and the new guard was 'set' to keep watch over Paul. It was not his part to query the duty allotted to him: such decisions were made by another mind in another place. For himself, a soldier might well have planned his service in more exciting, more apparently worth-while, enterprises. Nevertheless, this was what was required of him; it was in this situation that the traditions of the regiment must be upheld and his superior's praise merited. And Paul considered himself 'on duty' in these terms. He did not see his suffering as an act of divine forgetfulness ('Why did God let this happen to me?'), nor as a dismissal from service ('I was looking forward to years of usefulness, and look at me!'), nor as the work of Satan ('I am afraid the devil has had his way this time'), but as the place of duty, the setting for service, the task appointed. When the soldier came 'on duty' to guard Paul, did the apostle smile secretly and say to himself, 'But he doesn't know that I am here to guard him – for Christ'? The great ambassador is no longer free to range over land and sea with the good news, but he has not ceased to be an ambassador. The form of his ambassadorship has changed but not its purpose and duty. He is 'an ambassador in chains'.[2]

Paul relates his experiences with such a light touch that we might be deceived into thinking that what is easily told was easily accomplished. But why should it have been any easier for Paul than it is for us to leave the path of self-pity, to talk more of Christ than of our complaints and to accept each and every circumstance as the place of duty he has appointed? Such notoriously difficult attitudes of mind and heart are brought about only by practice, by hard-won choices in the very heat of that tribulation which works patience.[3]

Two friends were talking together, one older and wise, the other younger and passing through a severe testing-time. The older friend, with loving wisdom, said, 'No moment will ever again be like this; let there be something for Jesus in it.' It is not 'something for Jesus' if we dwell on our miseries; nor if we let opportunities pass without a word about our Lord; nor if we think that any hand other than his brought us to that place. It is 'something for Jesus' if we think and speak about him and his glory; it is 'something for him' if we acknowledge and trust his all-sovereign will.

[2]Eph. 6:20.     [3]Rom. 5:3.

As Paul looks forward into the future, he expresses what is in fact his abiding attitude (verse 20): *now as always Christ will be honoured* ('magnified'). How that word 'now' needs to eat its way into our minds and hearts and wills! It is *now* that we must show how great Christ is. Never again will we have the chance to live for him through *this* moment, to please him in *this* circumstance, to gladden him by trusting in *this* ordeal.

Such sentiments elate the heart, but there can have been small elation for Paul as he looked at his chain and his flesh worn by its chafing. No elation – but a resolve: *now as always!*

# 1:15–18
# 7. Divisions

*Some indeed preach Christ from envy and rivalry, but others from good will.* [16]*The latter do it out of love, knowing that I am put here for the defence of the gospel;* [17]*the former proclaim Christ out of partisanship, not sincerely but thinking to afflict me in my imprisonment.* [18]*What then? Only that in every way, whether in pretence or in truth, Christ is proclaimed; and in that I rejoice.*

As Paul viewed the Roman scene from the vantage-point of his hired house, it was not wholly to his liking. In verse 14 we sense Paul's delight in the forward move of the gospel through the ministry of an awakened church, but verses 15–18 open other windows into the state of affairs, and we learn that all was not quite so rosy.

The first of the disquieting facts is that Paul observes people whose hearts were at war with their testimony. The preachers in the Roman church were of two sorts, differentiated by their attitude towards the apostle. The one group consisted of those who felt genuine goodwill towards him, and all their Christian activity was motivated by love for him, springing out of their knowledge that he was *put* (there) *for the defence of the gospel* (verse 16). On the other side stood those who worked in order to *afflict me in my imprisonment* (verse 17).

We cannot take the easy way out in this distinction, and say that the one group was Christian in both name and reality while the other was Christian in name only, or even heretical. Some commentators have, indeed, taken this line, urging that we have here some sort of sect, or break-away group, possibly 'Judaizers', or 'Christ-plus' people, who added requirements like circumcision or other Mosaic precepts as essential for salvation.[1] But it seems certain that whoever they were, they cannot have been Judaizers, for there is nothing here of the stern language which Paul felt obliged to use when he proclaimed an anathema upon such troublers of the church, not hesitating to call them 'dogs'.[2] On the contrary, he approves the message these people preached – *Christ* was *proclaimed* (verse 18). Paul felt nothing but joy in the fact.

They were Christian preachers, then, but divided people. And not just divided from other Christians, but divided internally; their hearts were at war with their testimony. For even while they preached Christ they nourished emotions inimical to the gospel.

Paul tells us of their *envy and rivalry* and of their *partisanship* (verses 15, 17). Why were they envious? Why were they moved to oppose him (*rivalry*) and to fight for themselves (*partisanship*)? He does not say. He is as reticent here about the sins of others as he was in verses 13–14 about his own sufferings. He fills in no detail: love is not resentful; 'it keeps no record of wrongs'.[3] Did they envy Paul's great gifts or the success that had attended his ministry? Were their noses out of joint because when he came to Rome he rightly became an apostolic focus for the church there? We could go on guessing, but arrive at nothing more than a guess, for Paul shares no tittle-tattle. All we know is that they presented the truth about Christ in such a way as to express their animosity against the apostle.

There is great grace in Paul's silence, and great wisdom too. For if he had told us the details we should of course know more about the then church at Rome, but we might also be able to distance ourselves from the situation. Paul, however, deals in generalities, for it is still true that those who claim to love and preach the same Lord find opportunity at the same time to snipe and hint and denigrate. It is (it seems) all too easy for a

[1] See Acts 15:1, 5; contrast Acts 15:8–9, 11.
[2] Gal. 1:6–9; Phil 3:2.     [3] 1 Cor. 13:5, NIV.

new minister to establish his own reputation at the expense of his predecessor; the most regrettable aspects of sectarianism and denominationalism have always established their own identity and security by rebutting others and giving rein to the same spirit of envy, rivalry and partisanship which Paul noted.

But Paul does not stop short of invading the realm of motive: they do not preach *sincerely*, for as well as seeking the glory of Christ in the conversion of sinners and the edification of saints, they also thought *to afflict me* (verse 17). Observe again Paul's reticence. Magnificently he passes James's test![4] His tongue is controlled. Was he not hurt by what they were saying? Of course he was – he knew the biting sadness of danger from false brethren.[5] But he does not dwell on what they did to him, and to this day we cannot be certain what it was.

All we know is that they committed a cardinal sin of the preacher, to use the pulpit to make sly innuendoes and veiled attacks and concealed, damaging hints. And they exposed themselves to the danger of spiritual schizophrenia. On the one hand they were apparently faithful gospel preachers, committed to declare a selfless, self-sacrificing, unself-seeking Christ, a Christ intent upon the eternal good of all whom he died to save. On the other hand they privately and secretly indulged a different set of values, self-seeking, self-regarding, moved by desire to hurt one whom Christ had died to save. They were double-minded. Their public lives warred with their private lives, and their tongues with their thoughts.

The Bible is very emphatic in its warnings of the spiritual peril of such a double life, not least, for example, when Proverbs counsels to 'keep your heart with all vigilance; for from it flow the springs of life', or when Paul orders the Romans to cast off not only the bodily sins of 'revelling and drunkenness ... debauchery and licentiousness' but also the sins of the spirit, 'quarrelling and jealousy', and those of the mind when he says, 'Take no forethought (make no provision) for the flesh'.[6] Indeed, in the present Epistle he calls the Philippians to cultivate 'the same love, being in full accord', doing 'nothing from selfishness or conceit'.[7] But in the present

---

[4]Jas. 1:26.    [5]2 Cor. 11:26.    [6]Pr. 4:23; Rom. 13: 12–14.
[7]Phil. 2:2f.

passage he does not even pause to issue warnings. He is describing what he finds, and in so far as he has a purpose in his description it is not to denounce the divided loyalties of his opponents, nor their deceitfulness, nor to point them to a remedy. His purpose rather is to show how a Christian ought to behave when faced with a divided church, what things may be ignored, what deserves priority, to what principle an appeal may be made, and what is to be left out of account.

We must move on, then, with the apostle. Later verses will raise again the topic of divided loyalties and the bearing of vices such as faction and self-seeking upon the constitution and witness of the church, but at the moment we must look through the apostle's eyes at what is a very familiar situation today.

The church was divided within itself. There were Paulinists and anti-Paulinists (verses 15, 17). He does not describe them; we do not know how either side behaved to the other. And the result of his silence is that the passage is not limited to a by-gone situation, but raises great and abiding Christian issues in their simplest form and lays down an equally great and simple approach to them.

Divisions in the church remain one of the features of our own day, whether we think of individual differences and even antagonisms within a local church, or of the proliferation of denominational and other groupings. To mention again the list of sins in Romans 13:13, it is likely enough that few local churches today are greatly bothered by revelling and drunkenness, debauchery and licentiousness, but it is equally likely that many local churches are harbouring quarrelling and jealousy. Indeed, all too often this state of affairs is tacitly accepted as a feature of church life. In parallel to this, we have all grown up amid the present multiplicity of denominations; denominational titles have from the first been part of our Christian vocabulary: I am this, he is that, she is the other. The scandal has become domesticated. In this passage in Philippians Paul helps us to see in miniature, in one local church, what faces us locally and world-wide: two sets of people, each claiming the name of Christ, but not at one, not easy with each other, divided.

The passage speaks most plainly to us at the individual level. As we have seen, the situation was first and foremost one of personal animosity against Paul. How did he react? On the one hand, there is no way in which he would condone envy, rivalry and partisanship: such things are sins and are listed as characterizing those who reject God, as belonging to the works of the flesh, as evidence of unspiritual Christianity.[8] How Paul must have lamented such things in his fellow believers and longed to see them vanish! Given a divinely sent opportunity, he would surely have tried to minister to these Christians in their sinful bondage.

As Paul approached them in such contacts as came his way, he did not compare their degree of sanctification with his own. He did not say that if only they were more holy they would not think about him in this way, and that the cause of their hostility would thus disappear – true though that must be, for if all Christians were completely Christlike there would be no disputations. But in the present stage of the divine purposes, this is not the way forward. When we see him we shall be like him,[9] but that is still for the future. No doubt Paul would have readily admitted that in some of their feelings about him they were justified, for he knew that he had not 'already obtained' and was not 'already perfect';[10] no doubt, too, even those who loved him (verse 16) were not always lovable. Unity among Christians, the healing of divisions, has to be achieved in spite of imperfect sanctification. Paul did not condone unholiness but neither did he indulge in that recurrent 'crying for the moon' which church history has evidenced, when fellowship is made to depend upon personal holiness.

There is another negative truth which will enable us to clear the ground: Paul does not propose an organizational solution to the disunity he saw around him. There is a narrow and erroneous concept of apostolicity held today by Christians within the 'Catholic' tradition but absent from the New Testament and very effectively silenced by this passage. Paul, writes H. C. G. Moule, 'is apparently quite unconscious of the thought that because he is the one apostle in Rome grace can be conveyed only through him, that his authority and commission are necessary to authenticate teaching and to make ordinances

---

[8]Rom. 1:29; Gal. 5: 19ff.; 1 Cor. 3:3; cf. 2 Cor. 12:20.
[9]1 Jn. 3:2.    [10]Phil. 3:12.

effectual'.[11] This defective understanding of apostolicity, focusing on questions of valid exterior order and the authentication of the 'true' church by a supposed 'apostolic succession', seems to be beyond Paul's horizon of interest and teaching. For here there is no thought in his mind to disfranchize or excommunicate or declare invalid the ministry of those who have made public their repudiation of him and their desire to hold aloof from him.

On the contrary, the focal point of Paul's understanding of apostleship[12] becomes plain in the positive principle which he applied and followed through during his Roman imprisonment.

He invites us to consider how his experiences have fallen out for the advancement of the gospel (verse 12), how his sufferings have encouraged the brethren to speak the word of God with boldness (verse 14), to preach and proclaim Christ (verses 15, 17–18). He gives the weight of his authority and approval not to their devotion to Christ as such, nor to their concern for the unconverted as such, but to the fact that he agrees with and authenticates their message.

There is no true unity where there is no unity in truth.

We ought to notice that in this passage it is not even the person of Christ which occupies Paul, but the proclamation of Christ. There is the possibility that Christians can come together into an amorphous grouping around a common acknowledgment of the Lord Jesus Christ, but how can this be called Christian unity unless there is agreement as to what is true about the Lord Jesus Christ: that 'Lord' points to his unequivocal and eternal deity, 'Jesus' to the Word made flesh, the God-Man, and 'Christ' to his office as divinely endowed Saviour of sinners? If the name and title mean different things to different people, then it is a sign of their variance, not their unity.

There is a truly pathetic quality about the insistence on unity in order which has dominated interdenominational discussion and endeavour over the last quarter of a century. The Roman Catholic Church refuses to recognize Anglican orders, regarding them as outside the supposed succession of Peter and the

[11]Moule, *ad loc.*    [12]See chapter 2, above.

apostles; Anglican leadership has insisted on episcopacy (as it is said) within the apostolic succession as the essential point of agreement between uniting bodies. Yet in neither of these episcopal denominations has the presumed succession in order secured a true internal unity: each alike is a conglomerate of irreconcilable opinions. Unity must be unity in the truth. And to Paul, as Philippians reveals him, this means, at centre, unity in gospel truth, unity in the evangelistic message, unity of understanding of Christ, his person, mission, death and resurrection. Let Bishop Moule speak again:

> Paul would far rather have order, and he knows he is its lawful centre. But the announcement of Christ is a thing even more momentous than order . . . If even a separatist propaganda will extend the knowledge of *Him*, His servant can rejoice . . . Surely even in our day, with its immemorial complications of the question of exterior order, it will tend more than anything else to straighten crooked places . . . if we look, from every side, on the glory of the blessed name, as our supreme and ruling interest.[13]

In so far as the denominations cater for legitimate diversity of practice and belief among the people of God, they serve a good purpose. The purpose turns sour when living under the rule of Scripture is made to mean 'living under the rule of my understanding of Scripture' and becomes an occasion for dismissing all who espouse a different interpretation. The sad conflicts which have arisen over the doctrine of baptism are a notable case in point.

We return, finally, to the individual level. Differences of personal like and dislike will remain in the church; different stages of sanctification will mark individual Christians; different appreciations of what constitutes the will of God for a person's life will continue to be expressed. But all these are secondary – secondary to the grand truth of individual redemption by the blood of Christ,[14] of being accepted by God in Christ,[15] and, what grips and controls Paul in his Roman

[13]Moule, *ad loc.*    [14]*Cf.* Rom. 14:13–15; 1 Cor. 8:11.
[15]*Cf.* Rom. 14:1–3.

jail, common possession of the saving truth of the gospel. If there is anything which, for us, fails to pale into insignificance, compared with the scriptural knowledge of Christ, then we are not living by the priorities of God.

## 1:19–26
## 8. Looking forward

*Yes, and I shall rejoice. For I know that through your prayers and the help of the Spirit of Jesus Christ this will turn out for my deliverance, [20]as it is my eager expectation and hope that I shall not be at all ashamed, but that with full courage now as always Christ will be honoured in my body, whether by life or by death. [21]For to me to live is Christ, and to die is gain. [22]If it is to be life in the flesh, that means fruitful labour for me. Yet which I shall choose I cannot tell. [23]I am hard pressed between the two. My desire is to depart and be with Christ, for that is far better. [24]But to remain in the flesh is more necessary on your account. [25]Convinced of this, I know that I shall remain and continue with you all, for your progress and joy in the faith, [26]so that in me you may have ample cause to glory in Christ Jesus, because of my coming to you again.*

As we saw in our outline of this section of the letter, Paul follows his review of past events (verse 12), and his account of present circumstances (verses 13–18), by an attempt to peer forward into the future (verses 19–26). In studying this latter division more closely, we find Paul characterized by *certainty* and *uncertainty*. He is quite sure about some things: he says *I know* (verse 19), and speaks of *my eager expectation and hope* (verse 20; we must recall that the New Testament word 'hope' is full of confidence and contains nothing of the unsureness which modern usage has imported into it). Equally, in some things he is uncertain saying, *Which I shall choose I cannot tell* (verse 22). Examination will show that his certainty belongs to the realm of *ambition*: he knows what he is heading for; uncertainty belongs to the realm of *out-working*: he is not sure just how things will work out.

## 1. The Christian's ambition (1:19–20)

*Yes, and I shall rejoice. For I know that through your prayers and the help of the Spirit of Jesus Christ this will turn out for my deliverance,* [20]*as it is my eager expectation and hope that I shall not be at all ashamed, but that with full courage now as always Christ will be honoured in my body, whether by life or by death.*

Paul opens up his attitude towards the future by speaking of his 'salvation' (verse 19, RV). By translating this word (*sōtēria*) as *deliverance*, RSV narrows its reference so that it points only to the ending of the apostle's imprisonment. There is great value, however, and indeed greater accuracy in context in the translation 'salvation'. The word 'salvation' and the verb 'to be saved' have a threefold reference, as a glance at a concordance will show. They look back to the past, as Paul does when he reminds the Ephesians how they 'heard the word of the truth, the gospel of your salvation'.[1] From that time, many at Ephesus could look back and say: 'On that day, I was saved.' Paul reflects this past aspect of salvation when he says 'By grace you have been saved',[2] but by using the Greek perfect tense he adds a new and up-to-date dimension to salvation: 'You have been and are saved.' It is in the same spirit that he later exhorts the Philippians to 'work out' their own salvation,[3] for salvation is a present possession whose riches they may and must explore and enjoy, day after day. But the full experience of all that salvation means lies in the future. To this Paul looks forward when he says that 'salvation is nearer to us now than when we first believed',[4] and it is in this third sense that he speaks of salvation here.

Three things promote the attaining of this future salvation.

[1]Eph. 1:13.  [2]Eph. 2:8.  [3]Phil. 2:12.  [4]Rom. 13:11.

## a. The outworking of events

Paul says, 'This will turn to my salvation' (verse 19, RV). What does he means by 'this'? Certainly he includes 'the greater spread of the preaching';[5] surely also he intends 'this state of things, these perplexities and annoyances'.[6] But would it not be best to allow 'this' to have as wide a scope as possible? For 'all things contribute to the advantage of God's true worshippers'.[7] This is without doubt true to the view of things which Philippians teaches. More and more we come back to 1:6 as to a basic truth: 'He who began a good work in you will bring it to completion at the day of Jesus Christ.' Each item in Paul's experience is but another of the Father's finishing touches, and all will result in the full enjoyment of salvation. This is a sure faith for Paul and for us also. The Christian need never fear the outcome of events. Life brings (as we say) its daily pressures. Many of them are unexpected; often they seem uncalled-for; from time to time they are traceable to the malignity of wicked people (and there is no doctrine of divine sovereignty which relieves such people of a heavy guilt in the matter; the doctrine of sovereignty rather guarantees their punishment).[8] But God is over all, and there is no point in believing in a sovereign God if he can be tumbled off the throne by human or satanic agency! Philippians 1:6 tells us about this God, beginning, completing, and purposing to finish his good work in and for us. Romans 8:28 tells us about our personal history in which 'in everything God works for good'. Paul takes and accepts this great and comforting truth in a precise and unpleasant period of his life: *This shall turn to my salvation* (verse 19, RV).

## b. The prayers of other Christians

The Christian, however, is not a cork on the waters, carried along by the tide of circumstances. He is a person in need of help from God if he is to sustain the pressures of life and live for Christ through them. Such help is there for him. Paul calls it *the help* (RV 'supply') *of the Spirit of Jesus Christ* (verse 19).

[5]H. Alford, *The Greek Testament* (Rivington, 1880), *ad loc.*
[6]Lightfoot, *ad loc.*
[7]Calvin, *ad loc.*     [8]*Cf.* Acts 2:23.

'Supply' has a 'plus' element in it; it is the 'full, sufficient supply'. 'Of the Spirit' means either that the Spirit brings us the full supply in his great office of making real in our experience all the benefits and blessings of faith in God,[9] or else that the Spirit himself is the full supply as he indwells the believer. He is called 'the Spirit of Jesus Christ' because his presence in us and his gracious work for us have been purchased by the saving work of Christ.[10] Thus, God not only rules our lives from the throne, but he also sustains our lives from within.

This, however, is in answer to the prayers of other Christians. The two thoughts of intercession and supply are bound so closely together by Paul that we could, without violence, translate the Greek 'your prayers and the consequent supply . . .'. Paul could have asked for the Spirit for himself, and no doubt often did. It is a God-given privilege to ask for the Holy Spirit, and we are all invited to do so.[11] But Paul turned the matter in another direction: he showed himself concerned for the spiritual welfare of the Philippians, and his love for them issued in prayer.[12] He also needs and asks for their prayers. This is our responsibility to one another and something for which we depend on one another. We have an obligation to put one another's spiritual growth in the very forefront of our prayers, and to take the responsibility very seriously. Paul even sensitively suggests that the sufficient supply of the Spirit of Jesus Christ for my brother or sister in Christ depends directly on my prayer for them, and that failing my prayer the supply will dry up also.

### c. The Christian's personal efforts

Paul comes to his own responsibility in this matter of final salvation. God will bring him there; the prayers of Christians will sustain him on his way; meanwhile he himself pursues his great ambition. Paul here emphasizes three elements in his make-up.

He is absorbed in an *eager expectation*. The single Greek word here has three elements in it, 'away', 'the head' and 'to

[9]*Cf.*, *e.g.*, Rom. 8:11.    [10]*E.g.* Jn. 7:39; Acts 2:33; Gal. 4:4–6.
[11]Lk. 11:13.    [12]Phil. 1:4, 8–9.

watch', and these are combined to give the idea of 'watching something with the head turned away from other objects'. Paul's attention is wholly occupied with one thing, to the exclusion of others. This is essentially the same picture as he gives when he sees himself as a runner[13] expending every effort as he speeds to the tape. This *eager expectation* rests upon *hope* which in the New Testament means something whose coming is certain, but whose timing is uncertain. He does not tell us now the ground of this certain hope, for he has already made it plain. What can it be but that he is confident that God will see him safely home, and that Christ will prove sufficient for every eventuality on the road?[14]

The efforts which the Christian makes are not the doomed attempts of the unsaved to merit glory. They are the appointed avenue along which we express outwardly the new life in Christ which we already possess, and the means by which we come to enjoy that new life more completely. We can understand, therefore, the determination which Paul shows in pursuing his goal. It has three aspects. First, it is a determination to keep his conscience clear – *that I shall not be at all ashamed* (verse 20). Second, he is determined to maintain a plain, full testimony with confidence and courage. The word which RSV translates as *courage (parrēsia)* means boldness of speech as often as it means confidence of demeanour, and on a number of occasions is best served, as here, by allowing both senses to play their part. Thirdly, Paul is determined to maintain an unblemished record: *now as always* (verse 20).

On what is his determination concentrated? On the Christian's greatest of all ambitions for the future: that *Christ will be honoured in my body, whether by life or by death* (verse 20). The literal translation is, if anything, more striking: that 'Christ will be enlarged in my body', shown in all the dimensions of his greatness (*megalynō*). This is what God is aiming at as he prepares the saints for the great day; it is what he is doing as he rules and overrules the circumstances of his people,[15] and it is what he expects us to do through the constant and demanding efforts of our conscience and our will as we obey him.

---

[13]Phil. 3:13f.    [14]Phil. 1:6, 11.    [15]Phil. 1:6, 12, 19.

## 2. The Christian's indecision (1:21–26)

*For to me to live is Christ, and to die is gain.* ²²*If it is to be life in the flesh, that means fruitful labour for me. Yet which I shall choose I cannot tell.* ²³*I am hard pressed between the two. My desire is to depart and be with Christ, for that is far better.* ²⁴*But to remain in the flesh is more necessary on your account.* ²⁵*Convinced of this, I know that I shall remain and continue with you all, for your progress and joy in the faith,* ²⁶*so that in me you may have ample cause to glory in Christ Jesus, because of my coming to you again.*

Christian hope makes the outcome certain but leaves open both the time of fulfilment and the means by which the goal is reached. Therefore, at the end of verse 20, Paul can do no more than express alternative possibilities, *life . . . or . . . death*. He knows nothing of the future other than that it must be one or the other of these.

### a. The equal desirability of life and death

What does Paul mean when he says that for him *to live is Christ, and to die is gain*? In 3:4–8 he uses the word 'gain' in a way which illuminates his meaning here. In that passage he is looking back to the day when Christ became everything to him. He had candidly added up all that might have been counted as valuable; he had found Christ more valuable, and gladly surrendered all to and for him. But this attitude persists. Paul turns to a present tense: he is still 'counting' and still finding the surpassing worth of Christ, so that his whole life may be summed up as the progressive abandonment of everything else in the interest of possessing more and more of Christ.

'Gaining Christ', then, is another way of expressing the Christian's progressive experience of sanctification, growth in grace, or becoming more and more like Jesus. Returning to 1:21, Paul defines his life as gaining Christ, and death as the ultimate gain itself. In life he is absorbed and determined in consecrated living for Christ; in death he expects to possess Christ totally. We could paraphrase and extend his thought by saying, 'Life means Christ to me, as I more fully know and love and serve him day by day; death means Christ to me, when I shall finally possess and eternally enjoy him.'

What, then, is he to choose? He confesses, *I am hard pressed between the two* (verse 23). The benefits, as he sees them, are evenly balanced, for against the immediate gain of Christ which death brings, he finds he must take into account the increased fruit for Christ which continued life will bring (verse 22). This seems to be the broad meaning of verse 22, though the Greek is difficult. In language that is somewhat broken because of his intense feelings, Paul begins to discuss in verses 22 and 23 the alternative courses stated in verse 21. *To live is Christ*; very well, 'if my lot is to be life in the flesh, that means fruitful labour for me. Then which I shall choose I cannot tell.' To die is gloriously to possess Christ; to live is gloriously to bear fruit. He finds the choice pulls him in two.

### b. The preference for death

Faced with this double possibility, Paul attempts to assess what is involved in each course, and confesses that his *desire is to depart and be with Christ, for that is* (very) *far better.*

This is a very full and remarkable statement about the death of a Christian. He teaches us first about the nature of a Christian death: it is 'to depart'. This may be a camping metaphor. Paul, the old 'tent-maker',[16] resorts to the language of his trade. In this case, death for the Christian is the end of what was at best a transitory thing, a camp-life, in which he travelled without permanent resting-place. This is to be exchanged for the 'house not made with hands, eternal in the heavens'.[17] Camp-life is exchanged at death for home-life with Christ. But the other possibility is that this 'departing' is a 'weighing of the anchor', a 'setting sail'. Bishop Moule speaks of 'that delightful moment when the friendly flood heaves beneath the freed keel, and the prow is set straight and finally towards the shore of *home*, and the Pilot stands on board, at length "seen face to face." And, lo, as He takes the helm, "immediately the ship is at the land whither they go" (Joh. vi. 21)'.[18]

[16]Acts 18:3.    [17]2 Cor. 5:1ff.
[18]H. G. C. Moule, *The Second Epistle to Timothy* (*The Devotional Commentary* series, Religious Tract Society, 1905), p.140. The verb is

When a Christian dies all the uncertainties and dangers lie behind: the uncertainties and dangers whether of camp-life or of temporary stay in a foreign port.[19] All the certainties and safeties lie ahead in the presence of Christ. And this, in the second place, is the blessedness of Christian death. The Christian goes to *be with Christ*. Scripture leaves so much about life after death undescribed, but on this central fact there is no hesitation: the Christian dead are 'with Christ'.

Paul takes the matter a stage further. He declares that death to the Christian is (literally) 'by far the best'. Suppose we had been with Paul in Rome just then, and had seen him as he was, a man of immense vigour of mind and body, with gigantic gifts, a man irreplaceable in the church. How keenly we should have felt the loss were he to be executed! What an untimely death! – and all the other things we hear said when a notable Christian dies unexpectedly. But what is the reality for the person concerned, for Paul? He is not the loser; he is not 'poor Paul'. For him it is better by far than anything else that could have happened or could be imagined. Indeed, even while the church mourned his loss, he would possess unimaginable riches.[20] For him, as for us at our death too, it is *far better*.

This is not, of course, to say that mourning is out of place for the Christian when loved ones go to be with the Lord. The fact that they are experiencing the supremely best lightens but does not take away the fact that *our* experience is of loss, loneliness, and great joys now irretrievably gone – however much we know that they will be transcended by the 'joyful reunion in the heavenly places'. It is a very beautiful thing that in this same

---

*analyō*, elsewhere used only in Lk. 12:36 in the sense 'to come back home'. The noun *analysis* occurs only at 2 Tim. 4:6.

[19]C. S. Lewis puts this beautifully, in the terminology of Narnia: 'Then Aslan turned to them and said: 'You do not yet look so happy as I mean you to be." Lucy said, "We're so afraid of being sent away, Aslan. And you have sent us back into our own world so often." "No fear of that," said Aslan. "Have you not guessed?" Their hearts leapt and a wild hope rose within them. "There *was* a real railway accident," said Aslan softly. "Your father and mother and all of you are – as you used to call it in the Shadowlands – dead. The term is over: the holidays have begun. The dream is ended: this is the morning." ' (*The Last Battle*, Bles, 1956, p.165).

[20]1 Cor. 2:9.

letter in which Paul sounds the note of confident expectation in the face of death he also expresses the desolation which bereavement brings: 'sorrow upon sorrow'.[21] And how true that is! In bereavement every tearful memory waits to be replaced by another, every sharp pang of loss is succeeded by a greater. Tears are proper for believers – indeed they should be all the more copious, for Christians are more sensitively aware of every emotion, whether of joy or sorrow, than those who have known nothing of the softening and enlivening grace of God. In this too we follow the example of him whose tears were not restrained at the graveside.[22]

These two 'poles' of confidence and tears should mark our attitude to death, yet they are always and equally under threat. It is, of course, proper that we should face death 'triumphantly' – but not with that heartless and glossy triumph which can amount to denigrating the goodness and grace of God in this life. We face our own death with triumphant assurance, but surely not without a pang for all we enjoy in this life and which will then be past for ever. We face the death of our loved ones with triumph, but surely not without a tear because they are gone. Paul can speak of Epaphroditus' continuance in *this* life as a 'mercy' from God.[23] How right that is!

But there is a more grievous loss when Christians fail to grasp the concreteness of eternal security in Christ and resort to requiem masses and prayers for the dead, as though some uncertainty attended the condition of those who die in Christ. This deeply denies the effectiveness and finality of the saving work of Christ, a work so complete that Paul speaks of Christians as (here and now) 'qualified', by no less than the Father himself, 'to share in the inheritance of the saints in light'.[24] This same confidence breathes through our present passage in Philippians and we praise God for it.

[21]Phil. 2:27.

[22]Jn. 11:35. Our poor sense of proportion has distorted the elements in Jn. 11. It can hardly be called 'miraculous' that the Son of God should raise the dead: indeed, seen like that, it rather 'stands to reason'. The 'real' miracle in Jn. 11 is that the Son of God, full of authority and power to raise the dead, first stooped to identify himself without reserve with our condition, mingling his tears with those of Mary.

[23]Phil. 2:27.      [24]Col. 1:12.

## c. The motive for living

With all his heightened sensibilities Paul saw and savoured the prospect of being with Christ. He loved the Lord with an abounding love and yearned for his company. Yet, over against all that, he writes three words (two in Greek) which change the whole picture: *on your account* (verse 24). As far as personal enrichment was concerned, death would win hands down. But there is also the Philippian church and all the others who fill the loving imagination of Paul. What of them? They still need (as he sees it) his apostolic ministry. Paul believes it to be the will of the Lord that this need should be considered paramount (verse 25). Furthermore, such is his love for his fellow-believers and his desire for their spiritual advantage that he is ready for it to be so. What a man the apostle was! The fruitfulness of remaining in this life could sway him as against the joy of living with Christ; the needs of the church were met by a love which, for the present, was willing to postpone heavenly glories.

No doubt they would *glory in Christ* (verse 26) if and when Paul was restored to them, and congratulate him, too, on 'winning his case'. But for him, it all came down to two dominating motives: I live on so that others may grow in Christ and that Christ may be glorified in me.

# 1:27–30
# 9. The steadfast church

*Only let your manner of life be worthy of the gospel of Christ, so that whether I come and see you or am absent, I may hear of you that you stand firm in one spirit, with one mind striving side by side for the faith of the gospel, [28]and not frightened in anything by your opponents. This is a clear omen to them of their destruction, but of your salvation, and that from God. [29]For it has been granted to you that for the sake of Christ you should not only believe in him but also suffer for his sake, [30]engaged in the same conflict which you saw and now hear to be mine.*

Paul's confidence that he would be acquitted at his trial and set free (verses 25–26) inevitably fell short of an absolute certainty. He apparently so judged the needs of the church that he was as near sure as anyone could be that he would again visit Philippi. Nevertheless, he must prepare the church for either eventuality. Strikingly, one set of instructions was enough: absent or present, he required that their life should be *worthy of the gospel of Christ* (verse 27).

This requirement was both exclusive and absolute. The force of the word '*only*' is tremendous, as if Paul had said, 'This one thing and this only'. Nothing else must distract or excuse them from this great objective; it must be their all-embracing occupation whether Paul was there or not. An apostolic church is not necessarily a church in which an apostolic person is resident, but it must be a church cast in the apostolic mould.

Paul's own aim, as seen in verses 12–26, was to live 'worthily of the gospel of Christ'. He saw the interests of that gospel as the key to his past (verse 12); he came to decisions in present circumstances by asking what would best help the preaching of Christ (verses 14–18); he made exalting Christ the focus of his future (verse 20). He required the Philippians to do no less. They must be apostolic.

Paul exhorted the Philippians in a way which would have appealed to them. What he said, literally, was: 'Exercise your citizenship worthily of the gospel of Christ.' Philippi was a Roman 'colony', a title seen as one of the coveted prizes of the Roman empire.[1] 'Colonial' status meant that the people of Philippi were reckoned as Roman citizens. Their names were on the rolls at Rome; their legal position and privileges were those of Rome itself. They were a homeland in miniature. But all this is also true of them spiritually as men and women in Christ. Grace has made them citizens of a heavenly city; in their far-off land they are the heavenly homeland in miniature; heaven's laws are their laws, and their privileges, its privileges. The life *worthy of the gospel* is an inescapable obligation: it is the essence of the homeland where the Lamb standing, as though it had been slain,[2] forms the focal point of all life.

This is the third of three cords of the gospel which Paul weaves together in this chapter: there is the defence of the gospel (verse 7) for which the Philippians were notable, and the proclamation of the gospel (verses 13–18) so evident at Rome. But here is the adornment of it by worthy living (verse 27; *cf.* Tit. 2:10). This was where some of the Christians at Rome failed so conspicuously, and where the Philippians evidently needed a reminder.

All three responsibilities rest equally on those who love the gospel, but nowhere do they rest more heavily than where the honoured title of 'evangelical' is claimed. We have not succeeded wholly in any one of the three. Maybe we have been

---

[1] On Roman citizenship, see the Introduction, above, p. 15. The verb *politeuomai* makes its other New Testament appearance in Acts 23:1, 'I have exercised my citizenship before God', *i.e.* his possession of the privileges and duties of Israelite citizenship. *Cf.* the noun *politeia*, Acts 22:28 (Roman citizenship), Eph. 2:12 (Israelite citizenship).

[2] Rev. 5:6.

forward to defend the gospel, but we have too often marred our defence by an unloving controversy or a haughty pride. Often we have majored on proclamation and God has honoured our endeavours in ways in which we rejoice. But are we notable for living the life worthy of the gospel? Why should people believe our defence of the cause of Christ if they cannot see Christ in us, or take any notice of our offer of a saving Christ if they do not see the fruits of salvation in the beauty of holy living?

## 1. Steadfastness is grounded in unity

There was one thing which Paul specially wished to hear in connection with their living of the worthy life: that they were steadfast under attack. He had himself found Philippi a place of suffering and, in general, the apostolic church was a church under fire. The reminder to be unyielding was therefore timely.

The worthy life, then, is not a 'fugitive and cloistered virtue'. It is exposed, vulnerable. Three things follow in sequence: live worthily, stand firm, be united. The life worthy of the gospel is like a jewel in a double setting. It is encased in the opposition of a hostile world, against which it must *stand firm*. It is enabled to do this because of its second setting, in the unity of the church. This is a most important point in Paul's teaching, so for clarity we will put it another way. If we may paraphrase him, Paul is saying this: 'My objective for you is that you live worthily of the gospel. Whether present or absent, then, I look for the same news – that you are standing firm under attack. But remember this: that standing firm under attack, while it requires stern resolution on the part of each individual, is a corporate matter, an activity of the fellowship. Steadfastness requires your unity of spirit and soul, your co-operative battling for the faith you hold in common.'

Steadfastness is thus grounded in unity. When we examine the unity which Paul is here speaking of, we find that there are four elements in it. To begin with, he speaks of it as *unity of the Spirit*: *stand firm in one spirit*. It seems best to take this as a reference to the Holy Spirit, for two reasons: negatively, if it does not refer to the Holy Spirit it is very difficult to distinguish it from the following words 'with one mind'. Of course it could be that Paul is using a phrase like our 'heart and soul', that is, with complete dedication and enthusiasm, but the repetition of the word 'one' is against this. He seems to be enumerating distinct aspects of the unity he desires for them. Positively, the phrase *stand firm in one spirit* is paralleled in 4:1 by the phrase 'stand firm . . . in the Lord', and, as we shall see, the over-all movement and teaching of that later passage is virtually identical with that of the present verses, which makes the parallelism more significant. In 4:1 their steadfast stand is grounded upon the Lord Jesus. He has them 'in' his possession; they are the recipients of his grace; he is the object of their love and faith, and their common individual and joint possession. In the present passage the same truth is expressed by the words 'in one spirit', except that, if anything, there is greater emphasis upon what God has done and is doing for them, to the virtual exclusion of the element of responsive love and faith.

In the balance of New Testament teaching, the Father is the great Architect of salvation, the Son is its Accomplisher, and the Spirit applies to the individual and to the church the benefits which the Father planned and the Son actualized.[3] In the light of this, when Paul speaks of their unity in the Spirit, he is directing attention to the blessings bestowed upon them by the Spirit who has incorporated them into the church,[4] regenerated them into new life,[5] and indwells them in the fullness of divine power.[6] Their unity is thus something which God has accomplished. It is a given fact about Christians, and as they view a hostile world and wonder about their ability – singly or together – to meet its assaults, Paul counsels: 'Remember what God has done for you; live and grow together in the good things which are your common possession in Christ.'

Paul now proceeds to speak of a *unity of heart and mind: with one mind*. The word translated 'mind' here (*psychē*) refers to the sphere of the affections and moral energies. It points to what we feel about things and how we react to them. It raises the question of what things we consider valuable and what constitutes a worth-while objective in life. It is a single description of that complex of heart, mind and will which is our

---

[3]*Cf.* Eph. 1:4f., 7, 13f.; Tit. 1:2; 2:11; 3:5.    [4]1 Cor. 12:13.
[5]Jn. 3:5; Tit. 3:5.    [6]Rom. 8:11.

experience of ourselves 'on the inside' day by day. In other words, Paul is calling them to *unanimity*, a oneness of emotion, decision and ambition. When Paul wrote these words he was not, himself, experiencing the benefits of a church animated by 'one mind'. Many Christians at Rome were very far from this sort of unanimity with Paul.[7] In that earlier passage he taught us that the reality of unity is something other than the feeling of oneness. He directed us away from the diversity of emotion to the singleness of the message. Yet unity without mutual love, common interests and agreed values could be as cold as a marriage of convenience. While it remains an essential unity, and has grasped that one thing without which there is no unity at all, it falls far short of that ideal which Paul holds now before the church at Philippi, as he urges, 'Strive also to feel for each other, to be one in emotion and desire and decision.'

Easily, now, he passes on to *unity in action*: *striving side by side*. The church which is experiencing unity must be a church without passengers. Is there unity where there is the tacit or spoken attitude, 'I agree with you but I will not do anything for you', or 'I agree with your aims but I will not go with you to fulfil them'? Acquiescence is not unity; consent is not co-operation; approval is not partnership; a *nem. con.* vote is not enough.

Finally, there is the fourth element in the unity which enables the church to face the world unmoved. It is *unity in the faith*: *the faith of the gospel*. This phrase is capable of two meanings. On the one hand, 'faith' could mean 'believing', and the call to the church is to strive together to bring others to believe in the gospel of Christ, the primary reference being to personal experience. On the other hand, we could understand 'the faith' as the body of belief in which the gospel is defined, and the call to 'strive for the faith' would be equivalent to 'strive for the truth'. But these two are not exclusive alternatives. They have a common denominator. Whether the church goes out to bring others to faith or is viewed as a body of people holding certain things as true, they are agreed as to what the gospel is. Before anyone can preach and invite others to believe, he must know what to preach. There is no agreement unless there is

[7]Phil. 1:15–17.

agreement as to what constitutes the gospel. Paul here returns, therefore, to the essential and definitive position adopted in verses 15–18. Indeed, he is doing no more than stress what the New Testament declares throughout, that the unity of the church is a unity in the doctrine and the experience of salvation.

## 2. Steadfastness issues in conviction

The united church is capable of a resolute stand against the most terrifying opposition. Paul, taking his teaching further, sees the Philippians as *not frightened in anything* by their *opponents.* The word translated *frightened* (*ptyromai*) is found only here in biblical Greek and denotes 'the uncontrollable stampede of startled horses'.[8] Against such an outcome of the encounter between the church and the hostile world, Paul writes a majestic emphatic (in Greek, double) negative: *not . . . in anything.*

Can this be true? It sounds unlikely, yet words could hardly be clearer. The world rises up in a display of opposition designed to put the church to total rout, but the church responds with a rock-like immobility – simply because it is a united church. The often lack-lustre tedium of interdenominational conversations would not quickly suggest that such a momentous matter was at stake; the readiness of many evangelical groups to hold aloof from a wider unity than their own small coterie betrays a similar lack of urgency. To be sure, Paul was addressing a local church and affirming that the power of a united local congregation will prove to be just what he promises here, but our Lord Jesus had wider ambitions along the same line when he prayed 'that they may all be one . . . so that the world may believe'.[9] Sadly we accept divided local fellowships as normal and world-wide divisions as standard – and then wonder why, for the most part, the church is steadily withdrawing from the opposing world!

But, says Paul, let the church face the world from a position of true unity, and conviction follows for both parties.

[8]Martin, p. 86.    [9]Jn. 17:21.

### a. The world sees its true spiritual state

*This* (the unmoved church) *is a clear omen to them of their destruction.* The problem of producing real spiritual conviction in the unconverted is a daunting one: it is a humbling exercise to estimate the ratio of the number of sermons preached to the number of souls won for Christ, or of the number of churches in our cities to the level of interest, never mind concern, for spiritual values in the general public. Paul sees the problem and offers a solution. He locates the problem in the church: is the church concerned for the glory of Christ and the honour of the gospel? Is the church experientially benefiting from its true inner unity in Christ? Is the church, consequently, facing opposition undaunted? It is from this spring that convicting power flows to challenge the world.

And a genuine conviction too! Not a passing impression but a real dawning of eternal truths, *a clear omen . . . of . . . destruction.* This is conviction indeed. So often the last bastion of hope in the unconverted is that somehow all will be well after death. The truth that will not be faced is the eternal judgment of God. It was the first ploy of the tempter to deny a God of judgment,[10] and human eyes remain sealed to this conviction until they are opened by a true spiritual conviction. We need not debate the issue of the nature of this judgment. Is it an endless, conscious separation from God or, as some hold, an 'annihilation', a total cessation of existence? It is, in any case, the opposite of salvation, an eternal and irrecoverable state, with God, hope, paradise, joy, satisfaction, fulfilment, gone for ever.[11]

Here indeed is conviction of sin: a person gripped by the awfulness of eternal loss. It arises from seeing a church

[10]Gn. 3:4.

[11]*Apōleia* is the opposite of 'life' (*zōē*) (Mt. 7:13–14); it expresses 'loss, waste, contradiction of proper use or purpose' (Mt. 26:8); every aspect of departure from Christ or siding with Satan, spiritual loss (Jn. 17:12; Acts 8:20; Rom. 9:22); the lot of those who are enemies of the cross (Phil. 3:19); the characteristic of the man of sin (2 Thes. 2:3); the result of denial of the atoning Lord (2 Pet. 2:1–3); a feature of the end (2 Pet. 3:7); as the fate of 'the beast' (Rev. 17:8, 11) it is equated with the continuing experience of the 'second death' (Rev. 19:19–20).

standing for Christ, standing for eternal things, enduring worldly loss and disrepute for the greater riches found in the Spirit and, throughout all, standing united.

### b. Christians see their true spiritual state

Assurance comes to the Christian from the same experience as brought conviction to the world: an *omen, . . . of your salvation, and that from God* (verse 28). Salvation here has the same comprehensive meaning which we noted in 1:19. It sums up all the blessings that are ours in the plan of God, through the cross of Christ and by the agency of the Holy Spirit. And the Christians to whom Paul speaks in verse 28 have come to the conviction that all these are theirs, and that some glad day they will consciously possess an immense spiritual wealth which now, though really possessed, is only partly experienced. What is it that brings this assurance?

It comes, first, from evidence of the reality of the work of grace. This is stated in the explanation in verse 29; the word *for* looks back to the word *clear omen*. You have a clear proof that salvation has come to you from none other than God himself, *for it has been granted to you that for the sake of Christ you should not only believe in him but also suffer for his sake.* The evidence which Paul offers here is twofold: believing in Christ and suffering for Christ. To believe is possible only through God's gift of faith, 'for by grace you have been saved through faith; and this is not your own doing, it is the gift of God'.[12] *It has been granted to . . . believe*, or as we may translate, 'It has been given freely and graciously as a favour of God . . . to believe on him.' But alongside this evidence, which surely we find clear enough, Paul places another evidence which we would hardly have considered in this light: 'God has given you grace to believe . . . also to suffer for his sake.' The suffering which comes to a Christian as a Christian, far from being evidence of divine forgetfulness (as we in our easy rebellion often understand it), is rather 'sign, omen and proof' of the

---

[12]Eph. 2:8. In Phil. 1:29, *granted* is the word *charizomai*, which contains the component of *charis*, 'grace', and ordinarily means 'to give graciously, freely'.

reality of the work of grace, for 'all who desire to live a godly life in Christ Jesus will be persecuted'.[13]

Christian confidence of salvation comes, secondly, from comparison with apostolic experience. When the Philippians are *engaged in the same conflict which you saw and now hear to be mine* (verse 30) they will know that their experience of the hostility of the world and of the ability to stand against it is one of the hallmarks of apostolic Christianity. The life worthy of the gospel of Christ could not be a sheltered experience for them any more than for him. Conflict would be the order of the day, but when out of conflict they purchased victory, standing in one Spirit, with one mind, jointly contending for the faith of the gospel, they would not only see that gospel eating with convicting power into the opposing world; they would also find the Spirit witnessing with their spirits that they were indeed the children of God, and if children, then heirs, heirs of God, joint heirs with Christ, now suffering with him, but soon to share his glory.[14]

[13]2 Tim. 3:12.    [14]Rom. 8:16f.

## 2:1-4

# 10. The worthy life

*So if there is any encouragement in Christ, any incentive of love, any participation in the Spirit, any affection and sympathy, ²complete my joy by being of the same mind, having the same love, being in full accord and of one mind. ³Do nothing from selfishness or conceit, but in humility count others better than yourselves. ⁴Let each of you look not only to his own interests, but also to the interests of others.*

There is always a blessing to be had from the word 'therefore' (RSV *so*, verse 1) in the Bible. It makes us stop and look back to the preceding cause before we move on to the ensuing effect.

Behind 2:1 lies Paul's discussion of the worthy life in 1:27–30. In that passage his concern was more with the fruits or effects of the worthy life – how it issues, for example, in the steadfast stand. When, at 2:1, he writes the word 'therefore', he is returning to take up the great theme again – the theme of worthiness.

A paraphrase of 1:27 – 2:2 will help: 'I have a single desire that your daily life should match the worth of the gospel. Without such a life you will never hold your ground against the world, strong in what God has done for you, unanimous, jointly working for your common faith. But such steadfastness has great results: it convicts the world and convinces you; it condemns the world; it confirms the church. Therefore make my joy full by being of the same mind . . .'

By this summary we see that the word 'only' in 1:27 is

repeated in another form by *complete my joy* in 2:2, and the *so* or 'therefore' links the two together. We see also what the central characteristic of the worthy life is: 'Only (1:27) . . . complete my joy by being of the same mind' (2:2). It is the life of unity.

Two things help us to feel how important this was to Paul, and if we can start by sharing his point of view it will lead us to a more urgent consideration of what he is teaching us. First, he has already dwelt on the topic of unity in 1:27 as the necessary equipment against a hostile world, but now he returns to it again. It was not enough to say it once; it must be said again, and said in a different way. For if 1:27 is all we are told about unity, then it is simply an aspect of Christian expediency, a tool for a task: unity in order that the world may believe. Paul's repetition of the subject not only underlines its importance but lifts it to a higher level: unity is not just a useful weapon against the world, but rather it belongs to the very essence of Christian life, for it is the way in which Christians display outwardly what the gospel is and means to them. Unity is the gospel's hallmark; it says to all who examine it, 'This life is worthy of the gospel.'

Secondly, Paul says, concerning the life of unity, *complete my joy*. What a man the apostle was! If we were in prison, chained, guarded, unjustly accused, vilified by those who ought to be our friends, with no comforts and no guaranteed future, what would our joy be? Paul's was first spiritual, secondly occupied with the welfare of others, thirdly engrossed in the topic of unity. 'I will need no further happiness,' he says, 'if only I can hear that you are a united church.' It may well be that he sensitively felt the damage and disgrace of the disunity at Rome (1:15ff.). It may well be that he dreaded further growth of disquieting features of Philippian life (4:2). Leaving all such speculations aside, what we are positively taught is this: the life worthy of the gospel is a life of unity; the life of unity matches the apostolic ideal for the church.

Needless to say, Paul meant a very specific sort of unity. It was not his way to leave abstract notions like unity without definition, and his procedure in the present case is typical of what he does many times over in his letters: first the facts and then the exhortations. Verse 1 gives us the facts, for the word 'if' does not imply uncertainty: Paul means 'If, as is certainly the case . . .'. He proceeds to declare four things which are true about every Christian and which lay a factual foundation on which the life of unity is raised up. The exhortations begin in verse 2 and are at first corporate, and then (verses 3–4) individual.

## 1. Christian oneness

Before the life of unity can be lived there are certain things which can be assumed as true about those who are to live at one. These things exercise a pressure upon those to whom they apply, urging them into united living with each other. In order to illustrate this, take as an example one of the four items. When he says 'if there is . . . any participation in the Spirit', or, better, RV 'any fellowship of the Spirit', Paul is saying this: 'the work of the Holy Spirit is to create a fellowship both between the believer and God, and between believers; if such a fellowship has been created in Philippi (and I know it has), then can you resist my appeal to live at one?' The fact of a divinely created fellowship carries with it the implication of a church at one with itself.

We note then, that the order of the first three items in the verse is the same as that of the 'grace' in 2 Corinthians 13:14, 'Christ . . . love . . . Spirit . . .' Indeed, the concluding phrase 'fellowship of the Spirit' is virtually identical. May it not be, therefore, that Paul is reminding the Philippians here of the great Trinitarian activity of salvation whereby they are 'in Christ', experience the reality of God's love, and have been woven into a fellowship of which the Holy Spirit is both Author and Indweller?

He separates this out into three strands and allows each one in turn to exercise its 'pull' on his readers. If they are in Christ, there is a 'comfort' or *encouragement* which they have experienced. If they know the love of God, they know the truest consolation and the gentlest *incentive*. If they have been made into a fellowship (RSV *participation*) by the Spirit, can they live in any other way than fellowship together?

Both of the words *encouragement* (*paraklēsis*) and *incentive* (*paramythion*) are full of gentleness in their New Testament

103

usage. They share the idea of a true 'concern', itself the product of love for the needy and productive of those words and deeds designed to lead folk out of their need into a fuller life. *In Christ* Christians experience the loving concern which has reached out to them in their need, which was unwilling that they should remain needy, and which gently invites and encourages into a new life. In the love of the Father, they have found deep consolation, the voice that speaks to their sorrows, the hand that touches their hurts. And, as Paul would have us see them, these blessings now encourage us to be to each other what God in Christ has been to each of us. This experience of the Son and the Father has come to us through the Holy Spirit, who is himself the eternal bond of fellowship within the Trinity. In Christ, he pours this aspect of the divine nature, fellowship, upon the church. To have received the gift of fellowship but to fail to exercise it must be a central denial of saving truth.

What, now, of the fourth item, *affection and sympathy*? In relation to each other, these words are root and fruit. *Affection* (*splanchna*) is the inner source of the emotions, equivalent to our use of 'heart' as the seat of feelings. *Sympathy* (*oiktirmos*) is the feelings themselves, emotions reaching out towards their object. Paul has, in fact, turned to the subjective side of salvation. The person saved by Father, Son and Holy Spirit is made, by them, into a new creature with a new heart and new sensitivities. This too spurs them on to a new life with new relationships and new possibilities of identifying deeply with each other: another motive and spring of unity.

In verse 1, then, the doctrine of salvation is stated in its classical Trinitarian form as the work of Father, Son and Holy Spirit. If people do not agree in their acceptance and understanding of this, how can they be at one? It is essential to speak of 'acceptance *and understanding*', for the emphasis on *mind* in verse 2 forbids us to say that people can be truly united simply because in some undefined way they look to the work of God – understood by both head and heart, grasped as truth and lived as life. For this reason, Paul could not let things rest until he brought them down to the individual and personal level of *affection and sympathy*. A true agreement in doctrine naturally flows out through emotions renewed through the saving work of God in Christ.

## 2. Christian unison

A trained choir can sing in unison, but for the average congregation with varied and indifferent musical talent, the task requires a more conscious dedication. Paul saw unity as a by-product of the great truths on which the gospel rests, but he did not see it as coming about automatically or effortlessly. It is 'natural' in relation to the gospel, but it will not 'come naturally' – only by effort, obedience and deliberate cultivation. For this reason, the truths of verse 1 lead into the exhortation of verse 2.

We are at once struck by the 'inwardness' of Paul's requirements. By contrast with 1:27, where he included 'striving side by side', he is here preoccupied with *mind* (twice), *love* and *accord*. These things involve the inner attitudes of the individual Christian. There cannot be true unity if there is inner antipathy.

Does this contradict Paul's earlier rejoicing that Christ was proclaimed even by those whose motives were wrong? Are we not saying here that without complete sanctification we cannot be one with each other? This is true. The fellowship and unity of heaven will transcend even the best that we can know on earth for the very reason that it will be the fellowship of the sanctified. Sanctification is our *aim* on earth but not our *solution*. We cannot say, 'If only he were more holy I could get on with him', for with equal truth he could say the same of me! Therefore the objective realities of the doctrine and personal experience of salvation must be in the forefront of our thinking about unity, and form the basis on which we strive for the deeper unity among ourselves.

Paul emphasizes a unison of *minds*: *of the same mind . . . of one mind*, literally 'think the same thing . . . thinking the one thing'. The priority task is agreement in the truth. But within this there is unity in *love*: *having the same love*. Note that he does not say 'loving the same things', but 'possessing the same love'. What can this be but a love identical with God's love, his own love bestowed on us so that we act and react as he would do? It is also a unity of *accord*. Literally we are 'like-souled'. The 'soul' is the 'real person' and particularly his affections and will. If we allow the word 'love' to cover the emotional aspect of the unity we are to enjoy, then *accord* can be allowed to stress the volitional side. Paul's vision of unity includes mind, emotions and will.

## 3. Christian harmony

A new feature appears in verses 3 and 4, which, although not absent from verse 2 as we shall see, was not explicitly mentioned. It is the word *each*, which appears in both verses in RV. We could not draw out the meaning of verse 2 without speaking of 'me' and 'him', and so on. Nevertheless the verbs remained plural and the individual was still an implication. Now the individual is in the centre of the picture. The responsibility for the worthy life of unity is individual, personal, mine.

Actually verse 3 has no verb and could well be taken in with the plural of verse 2, as in the RV, 'doing nothing . . .'. It is better, however, to take it as part of the statement of individual responsibility. In this case we find in turn a wrong attitude towards oneself in the realm of aims (*selfishness*, 'faction' or 'self-seeking'), and in the realm of assessment (*conceit* or 'vainglory'). This is followed by a correct attitude towards oneself in the realm of assessment (*humility*) and in the realm of aims (each looking *to the interests of others*, verse 4).

Looking back, we can picture Paul's teaching from 1:27 to 2:4 as an upturned triangle. The long line at the top is the place where the church faces the world, finds it hostile but yet stands fast. But this steadfastness depends on the strength of the 'legs' which support it, and they are not 'splayed out' for strength, but triangle-wise come to a point – the point of individual responsibility. Paul does not leave the question of the worthy life which produces the steadfast stand until he brings it to rest on the worthy life as it is found in the individual, not self-seeking and conceited but with a correctly humble estimate of himself, seeking the welfare of others and putting them first. Steadfastness depends on unity, and unity depends on me.

We have already seen that there must be agreement in the

doctrine and experience of salvation before there can be the manifested unity of living in fellowship. That is a valid comment on verse 1, but if we are to be fair to Paul's development between verses 1 and 4, we shall need to look again at the relationship between truth and unity. To do justice to Paul's thought we could re-order the statement. Where there is agreement in the doctrine and experience of salvation there must be unity – 'must' not in the sense of automatic outgrowth but in the sense of an obligation which cannot be evaded. Paul himself was strikingly committed to this obligation. In his imprisonment, with all its trials and uncertainties, his fullness of joy (verse 2) was that his Philippians were living worthy of the gospel he had shared with them. Calvin rightly comments on 'how little anxiety he had as to himself, provided only it went well with the church . . . Before his view were tortures, near at hand was the executioner, yet all these things do not prevent his experiencing unmingled joy, provided he sees that the churches are in good condition.'[1] But Paul's joy is not in the wellbeing of the church in general, but specifically in a church living the gospel life of unity in mind, heart and will, devoted to the task of unselfish mutual care. Calvin later speaks of 'the chief indication of a prosperous condition of the church. . .'[2] – when mutual agreement and brotherly harmony prevail in it.

[1]Calvin, *ad loc.*    [2]*Ibid.*

## 2:5–8
# 11. The mind of Christ

*Have this mind among yourselves, which is yours in Christ Jesus, ⁶who, though he was in the form of God, did not count equality with God a thing to be grasped, ⁷but emptied himself, taking the form of a servant, being born in the likeness of men. ⁸And being found in human form he humbled himself and became obedient unto death, even death on a cross.*

The story of the cross of Christ is told in each of the four Gospels; the meaning of the cross is the preoccupying theme of the epistles. But the present passage[1] uniquely unfolds the cross as seen through the eyes of the Crucified, and allows us to enter into the mind of Christ. We tread, therefore, on very holy ground indeed. We do well to remember that this privilege is given to us not to satisfy our curiosity but to reform our lives.

If a friend does something which puzzles us, we might ask

[1] It is agreed on all hands that 2:6–11 forms a hymn or poem. Two studies by R. P. Martin are specially helpful, *An Early Christian Confession* (Tyndale Press, 1960) and *Carmen Christi, Philippians 2:5–11 in Recent Interpretation and in the Setting of Early Christian Worship* (Cambridge University Press, 1967). The older work by E. H. Gifford, *The Incarnation* (Longmans, 1911), is full of insight, and among more recent work the relevant section in J.–F. Collange, *The Epistle of Saint Paul to the Philippians* (1973; E.T. Epworth Press, 1979) stands out. Specialists remain divided whether the hymn was composed by Paul or used here as an apt quotation on which he was prepared to set his apostolic imprimatur. As in all true poetry, every word is weighed but the thought is often allusive rather than spelt out in detail.

what it was that he 'had in mind' in doing it. It is in this sense that Paul uses the word *mind* in verse 5. What was it that seemed important to Jesus? What principles did he cherish? What objectives? On what footing were his choices made?

The revelation of the mind of Christ is presented here as the story of a *great change*. It begins with one who was *in the form of God* (verse 6), that is, one who possessed inwardly and displayed outwardly the very nature of God himself.[2]

As is plain, verse 6 is speaking of the Lord Jesus Christ before his incarnation. We must, therefore, use such ideas as 'display outwardly' with care, for we know nothing of the conditions of his heavenly state: all we can affirm is that in Christ Jesus there was 'that expression of being which is identified with the essential nature and character of God, and which reveals it'.[3] What a change is expressed in verse 8 when he who was in the form of God *became obedient unto death*! Wesley put it justly when he wrote:

'Tis mystery all! The Immortal dies![4]

Mystery indeed, but at the same time the testimony of the Bible. How it could happen we cannot know; that it did happen we are assured.

There is great stress on the fact that this change came about by voluntary decision and in this we begin to enter into the 'mind of Christ'. Verse 7 says he *emptied himself*, and verse 8, *he humbled himself*. In each case the reflexive expression points to personal decision and action. In the first case the order of words (himself he emptied) makes this even

[2]'Form', *morphē*, only here in the New Testament, but *cf.* the verb *morphoōmai*, Gal. 4:19, where it refers to the inner development and outward manifestation of the life of Christ in the believer. *Morphē*, says Collange (*ad loc.*), 'indicates a most profound and genuine identity'; Moule speaks of 'an appearance which is a *manifestation*' (*ad loc.*). Interestingly, in English, we use 'form' to point inwardly ('Are you in good form?') as well as outwardly.

[3]Vincent, *ad loc. Cf.* 2 Cor. 4:4; Col. 1:15; Heb. 1:3; *etc.*

[4]C. Wesley, 'And can it be ...?' *Cf.* Acts 3:15, 'killed the Author of life'; 1 Cor. 2:8, 'crucified the Lord of glory'; *etc.*

clearer, for 'the emphatic position of "himself" points to the humiliation of our Lord as voluntary, self-imposed'.[5]

While we must tread with humility in any matter to do with heaven and touching on the Holy Trinity, we have in this passage a phrase which appears to bring us right within the actual decision which the eternal Lord Jesus faced and made. We read that he *did not count equality with God a thing to be grasped* (verse 6). It is not easy to pin Paul's Greek here to any single meaning. There are legitimate varieties of meaning, and they must have been more evident to him than to us. So we may surely allow each to contribute to the fullness of truth he desired to share with us. At all events, the problem centres on the word translated *a thing to be grasped*.[6] This might mean, first, 'something to be held on to at all costs'.[7] In this case the treasure would be the possession of (literally) 'equal things with God', the Son's co-possession with the Father of the eternal, divine glory, that glory which, in his incarnate, earthly life he longed to have restored.[8] To us, lacking categories of mind to appreciate heavenly realities, all this is 'mere words'; but to him? To him a known and loved reality which he freely surrendered. Is this 'the mind of Christ': to take what is best, greatest and most desirable to oneself, and to abandon it, freely, in the interests of a more cherished purpose?

Two other possible meanings may be mentioned together: 'a position which could be exploited (for self-advantage)' and 'a thing to be grasped for self as a robber grasps after loot'. The suggestion, either way, is that the Son of God, before the incarnation, could have used his divine nature as a stepping-

[5]Lightfoot, *ad loc.*

[6]The word, *harpagmos*, occurs nowhere else in biblical Greek. *Cf. harpagē*, Mt. 23:25, 'extortion'; Heb. 10:34, 'plundering'; *harpazein*, Mt. 11:12; Jn. 6:15, 'take by force'; Jn. 10:12, 'snatches'; *etc.*

[7]Vincent (*ad loc.*) says that in Greek usage the noun *harpagma* often occurs with the verb *ēgeisthai* (*count*, verse 6), in the sense 'to clutch greedily'. Lightfoot offers 'to set store by', 'a prize which must not slip from his grasp'.

[8]Jn. 17:5. *Cf.* Jn. 5:18 where Jesus was seen to have 'made himself equal with God'. The wording is almost identical, except that in Jn. 'equal' is the masculine adjective, *isos*, *i.e.* 'an equal person', while in Phil. it is neuter plural, *isa*, *i.e.* giving 'the expression a more legal air ... the equality of two powers, two functions' (Collange).

stone to further glories over and beyond those he already possessed. Let us walk here with care and reverence. Questions will become us better than suggestions. Could the Son have been tempted to usurp the Father? Was there a glory of the Father which, as Son, he might have sought to possess?[9] Or could it have been rather that the Son of God, being by nature Lord of all, could have grasped after a public and acknowledged exercise of that Lordship in advance of the Father's plan? Could he have wearied of the 'incognito' imposed upon him throughout the 'Old Testament' centuries?[10] How humanly, feebly, we are forced to speak when we venture upon the mysteries of God! Whether in fact such a choice was ever presented, we do not know. But we do know that he chose self-emptying, self-humbling, deliberately setting himself on the path of self-denial. Is this 'the mind of Christ'?

Having cleared some of the ground in this way, we can now try to come to closer grips with verses 6–8 as a whole. The 'great change' which we noted above was brought about in two stages. The parallel expressions *emptied himself . . . humbled*

[9]The Scriptures teach a 'primacy' of the Father within the Holy Trinity: Eph. 1:3, he is the *God* and Father of Jesus; Jn. 20:17, he is 'my God' to the risen Lord Jesus; Mk. 13:32 notes a rising scale of being, 'no one . . . not the angels . . . nor the Son . . .', *i.e.* lack of this knowledge was not an earthly limitation but a fact within the Holy Trinity; *cf.* 1 Cor. 15:28; *etc.* Without supposing that Phil. 2:6ff. is based on the Pauline doctrine of the first and second Adam, the Adam of Gn. 3 can be used *illustratively* here. He too, in his way, was the son, image and glory of God (Lk. 3:38; Gn. 1:26; 1 Cor. 11:7); but, when tempted, he did in fact use his privileged position as a ground of self-advantage; being in the image of God he grasped as a robber after the chance to be 'like God' (Gn. 3:5) – and grasping, died. Christ, by contrast, refused to grasp for himself; rather he laid hold on death that we might live.

[10]This is an attempt to summarize Collange's helpful discussion (*ad loc.*). It fits in well with the revelation of the incarnate Lord, manifestly possessed of all power and might but exercising his power only in subjection to the Father's will, *e.g.* Jn. 11:42. Jesus exercises his power to raise the dead as an answer to his prayer to the Father; it fits equally well with the ultimate granting by the Father of a universally acknowledged Lordship in response to the Son's total obedience (Phil. 2:9–11). We may here use *illustratively* the Lord's earthly temptations (Mt. 4:1–11) to exercise power for self-advantage (verse 3), to display power for self-glorification (verse 6) and to achieve power other than under the divine uniqueness of the Father (verses 8ff.).

**111**

*himself* describe the central action in the two divisions of the poem.[11] By the end of verse 7 Paul has traced the course of the Lord Jesus to the point of his birth *in the likeness of men*; he then takes this as a starting-point (verse 8, *found in human form*) and follows the great downward course to the very point of death on the cross.

## 1. The eternal God becomes incarnate

When Paul says that Christ Jesus *was in the form of God*, that is, in full possession of the divine nature, he underlines the fact by using, not the simple verb 'to be', but a stronger verb which in its characteristic usage has the force 'to be really and truly', 'to be characteristically', even 'to be by nature'.[12] In a passage like the present one, where it is plain that every word has been weighed and measured, the full meaning of the verb can be assumed: he was really and truly, in his own personal and essential nature, God.

But, being so, he *emptied himself*. The very notion of 'emptying' inevitably suggests deprivation or lessening, the loss of something that was possessed before. When Jesus *emptied himself*, did he diminish himself, and if so, in what way? Here is a thought which must obviously be handled with great care.[13]

---

[11]Commentators are much exercised about the best analysis of these compelling verses. See especially Collange, pp. 83–86, and Martin, *Carmen Christi*, pp. 22–41.

[12]*Hyparchein*. The participle (*ta hyparchonta*) frequently means 'possessions' (*e.g.* Mt. 19:21; 1 Cor. 13:3), indication that in itself the verb does not mean 'to be' purely and simply, but 'to be (in possession of)'. Often it seems, however, to have only the diminished sense of 'to be' (*e.g.* Lk. 8:41; 23:50; 1 Cor. 11:18), but its special force is well exemplified: *e.g.* Lk. 16:14; Acts 3:2; 5:4; 7:55; see especially Acts 16:3, 20, 37; 17:24; also Rom. 4:19; 1 Cor. 11:7; Gal. 1:14; 2:14; Phil. 3:20.

[13]The verb 'to empty', *kenoō*, in its noun-form *kenōsis* (not found in the New Testament), gave a name to a defective understanding of the incarnation which developed in the nineteenth century, namely that 'at the Incarnation, Christ divested himself of the "relative" attributes of deity, omniscience, omnipresence, and omnipotence, but retained the "essential" attributes of holiness, love and righteousness' (Collange, p. 102). In its crudest form the theory held that Jesus became no more

It is helpful to note, in the first place, the fact that the verb 'to empty' in every other New Testament instance means 'to deprive something of its proper place and use'.[15] 'Christ, indeed,' says Calvin, 'could not divest himself of Godhead; but he kept it concealed for a time . . . he laid aside his glory in the view of men, not by lessening it, but by concealing it.' Or again, 'Kenosis', according to D. G. Dawe, 'says that God is of such a nature that acceptance of the limitations of a human life does not make him unlike himself . . . he is free to be our God without ceasing to be God the Lord.' Or, more specifically, if we follow through the interpretation of Collange mentioned above, 'the kenosis was a voluntary deprivation of the exercise of Lordship'.[16]

Secondly, we ought to notice that in asking the perfectly natural question, 'Of what did Christ Jesus empty himself?', we are, in fact, departing from the direct line of thought in this passage. For the verb *emptied* is at once followed by an explanatory clause, *taking the form of a servant* (slave). Our eye, in other words, is removed from the realm of mystery (the relation between the new incarnate life and the eternal divine life) and focused on the realm of historical factuality, the reality of the eternal God becoming truly man. It is not 'Of what did he empty himself?' but 'Into what did he empty himself?' While it must be pointed out that this way of putting it arises from the flexibility of the English verb 'to empty' and does not reflect the Greek use of *kenoō* in the New Testament, it nevertheless catches perfectly the movement of Paul's thought: Christ Jesus brought the whole of his divine nature, undiminished, into a new and – had it not been revealed to us in Scripture – unimaginable state.

than a first-century Jew; at its best, kenotic theology is a serious attempt to safeguard the reality of the human nature of the Lord Jesus. Wrestling with the immensity of the doctrine of the incarnation continues, evidenced more recently by the books *The Myth of God Incarnate*, edited by J. Hick (SCM Press, 1977) and *The Truth of God Incarnate*, edited by Michael Green (Hodder, 1977); but see especially E. L. Mascall, *Theology and the Gospel of Christ* (Darton, Longman and Todd, 1977) and J. N. D. Anderson, *The Mystery of the Incarnation* (Hodder, 1978).

[14]*kenoō*: Rom. 4:14; 1 Cor. 1:17; 9:15; 2 Cor. 9:3.

[15]Calvin, *ad loc.*; D. G. Dawe, 'A Fresh Look at Kenotic Christologies', *Scottish Journal of Theology* 15 (1962), pp. 337–349; Collange, pp. 101f.

Yet it may be that 'Into what did he empty himself?' is not all that far, if far at all, from Paul's thought. The parallel between *he emptied himself* and Isaiah's word concerning the Servant of the Lord, that 'he poured out his soul to death',[16] is too plain to be resisted. The fundamental thought is that of a deliberate, conscious consigning of oneself to a foreseen situation: the Servant of the Lord brought himself voluntarily and totally into death; Jesus, in order to die, first brought his total being down to the condition of the Lord's Servant.[17]

Concerning the state to which the Lord Jesus consigned himself, Paul makes three points. First, the intention of the great change was obedient service; he took the form of a slave. Secondly, the sphere in which the service would be discharged was that of a true humanity; he was *born in the likeness of men*. Thirdly, his true humanity 'left room' for that other reality which he brought with him. It was a true humanity: Paul uses again the word *form*, already discussed; but this time of the slave-state. The Son became the reality of a bondservant. None of this reality is taken away by the careful phrase *in the likeness of men*: 'this leaves room for the other side of his nature, the divine, in the likeness of which he did not appear. His likeness to men was real, but it did not express his whole self.'[18]

Throughout all this there is the same revelation of the 'mind of Christ'. His are the eternal glories, both by nature and by right, but they are not a platform for self-display, nor

---

[16]Is. 53:12.

[17]For a discussion of the relation between Phil. 2:7 and Is. 53:12, Collange (pp. 100f.) refers to J. Jeremias, art. 'Pais', *TWNT*, V, pp. 654–717; he also notes the difficulty raised by G. Bornkamm that it cannot be proved that 'servant', *doulos*, refers to the Servant of the Lord. But if it is not a reference to the Lord's Servant, why is it there at all? There is no other way of making a link between the incarnation and the idea of a servant. If no reference to Is. 53 is intended, would not the poem read *morphēn andros labōn* instead of *morphēn doulou*?

[18]Vincent, *ad loc. Likeness, homoiōma*: for a similarly exact usage, see Rom. 8:3. J. A. Bengel, *Gnomon of the New Testament* (E.T. 1857) comments: 'Form (*morphē*) speaks of something absolute; likeness (*homoiōma*) speaks of the relationship to other examples of the same kind; fashion (*schēma*, v.8) refers to appearance.'

a launching-pad for self-advancement; they are all for self-denial. Self is something to 'pour out'.

## 2. The incarnate God becomes a curse

The story continues in the same vein. By the end of verse 7 a true incarnation has taken place, and at this point Paul picks up the narrative. Christ Jesus was *found in human form* (verse 8),[19] that is to say, those meeting him felt themselves to be in the presence of a man. They could say, 'Is not this the carpenter?'[20] How exactly true their observation was, but, equally, how much they missed! Well might Isaiah say, 'To whom has the arm of the Lord been revealed?' (53:1) – or, as we might paraphrase, 'Who would have believed, were it not revealed by God, that this is the Lord himself come down to save?' Notice how Paul says (verses 5–6) that it was *Jesus* who existed before the incarnation and possessed the very nature of God – but Jesus is the name of 'the carpenter'! The pre-existing and the incarnate Son of God were one and the same person:

> Lo, within a manger lies
> He who built the starry skies.[21]

He seems the same as other men but in fact is vastly different. The question therefore is, what will he do with this 'difference'? Will he use it as an occasion for self? Will it, in turn, become 'a thing to be grasped'?[22] Maybe this is the reason why the Lord spoke to Moses and Elijah on the Mount of Transfiguration of 'his departure, which he was to accomplish at Jerusalem'.[23] For, having received the plaudits of these two

---

[19]It is most unfortunate that RSV adopts here the translation 'form', inevitably confusing this with the entirely different word (*morphē*) in verses 6–7. NIV 'appearance' is more exact; *cf.* RV 'fashion'. See Bengel's comment above, note 18. The word *schēma* is 'the external appearance of the incarnate Son as he showed himself to those who saw him "in the days of his flesh" ' (Martin, *An Early Christian Confession*, p. 27). *Being found*, *i.e.* by any who chanced upon him or happened to meet him. The verb underscores the idea of the observer's view of the incarnate Son.
[20]Mk. 6:3.    [21]E. Caswall, 'See, amid the winter's snow'.
[22]See above on verse 6, and the note on our Lord's temptation, note 10 above.    [23]Lk. 9:31.

great prophets and the accolade from the Father himself, he could surely have chosen to step back into the personal glory of heaven.

What he did was, however, very different. He chose rather to take upon himself that one thing which, without his consent, had no power against him, death.[24] He was distinct from all others because of his divine nature. In particular, he possessed immortality, proper to God alone.[25] But he subjected his immortality to death and thus humbled himself; nothing has now been held back; all has been given up:

> Even his garments they parted
> When he hung on the cross of shame.

Paul tells us that this was done as an act of obedience to God. The English *obedient unto death* suggests 'obeying death', but the Greek cannot bear this meaning. It requires rather 'obedient as far as or right up to the point of death'.

Death was the mode, not the master, in his obedience; the obedience was yielded to his Father: this was 'the cup which the Father has given me'.[26]

Furthermore, the obedience which he rendered to God also achieved a purpose for man: it was *death on a cross.* Just as it was necessary to appeal to other scriptural evidence to establish that the obedience was a service offered to the Father, so here also Paul is using the succinct, allusive forms of poetry, not writing an itemized doctrinal thesis. When we ask why he proceeds from the fact of death (*obedient unto death*) to the mode of death (*death on a cross*), we must look elsewhere to discover what he intended. But the explanation is not hard to find. From one angle, the reference to the cross enhances the thought of his obedience, for 'cursed be everyone who hangs on a tree'.[27] Our Lord's cry of dereliction[28] shows how truly he entered into the place of rejection and with what horror he was enfolded in so doing: he who was in the form of God came down to earth, down to the

---

[24]Jn. 10:18.    [25]1 Tim. 6:16.    [26]Jn. 18:11.    [27]Gal. 3:13.
[28]Mt. 27:45–46.

cross, down to the curse – and he did it for us, for me! 'Christ redeemed us from the curse . . . having become a curse for us.'

> Though he was rich, so rich,
> Yet for our sakes how poor he became!
> Even his garments they parted
> When he hung on the cross of shame.
> All that he had he gave for me,
> That I might be rich through eternity.[29]

Finally, this Godward-manward act was undertaken by the will and consent of the Lord Jesus himself. No-one else did it: *he humbled himself.* This feature, so central to Philippians 2:6–8, must find its root in Isaiah 53, especially verses 7–9, where for the first time in the Old Testament we meet with a *consenting* sacrifice.[30] All through the long years of animal sacrifice the Lord had driven home the lesson that in the divine purposes there could be a transference of sin and guilt from the head of the guilty to the head of the innocent. Whenever a sinner brought his animal to the altar and laid his hand on the beast's head[31] the lesson was plain: this stands in my place; this bears my sin. Yet the substitution was incomplete, for the central citadel of sin, the will, was left unrepresented in the uncomprehending, unconsenting animal. Isaiah foresaw that only a perfect Man could be the perfect substitute and that at the heart of this perfection lay a will delighting to do the will of God.[32]

[29]E. H. Swinstead.

[30]Is. 53:7 offers a Hebraic equivalent to the 'himself' of Phil. 2:7–8. *nigas w<sup>e</sup>hū' n<sup>ca</sup>neh w<sup>e</sup>lō' yiptaḥ piw* (verse 7) . . . *al lō' ḥāmāṣ 'āsāh w<sup>e</sup>lō' mirmāh b<sup>e</sup>p̄iw* (verse 9). 'He was afflicted/ (tolerative niphal) he allowed himself to be afflicted and he on his part humbled himself and did not open his mouth . . . though he had done no violence (*i.e.* to anyone else) and no deception was in his mouth.' Verse 9 insists that there was neither public crime nor personal defect to justify his death; the reflexive verbs of verse 7, driven home by the emphatic pronoun ('he for his part'), bring out the voluntariness of the pro-ceeding; the unopened mouth represents the continuing element of self-restraint whereby at no point did he seek to hinder the progress of events. He was brought 'as a lamb', but unlike every lamb that ever was he came by conscious consent and voluntary decision.

[31]The recurring act of Lv. 1:4; 3:2; 4:4; *etc.* is explained in the central Day of Atonement ceremony in Lv. 16:21–22.

[32]*Cf.* Ps. 40:6–8; Heb. 10:4–9.

117

This was the 'mind of Christ'. He looked at himself, at his Father and at us, and for obedience' sake and for sinners' sake he held nothing back.

# 2:9–11
# 12. Responses, divine and human

*Therefore God has highly exalted him and bestowed on him
the name which is above every name, ¹⁰that at the name of
Jesus every knee should bow, in heaven and on earth and
under the earth, ¹¹and every tongue confess that Jesus Christ
is Lord, to the glory of God the Father.*

We are oddly choosy as Christians. Most of us would count
it odd not to celebrate Christmas Day in some form or
other, even though we know that the day itself is somewhat
arbitrarily fixed – and that by an ecclesiastical authority
which by no means all of us would recognize! Likewise we
do not let Good Friday and Easter Day pass unnoticed. But
Ascension Day? Did I hear you ask, *'Is* there an Ascension
Day?'

The Bible, however, makes much of the ascension of our
Lord Jesus;[1] not least the wonderful passage now before us.
We will, therefore, start by assembling the facts, using as a

[1]Jesus foretold it (Lk: 22:69; Jn. 7:33f.; 8:21; 14:1–4; 16:5–10); the
event is described (Lk. 24:50f.; Acts 1:9–11); it is referred to (*e.g.* in
Heb. 1:3; 9:12, 24; 10:12; *cf.* Lk. 24:26; Acts 5:31; 7:55f.; Eph. 4:10;
Col. 3:1; 1 Pet. 3:22); associated with the sending of the Holy Spirit
(Jn. 7:39; 16:7; Acts 2:33); the giving of gifts to the church (Eph. 4:8,
11); the certainty of our heavenly home (Jn. 14:1–4); Christ as our
Forerunner (Heb. 6:20) and his intercession for us (Rom. 8:33f.; Heb.
9:24); his role as Priest-king, hearer of prayer and bestower of grace
(Heb. 4:14–16); *etc.*

framework the five questions, Who, what, how, why and to what end?

## Jesus from beginning to end

The question 'Who?' might seem to be needless because, of course, the subject of the ascension was Jesus. The answer is correct but inadequate. The passage we have just studied (2:6–8) reveals first a pre-existent Jesus, a 'Jesus before Bethlehem' who was truly and fully God (verse 6); then, second, a Jesus who, without ceasing to be truly and fully God, became truly man (verse 7); furthermore, he experienced death and, in particular, a death of shame and rejection on a cross (verse 8). From beginning to end there was continuity of person, for it was *Christ Jesus* (verse 5) who was *in the form of God*, just as, at the other end of the process, it was *Jesus* (verse 10) who received *the name which is above every name* (verse 9) and to whom *every tongue* will yet *confess* (verse 11). One of the most practical truths of the ascension arises, as we shall see, from this observation.

## A value-judgment

*What* happened at the ascension? We must remind ourselves that we often express value-judgments – good and bad – by the words 'up' and 'down'. The schoolchild reports proudly, 'I am going up next term'; the erstwhile undergraduate admits he was 'sent down'; people go up and down in our estimation; the chosen few are 'elevated' to 'high positions'. Do we then imagine that our sons and daughters attend schools with the youngest on the ground floor and the eldest several storeys above? Do we draw the conclusion that all universities must be on hill-tops? Neither do we look on the narrative of the ascension as drawing a map of the universe, with heaven 'up there', earth here and hell beneath.[2] The great God is expressing a value-judgment about his Son: nothing will do but that he should be lifted up to the highest of all, for, in the Father's eyes,

---

[2] In so far as the ascension 'draws a map' it tells us that heaven is 'away', not here but elsewhere.

he is the highest of all. Therefore, before the eyes of chosen witnesses[3] the Father gave visible demonstration of his estimation of Jesus: that he is Lord of all, heaven, earth and hell alike, that his deity is unquestionable, for he is worshipped in heaven where none can be worshipped but God only, and that he has now emerged from incognito into his full and acknowledged possession of the divine name and Lordship.[4] The historical, physical event of the ascension is a moral and spiritual comment on Jesus.

### God in action

*How* did this event happen? *God . . . highly exalted him* (verse 9).[5] A passage like Hebrews 4:14 can speak of Jesus passing through the heavens, so to speak, by his own power and volition – as, indeed, he had every right to do. But the present passage says that the ascension was the act of God, and, as we learn elsewhere, not an act performed in haste or as a 'snap decision', but at the end of forty days:[6] a very deliberate, divine action.

### The divine response

But now, *why*? Why did God so lift Jesus up? According to our passage it was a response, something linked to what went before it by a *therefore* (verse 9). To what was God responding? A specific answer, calling attention to the *death on a cross* (verse

[3]The factuality of the event is guaranteed by observers and Luke underlines this in his narrative by using five different expressions for visibility and eye-witness experience in Acts 1:9–11.

[4]Comparison of Phil. 2:9–11 with Is. 45:22f. shows that it was the name 'Lord' (*i.e.* the revealed name of God, Yahweh) which was accorded to Jesus, not in the sense of 'conferring' what was not his before, but of calling attention to what he was and is now known to be.

[5]*Cf.* 1 Pet. 1:21.

[6]Acts 1:3. There are those who hold that the narratives of the resurrection and the ascension are stories told to express the mind of the church regarding Jesus. Apart from the fact that it is extremely odd to affirm events which you know not to have happened, the biblical claim is that the events express, not the assessment of man, but the mind of God.

121

8) would be biblical,[7] but not sufficiently accurate for this passage. For here death on a cross is but the last event in a continuous sentence which began in verse 5 with 'the mind of Christ'. The ascension is the divine response not to this or that aspect of the career of Jesus, but to the sort of person Jesus is, the way he looks at things, the values he cherishes, the principles he observes – his 'mind'. He was not grasping in relation to his glory (verse 6), defensive in relation to his deity, protective of his unique human experience: he *emptied himself* (verse 7) and *humbled himself* (verse 8). From the brightness of the glory to the dust of death and the place of the curse, from the glory of a true humanity down to the lowliest identification with our common clay, by his own self-humbling decision, Jesus showed both obedience and love to the uttermost. And the Father loves to see it so, for it is a principle with God that he who humbles himself shall be exalted.

## What shall it be when the King comes?

*To what end* is all this leading? Plainly, it is leading to the universal banishment of all that is 'incognito' about the Kingship of Jesus. In one of the great hymns of years ago we used to sing, 'Oh, the crowning day is coming, Is coming by-and-by . . .'.[8] It is exciting to sing, but factually not true! Jesus was crowned the day he ascended.[9] The crowning day has happened, it happened long ago! Yet so pitifully few know about it. The lovers of Jesus know it and rejoice, but the world's millions do not know that Jesus is King. But they will, on the day when the King comes.

On that day, *every tongue* will *confess that Jesus Christ is Lord* . How do we keep the succinctness of this poem in touch with the rest of Scripture at this point? By sadly recording that a confession made for the first time in response to the visible manifestation of his glory will not be a saving confession, but a grudging acknowledgment wrested by overmastering divine power from lips still as unbelieving as they were through their whole earthly experience. All will submit, all will confess, but not all will be saved.

[7]Heb. 2:9.     [8]El Nathan, 'Our Lord is now rejected'.
[9]Note the past tenses in verse 9; *cf.* Rev. 5:6–14.

### One Lord, one task, one life

These, then, are the facts which surround and open up the ascension of our Lord Jesus. So what, we may ask, does the ascension say to us?

First, and most clearly of all, the ascension proclaims the present reality of a reigning Lord. His exaltation has been long since achieved and remains true today. Among the millions who do not know this, we do know it. Jesus is Lord and King. According to the passage before us, there is a proper response to such a reigning Lord, for on the day when he is manifested in all his glory there will be something about that glory which will provoke, unbidden by anything save the glory itself, the bending of the knee in submission and the loosing of the tongue in confession (verses 10–11). It is by our homage gladly rendered and our spoken declaration of his name and nature that we, in our present situation, give evidence to all that he reigns and that we are his people.

Secondly, the ascension, as Paul has presented it here, speaks to us of the limits set to evangelistic opportunity. When the Master returns it is the day of accounting, not of continuing opportunity; it is the day when the door is shut; the day when eternal destinies are apportioned.[10] In the most telling of all phrases it is the day when books are opened[11] and when those whose names are not found in the Lamb's book of life stand before the throne, with nothing else to shield or cover them but the robe of the character fashioned by their deeds on earth, as those deeds have been recorded in heaven. Then, too late, they will find that death has wrought no marvel of transformation, but that, on the contrary, those who here held the Lord Jesus at arm's length will there do nothing else and will want nothing else; the filthy will be filthy still and the God-rejecting will reject for the last time. Not then but now is the appointed time, now is the day of salvation – nearer than when we first believed both in the bliss it brings to believers and the disaster it carries for the unbeliever. All that stands between our present unsaved friends and that dread day are our tongues telling about Jesus.

[10]Mt. 25:19; Lk. 19:15, 27; Mt. 25:10, 46.    [11]Rev. 20:12.

Not, of course, that our tongues work alone. The Bible's teaching about the God who is ceaselessly at work to bring to Christ all whom he would save belongs to other places in Scripture. Here the effective complement to the testifying tongue is the knee which bows before him, indicative of a life given to obeying him. What form should such obedience take? The third truth of the ascension emerges here: there is a way of life which bears the hallmark of divine approval. We noted above the continuity of the person of Jesus through the whole great career which took him from heaven's glory to Calvary and on to the supreme height. He is there, supremely exalted, because through it all he was the same – the one who, out of obedience to God and love for sinners, said 'No' to everything that might have been advantageous to self. He never ceased to look upward to the Father, seeking his approval, and outwards to others, seeking their eternal welfare. He held nothing back if, by yielding it up, he might more fully obey God and save the lost.

We return, then, to the point from which this great passage started: *Have this mind among yourselves, which you have in Christ Jesus* (verse 5) – the mighty description of the 'mind of Christ' (verses 6–8) is given both in order that we might know the life which matches our new nature and also in order that we might set ourselves to copy him.[12] For when the disciples of old did not know the way ('We do not know where you are going; how can we know the way?'), Jesus thought it sufficient to open his reply by saying, 'I am the way.'[13]

[12]Commentators follow one or other of these possibilities. For example, K. Grayston (*ad loc.*): 'Think this way among yourselves, which also you think in Christ Jesus, *i.e.* as members of His church . . . this attitude of mind . . . they are to have in their personal relations because it is the only attitude proper to those who are "in Christ".' And we might add, it is the attitude intrinsic to the new nature imparted 'in Christ': hence the words of J. I. Packer commenting on this passage (in an unpublished exposition), 'Identify with your new nature.' On the other hand the passage must at least also contain (even if it is not its first meaning) the interpretation espoused by Collange (*ad loc.*): ' "Behave this way among yourselves: for this is how it was in the case of Christ Jesus." '

[13]Jn. 14:5f.

# 13. Working it out

*Therefore, my beloved, as you have always obeyed, so now, not only as in my presence but much more in my absence, work out your own salvation with fear and trembling; [13]for God is at work in you, both to will and to work for his good pleasure.*

*[14]Do all things without grumbling or questioning, [15]that you may be blameless and innocent, children of God without blemish in the midst of a crooked and perverse generation, among whom you shine as lights in the world, [16]holding fast the word of life, so that in the day of Christ I may be proud that I did not run in vain or labour in vain. [17]Even if I am to be poured as a libation upon the sacrificial offering of your faith, I am glad and rejoice with you all. [18]Likewise you also should be glad and rejoice with me.*

God's 'therefore' (verse 9) is matched by the Christian's *therefore* (verse 12),[1] and that, in a nutshell, is what this passage is about. Just as God assessed and then reacted to the worth of his Son's life of obedience (verses 9–11), so the Christian must ponder the example of Christ and determine upon a worthy response (verses 12–18).

Behind the Christian's 'therefore' we note, first, that, in verse 4, Paul was stressing the crucial importance of right relationships between individuals within the church fel-

---

[1]The Greek words are different (verse 9, *dio*, 'therefore, wherefore'; verse 12, *hōste*, 'so then'), but the effect is the same.

lowship, for otherwise the church could never stand firm before a threatening world. At that point (verse 5) he adduced Christ, not only as our new life but also as the exemplar of the new life in practical terms. All this Paul recalls in the *therefore* of verse 12. He says, in effect, 'Let me tell you how to react if the great goal of wholesome relationships in the likeness of Christ is to be reached.' Thus we learn from the Bible not only what is true but also how to respond to the truth; not only what is the example of Jesus but also along what lines to make it real. Let us therefore sense the proper seriousness of what lies in front of us in 2:12–18, for Christlikeness is the Christian's greatest concern, and here is the procedure for attaining it.

Turning now to review verses 12–18, there is an obvious division between verses 12–16a (. . . *word of life*) which are full of *directives*, and verses 16b–18 which are concerned with *incentives*. But there is more to verses 12–16a than a list of commands; it is also a list of reassurances. There is a balance created between what we are to do and to strive to be and, on the other hand, what is already true of us. By statement or implication the directives are 'Obey', 'Work' (verse 12), 'Do' (verse 14), 'Be blameless', *etc.*, 'Shine' (verse 15) and 'Hold fast' (verse 16). The reassurances are 'God is at work' (verse 13), 'You are God's children', 'You are lights' (verse 15). This is the balance and testimony of the verses: the Christian life, growing in the likeness of Christ, is a blend of rest and activity – not alternating from one to the other, but a blend in which, at one and the same moment, the Christian is both resting confidently (for example, on what God is doing within) and actively pursuing (for example, the duty of being blameless). Let us try to see this in some greater detail.

## 1. Christian activity and the indwelling God

There is a worker in each of these verses: the Christian 'working out' in verse 12, and God 'working in' in verse 13.[2] This points to a blend, as we noted above, of commitment to what

[2]The neat contrast between 'out' and 'in' is more a coincidence of English idiom than an absolute requirement in the Greek. Nevertheless it does no violence as a translation, and could not be more accurate in balancing the teaching of the verses.

we have to do and reliance on what God is doing.

The work of the Christian carries the marks of obedience, responsibility and sensitivity. The emphasis on *obedience* comes first. In verse 12 Paul starts by looking back – obedience has *always* been in evidence in their lives; the words *as in my presence* carry the implication that were he now with them he would be looking for the mark of obedience just as he used to; *much more in my absence* creates the impression of a duty which not only belongs to all future time but becomes more important as the years pass. It stands to reason that it should be so, for the task of the Christian is to be made in all things like the Son of God who took his obedience even as far as death, death on a cross (verse 8).

Secondly, it is a *responsible* work in the sense that we are called, ourselves, to shoulder responsibility for seeing that the work gets done: *work out your own salvation* (verse 12). The care of the individual soul belongs to that individual; responsibility for personal spiritual growth is committed to the person – not at this point a work of God nor a work of the fellowship, but a work of individual responsibility, laying hold of grace, rejoicing in the benefits of fellowship. *My* responsibility for *me*.[3]

Thirdly, our work it to be *sensitive*: *with fear and trembling.* Is this a sensitive awareness of the preciousness of the salvation given to us, resulting in a trembling concern lest we fail to live up to our privileges and to enjoy the richness of the divine benefits? Is it a sensitivity towards other members of the

---

[3] *Your own salvation* is to be understood, not as an objective yet to be reached, certainly not as a benefit to be merited, but as a possession to be explored and enjoyed ever more fully. The proper models are the command of a schoolteacher to a class to 'work out a problem' – *i.e.* the problem (*e.g.* in mathematics) is possessed but waits to be unravelled; or the counsel to a newly-married couple to 'work at your marriage', for marriage once possessed is possessed in full but merits a lifetime of exploration, enjoyment, development and discovery. Translations like that of the Jerusalem Bible 'Work for your salvation' must be resisted, not because the verb (*katergazomai*) will not bear it but because the noun (*salvation*, here *sōtēria*) will not permit it. Reference to a concordance (Saviour, *sōtēr*; salvation, *sōtēria*, *sōtērion*; salvific, *sōtērios*; save, *sōzō*) will show that the New Testament position is accurately summarized by the affirmations of Eph. 2:4–8 and the negative safeguards of Tit. 3:4–5.

Christian fellowship towards whom, and for whose welfare, we are to *work out* those virtues of unself-regarding service which marked the life and ministry of Jesus? Or is it sensitivity towards God? For although

> The terrors of law and of God
> With me can have nothing to do[4]

there is a fear of God of which we know all too little and which we lose at our peril – a godly fear, growing out of recognition of weakness and of the power of temptation; a filial dread of offending God. This is not the fear of a lost sinner before the Holy One, but the fear of a true child before the most loving of all fathers; not a fear of what he might do to us, but of the hurt we might do to him. This last area of sensitivity is the deepest and would secure the values of the other two, for there is no failure in the lives of those to whom the Lord has given his full salvation which does not pierce directly to the throne of heaven.

We now turn to the other side of the coin. Our work, as obedient, responsible, sensitive believers, arises out of the internal work of God: *work*, says Paul, *for* ('because') *God is at work in you.* His is the basic activity; ours responds to what he is doing. His is the inner work of transformation and renewal; our obedience to him is how we enter into the benefit of his indwelling.

In the close-packed teaching of verse 13, the indwelling of God bears the marks of activity, effectiveness, completeness and free divine choice. Taking these in order, we note first that *God is at work*: he is *active*. Doubtless we have all heard sermons on the possibility of (say it reverently) 'neutralizing' the presence of God within. Christ was in the boat, but Peter took the helm and Jesus slept! We must never forget this side of the truth, or become insensitive to the moral and spiritual conditions on which we enjoy the indwelling presence of God. But, over against all that, there is the great, encouraging truth that God will never let his people go; he is always at work; he never sleeps; he is tirelessly active. We forget, he does not; we

[4]A. M. Toplady, 'A debtor to mercy alone'.

backslide, but we cannot halt, defer or deflect his work. He is the *active* indweller.

The note of *effectiveness* is sounded by the verb which Paul uses (*energeō*) and which characteristically describes work which achieves its purpose; the outcome is guaranteed in the deed. The verb is defined later in this same letter (3:21) when, using the related noun, Paul speaks of the 'effective working' (RSV 'power') by which he is able to subordinate all things to himself. God's working is effectual working: he cannot be deflected from his course nor fail to achieve his purpose. With our daily catalogue of failure and our not infrequent despair of ourselves, what unspeakable comfort lies in this truth!

The sense of comfort is enhanced when we turn to note the element of *completeness* which now emerges. In every action there are two aspects to be considered: the will and the deed, and one or other of these is often our downfall. Either we cannot bring ourselves to choose what we know to be right, or else, having chosen it, we fail to do it. Sin has corrupted both the power to choose and the power to accomplish. But God is effectually and ceaselessly *at work in you, both to will and to work* – to recreate our wills and to impart to us his own capacity for effectual working. For the same word is used: the effectual Worker would make us like himself.[5]

It is important to ask why he does it. If he works only where he finds a promising response, or if only where there is evidence of progress, or if only when we really desire him to do so, then none of us can entertain any hope of reaching the great goal. But it is not like that. He does it because he wants to. It is of *free, divine choice: for his good pleasure*. Nothing, then, can stop the ongoing divine work.

> The work which his goodness began,
>    The arm of his strength will complete;
>  His promise is Yea and Amen,

---

[5] This verse thus completes a trio of verses revealing that our salvation is all from God. In 1:29, the faith we placed in Christ was God's gracious gift. In 1:6, God's activity guarantees and brings about the completeness in Christ at which we aim. In 2:13, the divine Indweller is ceaselessly at work in the period between the beginning we remember (1:29) and the end we wait for (1:6).

> And never was forfeited yet.
> Things future, nor things that are now,
> Nor all things below or above,
> Can make him his purpose forgo,
> Or sever my soul from his love.[6]

Moses had a word for it which has never been bettered: 'It was not because you were more in number than any other people that the LORD set his love upon you and chose you . . . but it is because the LORD loves you.'[7] He loves you because he loves you! It is no explanation, and yet it is the greatest of all explanations, for it means that, though the reason is hidden from us, it is a reason which makes sense to him. He will never give us up.

## 2. Christian character and the outshining light

The opening words of verse 14 come like a shock of cold on a hot day. Paul's emphasis (verse 13) on the totality of the work of God has not prepared us for a command that we should *do all things*! Yet this is the scriptural logic which has been set out in principle in verses 12–13. Our obedience is the way we enter, in experience, into the totality of what God is doing in us. Since he, therefore, is doing all, we must *do all*: it is our total response to his all-sufficiency.

Though not so frequent today, the voice is by no means silent which calls Christians to an effortless sanctification based on some inner experience of God. The slogan 'Let go and let God' used to be popular, and found expression, for example, in the words of F. R. Havergal:

> Holiness by faith in Jesus,
> Not by effort of thine own.[8]

This is wholly contrary to the biblical mind. The new nature is ours by gift of God, but the activation of that new nature in terms of new character and new conduct is through the respon-

---

[6]A. M. Toplady, 'A debtor to mercy alone'.     [7]Dt. 7:7f.
[8]F. R. Havergal, 'Church of God, beloved and chosen'.

sive work of obedience, the hard graft of the daily warfare.

But another surprise awaits us. Having commanded us to *do all things*, Paul does not specify anything which we are in fact to do! He does not outline a *course* of action but calls for a *kind* of action: *without grumbling or questioning*; he does not specify a rule of life but a sort of person: *blameless . . . innocent . . . without blemish*; he focuses attention not on social involvement but on social contrast: *a crooked and perverse generation, among whom you shine as lights.*

We note, therefore, first, the outward display of an inner nature (verses 14–15a, . . . *without blemish*). The ungrumbling, unquestioning conduct of the Christian has an aim: *that you be* (better 'that you may show/prove yourselves to be') *children of God.* The great glory of Christian ethics is that it calls us to be what we are. *Children of God* describes neither wishful thinking, nor a fond hope, nor a target for supreme endeavour, but a present reality waiting to be worked out in our conscious, responsive behaviour. The Father has begotten us by his own will;[9] we are the sons whom he has brought to glory by his Son;[10] we are partakers of the divine nature,[11] as is the right of children. What, then, are we to do about it?

If it is the glory of Christian ethics to summon us to be what we are, it is one of the glories of Holy Scripture both to tell us what we are (*children of God*) and to declare our characteristic way of life. The *do all things* is thus not the expression of a Pauline whim but an authoritative exposition of the proper outgrowth of the life of God in the child of God. Just as it 'comes naturally' to our children first to crawl and then, not to crawl better, but to stand upright and walk, so there is a 'natural' expression of the life of God which we are to cultivate by deliberately adopted conduct.

There are three sides to it. First, the characteristic conduct of the child of God is *without grumbling or questioning*. *Grumbling* may be justified, but the example of the word in Acts 6:1 is a warning to us that when grumbling starts we are walking on thin ice. Nowhere does the self-centred heart of man more quickly take control than through the machinery of criticism and the promptings of self-interest. The word as used

[9] Jn. 1:12; Jas. 1:18.    [10] Heb. 2:10.    [11] 2 Pet. 1:4.

in the New Testament usually has an ethically bad sense: selfish complaining, unbalanced criticism of small matters, impatience towards what is not understood, grudging unwillingness to be helpful[12] – all expressed outwardly.[13] By contrast *questioning*[14] is wholly inward – an attitude and activity of mind and heart corresponding to the outward display of *grumbling*, so that the two words taken together cover all our actions towards others and our thoughts about them. Paul's use of the plural in each case makes his prohibition all-embracing: 'without carping, self-centred criticisms *of any sort*, whether spoken or silent.'

Secondly, Paul turns to something positive and personal: the child of God is to be *blameless and innocent*. The first word refers to a comment someone else might pass, and means 'above reproach'; and the second to a comment one might make upon oneself, knowing as we do our own inmost hearts, 'without any admixture (of evil)'. Just as, on the one hand, the Christian is not to entertain a carping criticism of others, so by the way we live we are to remove all cause of just criticism against ourselves. Does it matter what others think of us? Certainly it does! For Paul makes us accountable for seeing that no-one should have good cause to condemn us. And this applies equally to our hearts as they come under our own scrutiny. *Blameless* speaks of the unmixed goodness of character, the wholly clear conscience[15] of the true child of God.

The remaining dimension of the life of the child of God is the most searching of all. We call it, for convenience, the spiritual dimension, because it is concerned with how we appear before God. We are to be *without blemish*. This is what God had in mind when, in eternity, he chose us in Christ;[16] it is what, in the end, he will accomplish;[17] it was the perfection of the Passover lamb,[18] and is the unblemished character of Christ[19] – the character and life which not even the holy God himself can find

[12]Mt. 20:11; Lk. 5:30; Jn. 6:41; 1 Pet. 4:9.

[13]Noun *gongysmos*, *cf.* Jn. 7:12; verb *gongyzein*, *cf.* Jn. 6:61; 1 Cor. 10:10; another noun, *gongystēs*, is found in Jude 16, 'grumblers'.

[14]Noun *dialogismos*, *e.g.* Mk. 7:21 ('evil thoughts'); Lk. 5:22; 6:8; 9:46–47; Rom. 1:21; *etc.*; verb *dialogizomai*, *e.g.* Mk. 2:6; Lk. 3:15. The meaning is good or bad according to context.

[15]Acts 24:16; 1 Tim. 1:19.       [16]Eph. 1:4, 'blameless'.

[17]Eph. 5:27.

[18]Ex. 12:5.       [19]Heb. 9:14; 1 Pet. 1:19.

cause to criticize. Again, it is part of God's gracious salvation to us who 'have been sanctified through the offering of the body of Jesus Christ once for all';[20] and, again, it is appropriated as we become in experience what we are by grace, unremittingly living the life of obedience to which the saved are called.

Thus Paul sketches the outward display of an inner nature. But now (verses 15b–16a) he turns to his second theme in these verses: the discharging of a responsibility. He speaks of the setting in which the Christian lives (*in the midst of . . . among whom*), of the contrast between the Christian and that setting (*shine as lights*) and of the means by which the contrast is achieved (*the word of life*).

'Light' is a beautiful illustration of something that does what it has to do by being what it ought to be. It is therefore very appropriate in Paul's argument in these verses. Responsibility for the world around, outreach, making an impact, telling others about Jesus – these thoughts are entertained only after he has laid a foundation of Christian personal holiness. Like the light we must 'be' if we are to 'do'.[21]

We are not told anything specific about the world-darkness in which the light is to shine. The description *crooked and perverse* comes from the LXX of Deuteronomy 32:5, a general phrase for people turning away from the Lord and finding other gods. It is tempting to make *crooked*, 'bent', refer to activities, and *perverse*, 'distorted', 'topsy-turvy', refer to values. But it would not be safe to be over-specific: the world is astray from the true God, living the upside-down life of those who do not believe. By contrast, the Christian both 'holds fast' *the word of life*, just as a lantern hold within itself some radiant element, and also 'holds forth' *the word of life*, just as from a lantern a bright outshining dispels the surrounding darkness.[22]

[20]Heb. 10:10.

[21]*Lights* (verse 15): *phōstēr* has two meanings: a. the outshining of light, radiance (Rev. 21:11); b. a light-bearing body (LXX Gn. 1:14, 16); classically, a 'lantern'. Both meanings can be held together here in Philippians. The Christian is a 'radiance', an outshining of light; but also a 'lantern', holding and gleaming with a light imparted from elsewhere.

[22]No New Testament use helps us to decide between 'hold fast' and 'hold forth'. The verb is *epechein* (cf. Lk. 14:7; Acts 3:5; 19:22; 1 Tim. 4:16). Classically it is used of offering food or wine to somebody.

The *word of life* has thus two distinct sides. It is the message which both tells of life and also imparts the life of which it tells. It stands broadly for the total message of the Scriptures,[23] and specifically for 'the word of truth, the gospel of your salvation'.[24] Without this life-giving word Christian character is impossible. But at the same time, the light of Christian character is an uninterpreted parable if we do not speak about Christ. Equally, speaking about Christ is futile if our lives do not back up what we say.

It is important to see why Paul brings his teaching to this point of the inner light whose radiance shines out in the darkness. The brightest and most glorious light was that of Jesus, who, though he was in the form of God and equal with God, brought his light into this poor world for the sake of sinners beneath the curse. It is the very life of Christ which the life-giving word imparts to us. This life must have its way, shining out into *a crooked and perverse generation*, exposing and condemning, illuminating and transforming. Testimony is part of becoming Christlike.

### 3. Christian incentive: the day of Christ

The Christlike life, then, is a life of work, character and testimony. When the Lord Jesus lived out his distinctive life he had the encouragement of the joy that was set before him,[25] and Paul does not leave us without the encouragement of the forward vision as we seek to imitate our Saviour.

First, he shows us the intrinsic worth of the life he has outlined. He refers to *the sacrificial offering of your faith* (verse 17). The word *offering* points to our status as priests. We have no animal oblations to bring but we do have a sacrifice, appointed by God and acceptable to him.[26] The sacrifice of a life of obedience, character-building, holiness and witness – the life

---

Hence Moule, *ad loc.*: ' "holding out" . . . as those who offer a boon . . .'; Collange (paraphrasing) 'holding up the light to a world of darkness'. *Cf.* Kent (opting for both meanings): 'Those who hold out the word to others are understood to have first received it themselves.'

[23]*Cf.* Jn. 5:39; 2 Tim. 3:15.    [24]Eph. 1:13; *cf.* 2 Thes. 2:13–14.
[25]Heb. 12:2.
[26]Rom. 12:1; Eph. 5:1.

to which our *faith* prompts us. This is our priestly service to God.

Secondly, Paul encourages in following Christ by expressing his own apostolic approval of this sort of life. He has a forceful way of putting this in verse 17. We must remember that his imminent death was at this time a distinct possibility.[27] He speaks of it here as his being *poured as a libation*. The word refers to the 'drink offering' of the Old Testament. The regulations for this part of the sacrificial system are not absolutely clear, but we can at least say that the drink offering was the accompaniment of a larger sacrifice; it was the small thing which brought a major offering to completeness.[28] Paul says that he would count it nothing but joy that he had 'laboured to weariness' (for this is what the word means in verse 16), if by this means he can 'put the finishing touch' to their appointed sacrifice of work, character and testimony. He could hardly have rated more highly the life to which he calls them.

But he has, none the less, a still higher value to express. For, thirdly, he encourages us on our way by showing that the life of Christ-imitation is acceptable before Christ himself in the day of his coming. Paul looks forward to the joy that will be his when Christ returns (verse 16), if only his Philippians have held on to the course which he has outlined for them. Could he rejoice if Christ had to rebuke them at his return, if there was no 'Well done'?[29] But what joy will be his if and when he beholds Christ's favour towards them and approval of them! And the road towards that day and to a joyful standing before Christ at his appearing is this road of obedient work, patient pursuit of a holy character, and shining testimony to a dark world.

[27]Phil. 1:19ff.  [28]*E.g.* Nu. 15:8ff.  [29]Mt. 25:21; Lk. 19:17.

# 14. Model Christians

*I hope in the Lord Jesus to send Timothy to you soon, so that I may be cheered by news of you. [20]I have no one like him, who will be genuinely anxious for your welfare. [21]They all look after their own interests, not those of Jesus Christ. [22]But Timothy's worth you know, how as a son with a father he has served with me in the gospel. [23]I hope therefore to send him just as soon as I see how it will go with me; [24]and I trust in the Lord that shortly I myself shall come also.*

*[25]I have thought it necessary to send to you Epaphroditus my brother and fellow worker and fellow soldier, and your messenger and minister to my need, [26]for he has been longing for you all, and has been distressed because you heard that he was ill. [27]Indeed he was ill, near to death. But God had mercy on him, and not only on him but on me also, lest I should have sorrow upon sorrow. [28]I am the more eager to send him, therefore, that you may rejoice at seeing him again, and that I may be less anxious. [29]So receive him in the Lord with all joy; and honour such men, [30]for he nearly died for the work of Christ, risking his life to complete your service to me.*

In the wonderful variety of the Bible, we come from the deep and reverent picture of the Lord Jesus Christ, with which Philippians 2 opened, to this homely picture of three outstanding Christians with which it closes: Paul, disclosing himself by implication, and Timothy and Epaphroditus, whose characters he sketches as he commends them to the church. But the beginning and ending of the chapter, though contrasted, are not unconnected. What Paul was inspired to imply about himself and to state concerning the other two reveals them as men who have taken the example of the Lord seriously. The Lord so consecrated himself in obedient service to God that he poured himself out for the benefit of others. They so consecrated themselves to God that self was subdued in the service of other Christians. The Lord is the Christian's model; they are model Christians.

## 1. Paul and Timothy: father and son in Christ

These verses are a veritable window into the heart of Paul. He was a complex man. From other passages we know that, when necessary, he could stand on his proper dignity as an apostle of Christ, and on this issue he would brook no contradiction, or allow his authority to be diminished. In Philippians, however, we find, not a different Paul, but another facet of the same Paul. His proper dignity and authority as an apostle who could 'magnify (his) ministry'[1] is divorced from self-assertive haughtiness. The two things went together in a completely harmonious personality: the dignity and exaltation of office, and the humility and self-forgetfulness of one who modelled himself upon Jesus Christ.[2]

One turn of phrase in verse 22 aptly reveals this. Paul is speaking of Timothy, and offering proof of his excellence as a Christian. They are like father and son together. If we could close our eyes for a moment to what we know is written here, and try to predict what the parallelism requires, it would come out like this, 'as a son serves a father, so he served me'. They were father and son together. The one was the natural leader, the other the natural subordinate. But Paul does not say, 'so he served me'. To do this would be to exalt himself, to make himself a man to whom others ought to be subordinate. He says instead, 'so he served *with* me'. We were 'co-slaves'.

The idea of 'slavery' introduces, and at the same time sums up, Paul's attitude towards the Lord Jesus Christ, the slave's attitude of obedience. It is displayed in this passage in three

[1] Rom. 11:13.    [2] 1 Cor. 11:1.

ways. First, Paul was submissive to the Lord's ordering of his life. Concerning the proposed mission of Timothy (verse 19), he expresses *hope in the Lord Jesus*; and in verse 24, concerning his own future, *trust in the Lord*. One is a small matter – whether Timothy can go or not; the other is comparatively much more important – whether Paul lives or dies, whether he lives as a prisoner or as a free man. Each alike is resigned to the Lord's overruling. The extent of Paul's submission to the will of the Lord is especially seen in the second. Once more may we try to imagine what Paul might have said here? 'I trust in the justice of Roman law that I shall be released, for after all there is no real charge against me'; or, 'I trust in my position as a Roman citizen.' But he says neither of these. From the Roman court, he appeals to the highest court of all, the throne of God; from any assertion of personal prestige, he resigns to the authority of his Lord. Paul's *doctrine* taught him that a sovereign God rules all things: freedom, imprisonment, comfort, discomfort, sickness or health. Paul's *practice* was to accept without question what the Lord ordained. It was the Lord who had appointed him an apostle, and the same Lord would ordain the sphere and conditions of apostleship, be it the old free-roving commission to the Gentile world, the restrictive limits of a Roman jail or the sentence of death.

Secondly, Paul submitted to the Lord for service. Submission did not carry implications of inactivity, as when a defeated army submits and is consigned for the duration of the war to prison camp. Paul's was the submissiveness of obedience, submitting to do the Lord's will. And so, along with Timothy, he 'slaved for the gospel', matching the example of Christ who 'took the form of a slave'.[3] Those who are his must accept his pattern. The Lord Jesus became a 'slave' for obedience' sake to his Father and carried his obedience as far as death in order to serve us with the blessings of salvation; Paul's slavery was directed upwards towards Jesus in perfect obedience and outward to people in the slavery of the gospel. Obedience and evangelism are the normative poles of Christian slavery.

Thirdly, Paul obeyed the Lord Jesus by taking him as his example in his relationships with other people. Jesus took the

[3]Phil. 2:7, margin.

form of a slave and was made in the likeness of men as part of his pouring out of himself for the benefit of others. It was the same for Paul: his slavery to Christ issued in his self-forgetful regard for other folk, here seen in his relationships with other Christians. We do well to dwell on this, for (so it seems) it is possible to be devoted to the cause of Christ, the spread of the gospel, the winning of the outsider and the amelioration of the lot of a hungry world, and yet to fall down in our attitudes and actions towards other Christians. But Paul saw his Christian friends at Philippi as worthy of the best he had to give. He gave them Timothy, the man who was in a class by himself (verse 20) and who seems to have occupied the central ground in Paul's affections in a way no other did. The words were easily written, *I hope in the Lord Jesus to send Timothy to you*, but they were costly to put into effect. The same point comes out in Paul's willingness to send Epaphroditus back to Philippi. His own love and need for Epaphroditus is plain in verse 27, but the happiness of Epaphroditus himself (verse 26) and of the Philippians (verse 28) were overriding considerations.

We turn now from this incidental portrait of Paul to a carefully drawn sketch of Timothy. Once again the continuity between the example of the Lord Jesus and the true life of the believer comes out clearly. Both for the Lord and for Timothy the pre-eminent man (verses 19–22), consecration to God issued in service to the people of God.

*I have no one like him*, says Paul. The words may refer to Timothy's personal uniqueness: this suits the context, for Paul proceeds to bring Timothy into contrast with *all* who *look after their own interests*. On the other hand, the words may mean 'I have no one else who is so like me' – and this, too, suits the context, for Paul goes on to describe their happy unanimity in a father-son relationship. Or, again, Paul may have intended to say that he had no-one else so suited to the task in hand. This, too, would lead into what follows: Timothy *will be genuinely anxious for your welfare*.[4] If Paul was aware of this rich possibility of meaning (and surely he must have been), then Timothy well deserves the title of pre-eminent.

---

[4] The word which gives rise to such possibilities is *isopsychos*, lit. 'of equal soul', and it occurs only here in the New Testament.

In the first place, Timothy possessed a *genuine care for other Christians*. We might translate the latter part of verse 20 to say that he will be 'naturally and genuinely painstaking' for your welfare. The word *genuinely* contains the idea 'as a birthright', something possessed by spiritual parentage.[5] There was nothing forced or artificial about Timothy's concern: it was the genuine product of a regenerate nature and found expression in a true anxiety. The strength of this word can be felt by noting that it is used to describe both the excessive worry which beset Martha and the weight of care necessarily carried by Paul.[6] Timothy was a proper child of his spiritual father.

Secondly, we learn that Timothy *outstripped all in his devotion to the Lord Jesus*. The *all* of verse 21 must be taken as a generalization. It could not, for example, include Epaphroditus, who plainly put Jesus first. But what a sad generalization it is! The general run of Christians, as Paul saw them, put themselves first and Jesus next. But it was not so with Timothy.

The third mark of Timothy's character was his *ungrudging acceptance of second place: as a son with a father*. Paul, as we have seen, softened the relationship by the gentle way in which he said *served with me*, putting himself alongside Timothy in slavery for the gospel. But even so Timothy's subordinate place is clear. In terms of slavery he was a second-class slave. His task was to be a second-in-command. And he was ready for it to be so. He never usurped.

The fourth feature is implicit in what has just been said, but may be mentioned for completeness. Timothy was *a slave for the furtherance of the gospel*. He, with Paul, stands in the succession of him who took 'the form of a slave'. He was a person whose whole life was given to the gospel; but who accepted and obeyed its total claim upon himself.

But these four aspects of Timothy are not simply four

---

[5]See especially Lightfoot and Vincent. Collange insists that the word means 'legitimate', *i.e.* Timothy was the only one possessing a valid mandate from Paul to minister to the Philippians. But the possession of a paper-qualification like this would not make a proper contrast with those who look after their own interests. We need a reference to Timothy's personal qualities, not his official authorization.

[6]Lk. 10:41; 2 Cor. 11:28.

separate items. They are one whole, and the passage makes them identical. Verses 20–21, by the parallelism involved, equate being *genuinely anxious for your welfare* with 'looking after the interests of Jesus Christ'. Putting this positively, a Christian displays his pre-eminent devotion to the Lord Jesus by seeking the true welfare of others. It is necessarily so, for the Lord Jesus displayed his total obedience to God by pouring himself out wholly for others. Had he not done so, his consecration would have remained theoretical, if not hypothetical. Timothy was like his Lord.

In the same way verses 21 and 22 are linked together. The facts mentioned in verse 22 are the proof of the position adopted in verse 21: 'Do you wish to have proof of Timothy's pre-eminent devotion to the Lord Jesus? Here it is: he slaved in the furtherance of the gospel.' Thus, just as verses 20-21 identified seeking the good of other Christians with giving the prior place to the interests of Jesus Christ, so verses 21–22 identify giving the prior place to the Lord Jesus with being a slave for the gospel's sake. And this, in consequence, is the portrait of the pre-eminent Christian, cast in the apostolic mould and useful for the work. He puts the Lord first by seeking the spiritual good of others through a sacrificial gospel ministry.

## 2. Paul and Epaphroditus: brothers in Christ

Paul was not, as far as we know, bound to Epaphroditus by the special tie which bound him to Timothy, namely, that he had led him to Christ. Paul had been a proud Pharisee, and Epaphroditus at one time would have been no more to him than a Gentile 'dog'. But Christ had brought them into a relationship of true emotion (verse 27), perfect brotherhood and co-operation in the work (verse 25).

The relationship pictured here between Paul and Epaphroditus and the incidental revelation of Paul's attitude towards the Philippian church as a whole amplify what we have already noticed in Paul's relationships with other Christians. We saw that he was ready to give the best he had. But this was no merely formal copying of Jesus; it was not a detached exercise in dutifulness; his heart was full of *warm affection,*

141

*ungrudging praise and true concern.* Warm affection is implied in Paul's heartfelt outburst over Epaphroditus' narrow escape from death (verse 27). He expresses ungrudging praise when he heaps word upon word in his appreciation of Epaphroditus whom he loves as a *brother*, acknowledges as a colleague and welcomes as a *minister* (verse 25). His true concern shows itself in the words *eager* and *less anxious* in verse 28.

None of this is automatically true of Christians. We do not always love one another; nor are we always ready to acknowledge one another as *fellow workers* and *fellow soldiers*. We sometimes look on each other with suspicion; we hold aloof, fearful of guilt by association with those purchased by the same precious blood; we refuse to pray with those who call upon the same precious name. There are Christians who begrudge the gifts God has given to others and are afraid that praise deserved by a fellow Christian might threaten their own prestige. All too often self-concern dulls our hearts to the needs of the church. Our eagerness (verse 28) is directed to self-advancement, and our anxiety diminishes only as our personal security increases. The apostolic standard – which is the standard of Christ – is a target we have not yet reached and one which we are not always concerned even to hit.

Paul will soon say, 'Join in imitating me' (3:17). His unwitting self-portrait here is plain: he was deeply humble; he submitted his energies to the Lord; and he put the church's needs before his own. If the Lord Jesus is the Christian's model, then Paul was a model Christian. But what of the praiseworthy Epaphroditus? *Honour such men*, says Paul (verse 29). When we find the same lessons repeated we should recognize the Holy Spirit's insistence. Scripture does not repeat truth for the sake of filling up space, but to give it emphasis. And so now, for the third time, we are to be brought face to face with a man in whom the example of Jesus Christ shines, a man whose consecrated devotion to Christ was evident in the way he served other Christians and worked to spread the gospel.

In relation to other Christians Epaphroditus was marked by the fellowship he offered to them, by placing his gifts at the disposal of the church, and by his concern for their good. Paul found him a *brother and fellow worker and fellow soldier*. We do not wish to snatch at small indications of character and magnify them into something Paul did not intend, but, none the less, these three descriptions point to a man of harmonious disposition. Had he been a quarrelsome, nagging, restless person, ready to pick out faults and quick to criticize, he might still, in Christian charity, have been called a worker and a soldier, but he would not have been awarded those titles 'fellow worker, fellow soldier'.

Then, again, he was the one the church singled out as their messenger, and Paul commends him for the way he discharged his task. He was *your messenger* (verse 25), the one who completed the church's service of the apostle. We will dwell later on the whole-hearted way he accomplished his service, *risking his life to complete your service to me.* That phrase teaches us much about the man, but here it shows specially that he did not begrudge placing his gifts at the disposal of the local church. In the group of Christians with whom he was associated, he had the name for being trustworthy and willing. They were content to commit their trust to him, and he was ready to carry it out.

But he carried out this work in a very committed manner. It was not just a job to be done. He almost lost his life in his zeal to minister on the Philippians' behalf to Paul (verse 30), and this warm-hearted, self-forgetful regard for other Christians made him almost demented (verse 26). The word translated *distressed* (*adēmoneuō*) is used of the Lord's deep trouble of spirit in the garden of Gethsemane[7] and always denotes a strong perturbation.[8] This was provoked in Epaphroditus by the simple fact that they were anxious about him! Far from feeling gratified that he was the centre of attention back at home, it drove him to mental torment that he was being a worry.

Behind his sensitivity towards others there is his fundamental consecration to the Lord Jesus. In his service, he was a *worker* and a *soldier* (verse 25), no passenger. Effort, endurance and loyalty marked him – the effort of the work, the endurance and loyalty of the soldier. As a result *he nearly died for the work of Christ* (verse 30). Literally, 'he drew near to death'. In the Greek, the words 'to death' are identical with

[7]Mk. 14:33.    [8]Lk. 10:41; 2 Cor. 11:28.

'unto death' in 2:8. Epaphroditus was following in the great succession. The additional words *risking his life* tell us more of the man. The verb (*paraboleuomai*) occurs only here in the New Testament, but was elsewhere used as a gambling term. We might say that he took a calculated risk which involved the expenditure of all he had, his very self, in response to the worthiness of Jesus.

Well might we honour such a man; and well might we wish to be like him. But, indeed, that is the purpose of the portraits given here of Epaphroditus, Timothy and Paul. The grace of God had been at work in them. The effectual work of the indwelling God (verse 13) was changing them, in will and deed, into the likeness of the great Servant, the Lord Jesus Christ. They were varied characters, with varying gifts and diverse temperaments; their backgrounds could not have been more dissimilar; but they were each coming to resemble the Saviour; they loved him and followed his example.

What was true of them can be true of us; God has not changed.

## 3:1-3

## 15. Anger and joy

*Finally, my brethren, rejoice in the Lord. To write the same things to you is not irksome to me, and is safe for you.*

*²Look out for the dogs, look out for the evil-workers, look out for those who mutilate the flesh. ³For we are the true circumcision, who worship God in spirit, and glory in Christ Jesus, and put no confidence in the flesh.*

Is it justifiable for a Christian to be angry? Are controversy and argument a permitted activity for Christians? We can be both unduly sensitive and culpably insensitive on these matters. On the one side differences of opinion are regarded as a blot upon 'the fellowship' and therefore ought to be suppressed; and on the whole it is this attitude which prevails in the majority of Christians, and much offence is taken if any suspicion of heat enters into our discussions. On the other hand, there are those who pride themselves on 'speaking their mind', and whose virtuous regard for truth is often indulged to the detriment of the 'affection and sympathy' which should characterize our new nature in Christ.

Speaking broadly to this topic we see in the New Testament that there is a justifiable anger, but that its display is hedged about with warnings. James does not forbid anger when he says, 'Let every man be . . . slow to anger', but he hastens to warn that 'the anger of man does not work the righteousness of God'.[1] Likewise Paul, in a passage which dwells notably upon

[1] Jas. 1:19f.

145

sins of speech and the need to eradicate them,[2] admits that anger
has a place in the life of the Christian: 'Be angry.' But how
swiftly he adds, 'but do not sin; do not let the sun go down on
your anger.' It is as though he was erecting a warning sign at the
entrance to a dangerous path. Anger is always trembling on the
verge of sinfulness.

Sometimes Paul himself could be fired to controversy,[3]
especially when 'the truth of the gospel' was threatened. In this
regard his indignation is to be measured by the word 'accursed'
which he uses against those who preach another gospel. The
importance he attached to defending the true gospel is seen in
his opposition to Peter: 'I opposed him to his face'. In the cause
of the truth there can be no partiality. Neither is there room for
back-door tittle-tattle, smear campaigns or second-hand
dealing; there should be open, person-to-person encounter
before witnesses. The truth of the gospel must be known,
preached and defended and its opposite recognized, rejected
and opposed.

The same situation gave rise to the explosive material in the
opening verses of Philippians 3. The wording takes us by
surprise: *dogs . . . evil-workers*. They stand in pointed contrast
with the gentle and joyous language which characterizes this
letter, so much so that some commentators have urged that
having just started on what we call chapter 3 Paul was interrupted by news that old opponents of the gospel were at work
in Philippi. There is, however, no need of this hypothesis. The
matter can be explained smoothly and in sequence.

At 2:17f. Paul was dwelling on the topic of joy, but at that
point it was the shared joy of believers. He has more to say on
the subject and so, having paused to outline his plans touching
on Timothy and Epaphroditus, he now resumes his theme: 'To
proceed, then, brethren . . .' (3:1).[4]

[2]Eph. 4:25ff.    [3]See Gal. 1–2.

[4]Not 'Finally', as in so many translations. From the adjective *loipos*
('the rest/remainder of . . .') three adverbial usages arose: *to loipon*,
*loipon*, and *tou loipou*, all with the basic meaning 'as to what remains',
hence 'additionally', 'furthermore', 'from now/then on', 'to proceed',
*etc.* There is no place in the New Testament where the translation
'finally' is required, though it is plainly the most suitable translation in
2 Cor. 13:11 (*loipon*), where 'all that remains' to be said is also the
apostle's last word: in other words, the translation 'finally' is required,

The command which Paul gives in 3:1 acts as a bridge between what he has taught and what he is about to teach. Jesus has been glorified as God, Saviour, Example and Lord. So then, *rejoice in the Lord.* He is about to be displayed as the Christian's pride, choicest possession, ambition, pattern, possessor, the crucified and coming Saviour.[5] Should we not, then, *rejoice in the Lord*? The command may be understood better in the light of a similar phrase in 1:18. There Paul wrote, concerning the preaching of the gospel, 'in that I rejoice'. He meant, 'This is what brings joy to me' – this, and not that he should be well thought of by all, not that he should be released, and so forth. 'It is in this that I find my joy.' Similarly the command *Rejoice in the Lord* means, 'Let the Lord be the one who makes you happy,' 'Find your joy in him and in him alone.' The command is relevant, as we shall see, to the controversy into which the apostle plunges as he takes issue with those who would add to Christ other factors and conditions as necessary to salvation. This is the first and greatest threat to a true joy in the Lord. Or, to put the matter positively, the first secret of a joyous life is this: if we are to rejoice in the Lord, then we must be certain that we are holding and practising the true religion. Paul lays considerable emphasis on the importance of this teaching. Not only does he place it first, but (verse 1) he has previously dwelt on it, and he sees in it something that will be for the 'safety' of the Philippians: 'I do not find it irksome to return to old topics with you; indeed your safety requires it.' There are, in fact, three items which he says he is reiterating: a warning, 'Look out'; an assurance, 'for we are . . .'; and a definition, 'who worship . . . glory . . . and put no confidence'.

## 1. An assurance

It is striking that Paul, the great opponent of the retention of circumcision for Christians (*cf.* Acts 15), should choose this

---

not by the word used but by the place where it is used. For *to loipon*, see, *e.g.*, 1 Cor. 7:29 ( ('for what (time) remains . . .'); Phil. 4:8 ('Beyond that . . .'; 'In addition'); *loipon, e.g.* Acts 27:20 ('from then on . . .'); 1 Cor. 1:16 ('Beyond that . . .'); 2 Tim. 4:8 ('For the future . . .'); *tou loipou, e.g.* Gal. 6:17 ('From now on . . .').

[5]Phil. 3:3, 7, 8, 10, 12, 18ff.

particular way of asserting his assurance that he and the Philippians were in the right as against those whom he calls *the dogs. We*, he says, with deliberate emphasis, *are the true circumcision.* He could not have chosen a more suitable, biblical or instructive word.

In the first place, he meant that 'we are the covenant people of God', for circumcision was introduced into Abraham's family, and thence passed on to Israel, as a mark of the special relationship which God had established with them. It distinguished the covenant people.[6] This idea of a 'covenant' is the greatest of the unifying themes of the Bible. It is mentioned first to Noah[7] as that which preserves him from the calamity which overwhelmed his contemporaries. It comes to fuller flower in God's dealings with Abram,[8] when we are permitted to see that the covenant rests upon a sacrifice which God appoints.[9] It is embodied in the sign of circumcision,[10] and is the basis on which God was moved to save his people from Egypt.[11] It reaches its fullest flowering through Moses and the redemption from Egypt, for it is specifically the people who were redeemed by the blood of the lamb[12] upon whom God bestows covenant status and seals the relationship with blood at Mount Sinai.[13]

The covenant became the basis of prophetic predictions of the glorious future of God's people. Isaiah foretold an eternal 'covenant of peace'[14] wrought by the Servant of the Lord upon whom 'the chastisement of our peace' was laid.[15] Jeremiah looked forward to a 'new covenant' resting upon such a settlement of the sin-problem that God says, 'I will forgive their iniquity, and I will remember their sin no more.'[16] Ezekiel saw that there would come 'a covenant of peace . . . an everlasting covenant' of which the central blessing would be the eternal dwelling of God in the midst of his people.[17] The Lord Jesus brought this glorious sequence of prophecies to its climax: 'On the night when he was betrayed (he) took bread, and when he had given thanks, he broke it, and said, "This is

[6]*Cf.* Jdg. 14:3.    [7]Gn. 6:18.    [8]Gn. 15:18.    [9]Gn. 15:9–17.
[10]Gn. 17:10ff.
[11]Ex. 2:24; 6:2–8.    [12]Ex. 12.    [13]Ex. 24:4–8.    [14]Is. 54:10.
[15]Is. 53:5.
[16]Je. 31:31–34.    [17]Ezk. 37:26–28.

my body which is for you. Do this in remembrance of me." In the same way also the cup, after supper, saying, "This cup is the new covenant in my blood . . ." '[18]

When Paul says *we are the circumcision* he is claiming for himself and the Philippians the privilege of being the undoubted heirs of this age-long divine programme of salvation. But there is something more to it even than that, for Paul does not simply say, 'We are the covenant people.' He says, *We are the true circumcision.* What precisely does this imply? What is the relation of the sign of circumcision to the covenant itself? The key passage is Genesis 17, and the important point can be simply expressed. The covenant is God's promise. He goes on oath in certain specific matters. Abram is the recipient of the promise which is first personal: Abram becomes Abraham (verse 5), a vivid promise of regeneration or a new nature, for with the new name there is created a new man. Secondly, the promise is national, a multitude of nations (verses 5b–6). Thirdly, it is spiritual, 'to be God to you and to your descendants after you' (verse 7). Fourthly, it is territorial, the 'land of your sojournings' (verse 8); and finally, by way of emphasizing the most important point, spiritual again, 'and I will be their God' (verse 8).

But Genesis 17 also defines the covenant in a second way. We read in verse 10, 'This is my covenant . . . you shall be circumcised.' The covenant which is first (verses 4–8) a complex promise from God to a chosen man cannot suddenly change its nature. When, therefore, it is defined, secondly (verses 10–14), in terms of a sign, it must still speak of a movement of grace from God to man. Circumcision symbolizes the application of the covenant promises to those individuals whom God has chosen to receive them.

All this, Paul applies to himself, to his Philippians and to us when he says that *we are the true circumcision*: we are the chosen recipients of the promises of God. His words are, if anything, stronger than RSV allows them to be, for the word 'true' is not in Paul's Greek: 'We are the circumcision' – not the true as compared with the false, or whatever, but the only 'circumcision' there is. We are the only 'Israel', the sons of

[18]1 Cor. 11:23–25; *cf.* Mt. 26:28; Mk. 14:24; Lk. 22:20.

149

Abraham, the children of the covenant, the chosen inheritors of the promises. But of what promises in particular? We saw that Genesis 17 stressed one aspect of the divine oath: a promised spiritual relationship between God and Abraham and, thereafter, Abraham's children.[19] This came to be seen as the essential heart of the covenant promise and the most quoted verse in the Bible: 'You shall be my people, and I will be your God.' Paul, the Philippians, the whole company of Christian believers down the years – we are the chosen people of God, individually born again, individually and collectively heirs of the Lord's purposes of grace. It is as though Paul said: We may be sure that God has set his personal seal of choice and ownership upon us, for we are the circumcision.

## 2. A definition

Can such a glorious claim be true? In order to establish us in a real confidence that we are God's people and possess his promised blessings, Paul adds three defining clauses setting out the marks of membership: the experience of the Spirit of God, the right attitude towards Jesus Christ, and the refusal to rely on oneself. Here, in turn, are the upward, outward and inward aspects of true religion, for the Christian must always be careful to be at one with God, to behave correctly before others, and to guard his own inner life.

The upward aspect of true religion is that it is prompted and controlled by God's Spirit, '. . . worship by the Spirit of God'.[20] The word 'worship', both as noun (*latreia*) and verb (*latreuo*), as it is used in the New Testament, has an exclusively religious significance, and it holds together the two aspects of the word 'service' in our common usage. We speak of 'Christian service', but we also say, 'Are you coming to the service?' This conjunction of worship and work is interesting, and should warn us not to make an unnatural and unbiblical separation between what happens inside and outside our church meetings. All our life is worship. Prayer is worship, and so is the consecrated life of a body presented

[19]Gn. 17:7.    [20]Phil. 3:3, RSV margin; *cf.* RV.

to God.[21] Worship involves the character of the worshipper.[22] It must be carried on with a correct attitude towards God, and it requires enabling from above.[23]

All this is catered for by the words 'by the Spirit of God'. There is the touch of the supernatural upon the worship of those 'who by the inward presence of the consecrating and transforming Spirit offer the sacrifice not of dead victims but of a devoted and renewed life'.[24] Worshipping by the Spirit of God delivers from bondage to any special place[25] and from the burden of obligatory animal oblations.[26] Worshipping by the Spirit of God demands a heart that is right with him, a body that is a fit temple for the Holy Spirit.[27] But worshipping by the Spirit of God also speaks of the agency of that divine Spirit, at work in us, at prayer for us,[28] empowering worship acceptable to God. Worship is a holy thing of the deepest and most satisfying reality, for we have here the promise that in worship we are acceptable to God as his priestly servants through the operation of his Spirit.[29]

The outward mark of the people of God is that they *glory in Christ Jesus*. If we give this word more vigorous translation the meaning will be plainer, 'boast about Christ Jesus'. He is their joyous theme. The word indicates a buoyant satisfaction in him; they enthusiastically appreciate who he is and what he has done, and glorify him as alone worthy of all praise: the Lord Jesus Christ.

Thus God has reached down from heaven to take a people for himself. He has animated them by his Spirit, displayed before them the beauty and satisfactoriness of his Son and given them faith in him. But he has also shown them what they are in themselves, so that, alongside the experience of the life-giving Spirit and the truth of the atoning Son, they are aware that they totally lack any personal worth: they *put no confidence in the flesh*.

This is the negative counterpart of the preceding two great positives. If it is true that we are God's people only because the Spirit of God has quickened us from the dead,[30] what ground is

[21]Lk. 2:37; Rom. 12:1.   [22]Lk. 1:74; 2 Tim. 1:3.   [23]Heb. 12:28, RV.
[24]Vaughan, *ad loc.*   [25]Jn. 4:21–24.   [26]Heb. 10:15–18.
[27]Rom. 1:9; 1 Cor. 6:19.
[28]Rom. 8:26f.   [29]*Cf.* Eph. 2:18.   [30]Eph. 2:1.

there for self-praise? If Jesus alone is worthy to be boasted of, what room is there for self-glory? If the energy of the flesh can only consign us more and more certainly to the wrath of God, of what use is self-reliance? *Flesh* sums up what a person is apart from the grace of Christ – the human being as yet unchanged by God's regenerating and redeeming work. It covers man at his highest pinnacle of development and at his lowest point of failure: the unsaved sinner, as mean and wretched as he can be or as great and lovely as he often is: man without God. The vote of 'no confidence' in the flesh is a co-equal part in the creed of the Christian, so that we confess: 'I believe in the Holy Spirit who has given me new life, made me a priest of God and who leads me in true worship. I believe in the Lord Jesus Christ, the only Saviour, the only worthy object of adoring praise. I believe that in me, in my flesh, there dwells no good thing.'

## 3. A warning

The first root of joy, then, is true religion. But Paul, as a careful pastor, knows that it is not enough to declare the truth; it is necessary also to hedge the truth about with the denial of error. Therefore he erects a warning sign, 'Beware.' The word *dogs* is as insulting as could be found, and no doubt was as offensive in Paul's day as it seems in the anti-controversialist atmosphere of our own. Yet Paul does not hesitate to use it, which indicates that something crucial was involved, for such a word is not adopted lightly.

The point at issue is at once simple and decisive. Paul describes as *dogs* – as excluded from the fellowship of the people of God – those who put a plus-sign after Christ in their teaching about salvation. First they add 'works': they are *the evil-workers*, a phrase which rather means 'evil advocates of (the necessity of) works'. Next they add ceremonial: they are *those who mutilate the flesh*. He will not give them the name they would have chosen, 'the circumcision', for he sees that in their obsessive insistence upon this rite they have glorified the mere act, the mere ritual performance as such. Therefore he again perpetrates a deliberate rudeness, they are 'the mutilators'. These are the men in Acts 15:1 whose doctrine is that 'unless you are circumcised according to the custom of Moses, you cannot be saved'; and verse 5 adds another requirement, namely, 'to charge them to keep the law of Moses'. Thus salvation, while it includes the requirement of belief in Christ, equally needs personal works of righteousness, and the acceptance of a religious ceremony. Christ is not all their boasting; the church and its ceremonies take a quota; the self and its efforts bear a part. 'Beware', says Paul. Danger lies that way!

Living at a time when the capacity for moral and spiritual indignation is at a low ebb, it is not necessarily easy for us to identify with Paul's heat of spirit. What is the danger which makes him so urgent?

The opponents whom he attacked were detracting from the sole sufficiency of what Christ had done and, in this way, were threatening the doctrine and way of salvation. Those who 'add to Christ' are still with us – sects like the Mormons who say nice things about Christ but in fact make membership of their sect the real essential for salvation; ministers who, whatever their own personal trust in Jesus, yet by their ministry cause people to trust in rites and ceremonies and sacraments; and others even who add to the work of Christ some additional experience of the Holy Spirit as essential for full salvation. Similarly, those who corrupt the way of salvation are still with us, especially the pathetic multitude whose only confidence is in their own earned merits. And, in the same way, those who detract from the sole glory of Jesus are still with us. Within the Christian camp there are, in particular, those who challenge the reality of the incarnation and the resurrection, and those who would find salvation, for each according to his lights, in all the 'great' world religions.

To Paul, these things mattered. He insisted that what he preached was the truth, not an insight or facet of truth; the Christ he preached was the only and all-sufficient Saviour of sinners; and the gospel he preached – Christ alone, grace alone, faith alone – was the only gospel which ensured acceptance before God and eternal glory. Our determination, therefore, should be to identify with Paul's indignation, to love truth as he did, to glorify the Lord Jesus Christ as he did, and to rest on and share the gospel as he did.

'Anger and joy' thus proves to be the right title for this

153

chapter. Towards our Lord Jesus Christ and everything that speaks of him we should covet a true and pure jealousy which rejoices in his glory and is moved to indignation by anything that diminishes or detracts from the honour due to his name and his saving work. There is indeed a holy anger without which joy in the Lord is something short of what he intends it to be.

# 3:4–8

# 16. Profit and loss

*Though I myself have reason for confidence in the flesh also. If any other man thinks he has reason for confidence in the flesh, I have more: ⁵circumcised on the eighth day, of the people of Israel, of the tribe of Benjamin, a Hebrew born of Hebrews; as to the law a Pharisee, ⁶as to zeal a persecutor of the church, as to righteousness under the law blameless. ⁷But whatever gain I had, I counted as loss for the sake of Christ. ⁸Indeed I count everything as loss because of the surpassing worth of knowing Christ Jesus my Lord. For his sake I have suffered the loss of all things, and count them as refuse, in order that I may gain Christ . . .*

Paul knew the value of safeguarding his great positive statements by equally great negatives. In the present context he has amplified his command to rejoice in the Lord by showing the Philippians that, to obey it, they must hold and practise the religion which matched their status as God's covenant people. In relation to this he *affirmed* the work of the Holy Spirit and the centrality of the Lord Jesus; and in parallel terms he *denied* the legitimacy of trusting in the flesh (verse 3). His doctrine of salvation required the denial of any and every form of 'do-it-yourself' merit before God.

What is it, this 'flesh' in which the Christian is to have no confidence (verse 3), in which Paul thinks he might be confident were such confidence allowable (verse 4) and in which he sees other people placing their confidence (verse 4b)? It is a description of anyone who is lacking a personal relationship with the Lord Jesus Christ.

It must be a common enough business experience to carry through the adoption of a new method of book-keeping and accounting, and one can imagine a businessman recalling (whether with gladness or regret!) 'the year we introduced the new system'. Paul dares to look on Christ in precisely this way in these verses. He looks back to the time – rather, in the light of Acts 9, we should say the day, even the hour and minute – when his whole system of personal spiritual accountancy broke down, and all the accumulated 'profit' of the years slumped to rock bottom and to his astonished gaze there was presented Christ, whom he had hitherto despised and rejected, as a completely adequate 'credit' which would cover all his needs. *Whatever gain I had, I counted as loss for the sake of Christ* (verse 7).

We cannot but notice the personal nature of this transaction, its sheer individuality. When Christ met Paul, no-one else was with them.[1] Paul does not dwell, in Philippians, upon the suddenness of his conversion, but he could hardly make it more personal. Christ became his very own, as real as a cash transaction! This stress upon a glorious individualism in New Testament Christianity is vital to 'joy in the Lord'. We cannot believe that Paul introduced the note of personal testimony in Philippians 3:4 merely in an illustrative way, and certainly it was not for self-advertisement. It is rather because, if the 'we' of verse 3 is to have meaning (that is to say, if 'we' – the Christian church – are truly to worship by the Spirit of God, glory in Christ Jesus, and reject fleshly confidence), it can happen only when 'you' and 'he' and 'she' and 'I' find, possess and treasure Christ for our very own selves.

Now prior to such a possession of Christ, all is *flesh*. Paul, in verses 4–6, describes himself as *flesh*, for he has not yet come into personal possession of Jesus. In other words *flesh* describes our state from birth until God is pleased to bring us to the new birth.[2]

But Paul is even more specific, for *flesh*, as he uses it here, describes a man who has reached the very pinnacle of moral

[1]Acts 9:5–6; 22:9; 26:13f.    [2]*Cf.* Jn. 3:3–7.

and religious development. Present-day usage might confine 'flesh' to a description of the rather grosser aspects of immorality. But we learn what is our true state before God, and how incredibly marvellous is our Saviour, only when we dismiss this popular conception from our minds, and accept that it is not only man at his worst but also man at his best who is 'flesh' and therefore not yet acceptable to God.

We see first Paul's natural advantages (verse 5). He had the *ecclesiastical* advantage of full possession of covenant privileges from infancy, having been *circumcised on the eighth day*. And if we ask, 'What good is circumcision?', we can give Paul's own answer, 'Much in every way. To begin with, the Jews are entrusted with the oracles of God', or again, 'to them belong the sonship, the glory, the covenants, the giving of the law, the worship, and the promises'.[3] Paul was born to all this, and introduced to his inheritance on the eighth day of life. In addition he claimed the *national* advantage of pure Israelite descent. The descendants of Abraham included the impure line of Ishmael. Isaac was father also to Esau. But *Israel* was the transformed Jacob from whom sprang the twelve tribes of God's people. Paul's *ancestral* advantage is mentioned next; *the tribe of Benjamin*. While he was not of Judah, the royal tribe, he was of that tribe which gave the first king of Israel and which later, alone of the other eleven tribes, remained loyal to David and his successors. Finally among his natural advantages he mentions the *parental* benefit: *a Hebrew born of Hebrews*. He was the child of godly, convinced, zealously religious parents, with all the benefit that entailed.[4]

Add now to this list of natural advantages the *personal* additions which Paul claims to have made (verses 5b–6). He speaks of an attitude, an activity and an achievement. Towards the law of God he adopted the most respectful and responsive attitude possible. He was a *Pharisee*, 'the strictest party of our religion'.[5] His overriding concern was to live in conformity to what he believed were God's regulations down to every smallest detail of daily life. So firm was his belief that this alone was the way and will of God that he was zealously active in opposition to every apparent challenge to the dignity of his

[3]Rom. 3:2; 9:4.    [4]*Cf.* Lk. 1:6, 15.    [5]Acts 26:5.

religion, even to an extent which later so pained him, being 'a persecutor of the church'.[6] But he achieved his goal, for he saw himself *as to righteousness under the law blameless.*

There is no point in our saying, 'Ah, but it was only a legalistic and limited attainment in righteousness.' This is undoubtedly true, but what an attainment it was! Again, there is little point in saying that Paul was assessing his achievement through unregenerate eyes and that his standards were not high enough. This again is true, but what standards they were! Nevertheless it was all 'flesh', for 'flesh' defines the whole life of any and every man, woman and child who is without living, personal acquaintance with Jesus Christ. It suits those who have sunk lowest in sin, and those who have risen highest in moral, religious and spiritual rank. Of all alike, Jesus himself said, 'That which is born of the flesh is flesh . . . Do not marvel that I said to you, "You must be born anew." '[7]

Let us, however, follow Paul further as, having described what 'flesh' means, he turns to estimate its worth. Remember that his theme here is 'confidence', that is to say, What is it that can make a person confident in the presence of God? Undoubtedly his moral attainments were a great tribute to human endeavour; equally they may have been a superb influence and contribution to human social well-being: but of what worth were they in giving him confidence before God? Did they fit him for that test? They did not. Man at his most privileged, his most moral, his most religious, his most zealous and devoted, is yet not thereby made fit and acceptable to God. Paul had no recourse but to add up his advantages and achievements one by one and admit that the total was zero. *Whatever gain I had, I counted as loss for the sake of Christ* (verse 7). The word *gain* is plural in the Greek; that is to say, Paul has taken his advantages on the credit side item by item, forgetting nothing, omitting nothing, excluding nothing. All that could be put to his good account is there, his 'gains' each and every one. But when the accountant's eye travels down the list, and the sum total is reckoned, and the line is drawn beneath the completed sum, the answer is an uncompromising singular word, *loss.* After all has been said, there is nothing and less than nothing for his efforts,

[6]1 Tim. 1:13.    [7]Jn. 3:6–7.

and, for certain, no ground of confidence in the sight of God.

But now in the place of 'loss' there stands 'Christ'. How does a person come to possess Christ who alone is the ground of confidence before God? The positive answer, which is given in verse 9, can be brought into focus by the negatives which arise from the verses under review. We learn that Christ does not become ours by effort but by rejection of effort. No-one had ever striven for righteousness as did Paul, and yet he does not see Christ as the prize standing just above the top rung of the ladder of self-advancement. He cannot have Christ until he has totted up all his works of righteousness and admitted the answer to be *loss*. 'Not the labours of my hands can fulfil thy law's demands ... Foul (in spite of all my efforts), I to the fountain fly.'[8] Again, Christ is not gained by ecclesiastical ceremony. His circumcision will not save him, although it was a rite commanded by God,[9] any more than baptism could save Simon the sorcerer,[10] though that too is of divine origin. Even sacred rites and ceremonies simply trusted as such must become items in an addition sum to which the answer is 'loss' if Christ is to be ours.

And if we cannot have Christ we have no other hope. Paul, rejecting as useless all his inherited and acquired virtues, has nothing to put in their place but Christ. These 'I counted as loss *for the sake of Christ*'. He is the only replacement; he is altogether enough and he is Paul's and ours 'through faith' (verse 9). The great missionary John G. Paton, struggling to find a local word which would translate 'faith' and failing to find one, was interrupted by someone in great trouble and needing help. 'Please, may I come and lean heavily upon you?' he said. Faith is leaning heavily upon Christ: not labour but cessation of labour, not doing but ceasing to do; simply leaning the whole weight of our needs upon him, and finding in him acceptance before the presence of God, and a righteousness which could never be ours by our own works.

So Paul came to the end of all his costly striving after acceptance before God through simply believing in Christ. But at the moment of writing, that experience was long past. It

[8]A.M. Toplady, 'Rock of ages, cleft for me'.    [9]Gn. 17.
[10]Acts 8:13, 21–23.

belonged to a far-off day on the road to Damascus. Has Paul no fresh testimony to offer? We notice that present tenses appear in verse 8. Verse 7 records that *I counted*; verse 8 affirms that *I count*. It is really here, in fact, that Paul turns to explain what it means to 'glory in Christ Jesus'. He has by now cleared every other potential subject of glory out of the way. All personal merit, all acquired virtue, all efforts to attain righteousness, all that would be to the glory of man is gone. Christ stands alone on the stage, the *exclusive* (*i.e.* that which excludes all others) object of praise.

We are immediately struck by the fact that the years between the *counted* of verse 7 and the *count* of verse 8 have been, for Paul, years of progress. The verses seem to be framed in terms of a deliberate contrast: *whatever* – *i.e.* a more or less stated number of things – has become *everything*; *loss*, the estimate then placed upon self-righteousness, is now *refuse*, positively expressive of worthlessness; the bare mention of *Christ* has been filled out over years of experience of him, so that it is now *the surpassing worth of knowing Christ Jesus my Lord*. Glorying in Christ Jesus is not a static thing. Joy in the Lord keeps company with progress in the Lord.

There are four aspects in which Paul notes progress or increase in the years he has known the Lord Jesus. First, there has been a growth of *knowledge* of the Lord. How little he really knew about Jesus that day on the road to Damascus! As, indeed, how little any of us knew about him at the moment of our conversion! But conversion is not experienced through greatness of knowledge but through simplicity of faith, as the soul passes from darkness to light, and from the power of Satan to God.[11] In honesty, therefore, when Paul gives a testimony of that far-off day, he does not pretend something which was not true. *Christ* is a sufficient summary word. But now there is *the surpassing worth of knowing Christ Jesus my Lord*. The fullness and wealth of apostolic truth gathered by revelation over the years is in that phrase, as well as the apostle's own intense satisfaction in it and in the Lord. And now he cannot be content with the monosyllabic title. He must express the full glory of the Saviour: *Christ Jesus ... Lord*, and along with it his

[11]Col. 1:13.

conviction that he personally knows Christ – a conviction which has not diminished with the passage of time, or lost its savour: *my Lord*.

He has progressed in knowledge, and glories all the more in Christ Jesus because he knows him more. And because he knows him more, Paul has become more consecrated to him. At his first experience he reckoned as loss everything which he could otherwise have considered as part of his credit balance: *whatever* (verse 7). Now nothing is held back. For *the surpassing worth of knowing Christ Jesus my Lord*, he says, *I count everything as loss*. How does a Christian follow Paul in consecration? Progressively, through deeper and deeper knowledge of Christ, for the more we know him the more we see his glory and the more we gladly give all to and for him.

But a darker thread also was woven into Paul's progress over the years. They brought an increase of *suffering: for his sake I have suffered the loss of all things*. Paul's consecrated experience was not wholly voluntary. Sometimes he was forced to give up things for Christ: sometimes they were stripped off him by others. He lost the skin off his back through a Philippian flogging.[12] He lost his liberty in a Caesarean and then a Roman prison; yes, and so much else besides.[13] What he told others, he experienced himself, 'that through many tribulations we must enter the kingdom of God'.[14] To put it another way, we never truly glory in Christ without being, in some way and at some time, *tested*. The point is that glorying in Christ is not a Christian pastime or a summer sport, but a lifetime's preoccupation. The darker the day, the greater his glory when he finds us still rejoicing in the Lord.

Paul's understanding of suffering is very positive. First, whatever loss he has endured and however it has come on him – by his own decision, by the action of others or by turn of circumstances – it is all *for his sake* (verse 8). There is nothing in the whole catalogue of the years which he did not accept as being from and for Christ, understand as the sovereign outworking of his will, and endure for his glory. Secondly, everything he endured was also a step forward in enjoying Christ, an experience through which Paul grew more per-

[12]Acts 16:22f.    [13]2 Cor. 11:23–28.    [14]Acts 14:22.

sonally conscious of some facet of his relationship with Christ. Often Christians look back on a time of trial and can testify how near and dear the Lord became to them in it, and how they learnt lessons that could not have been learnt in any other way. It was like that for Paul all the time – the pin-pricks, the calamities, the smiles and tears, the encouragements and disappointments, the sicknesses and pains – everything was a door into the richness of Christ.

Paul's up-to-date testimony (verse 8) brings us a final word, *satisfaction*. He looks candidly at *everything* and acknowledges the suffering which has taken it away. And then he makes his assessment: *I . . . count them as refuse, in order that I may gain Christ*. Who would want to spend his life on a rubbish heap? Far from regretting that these things are gone or wanting them back, Paul no more desires to repossess them than he wants last week's refuse back, provided only that this is the way to more and more of Christ. It is Christ who satisfies; it is Christ that he would gain. He has possessed Christ since that first meeting (verse 7), but he is all the time hungry for more. We who are saved possess Christ and he cannot be taken from us; we who are being sanctified are consumed by the ambition to *gain Christ*, and this is the driving force in our lives. Christ is the only hope for salvation when our ceremonies, privileges, religion and works of righteousness produce only loss. The same Christ always remains the only satisfaction for the Christian. This is how we work out the command to make the Lord our joy (3:1). May we be like Paul in seeing Christ alone as our wealth, and in being determined to evaluate everything else in the light of the full satisfaction only he provides.

# 17. Satisfied

*... and be found in him, not having a righteousness of my own, based on law, but that which is through faith in Christ, the righteousness from God that depends on faith;* [10]*that I may know him and the power of his resurrection, and may share his sufferings, becoming like him in his death,* [11]*that if possible I may attain the resurrection from the dead.*

[12]*Not that I have already obtained this or am already perfect; but I press on to make it my own, because Christ Jesus has made me his own.*

'I can do no more than my best,' we often say. And yet, as we say it, we are so often acknowledging that, once again, our best has eluded us. It is a statement not of achievement but of failure. Even our own prejudiced and inadequate self-examination recognizes that there are heights and ideals which we have not realized. Few of us can say, with Paul, that 'as to righteousness under the law' we are 'blameless' (verse 6). But the Paul who could say it found no comfort in it, for it gave him no confidence or standing before God. So it was with alacrity and gladness that he counted all his do-it-yourself righteousness as loss, and trusted Christ.

We have been following Paul's testimony along these lines in Philippians 3:4–8. In verses 9–12 the themes remain the same, but the apostle turns from facts to explanations. In his testimony he has told us *what* happened; he now tells us *why* it must be so. Why is the *flesh* inadequate to provide us with acceptance before God? Why is Christ sufficient? And what is the nature of the satisfaction which he has found in Christ?

## 1. Satisfied to be found in him

Paul has just portrayed the Lord Jesus Christ as an all-sufficient wealth which he is determined, as time passes, to appropriate more and more (verse 8). He now changes the picture: the Lord Jesus is a dwelling so attractive that Paul cannot bear to be away from home. He wants nothing except to *be found in him* (verse 9). There was a similar phrase in 2:8 where it says that Christ Jesus was 'found in human form'. This means that to any chance observer coming upon him at any time, the Lord Jesus presented a human appearance and would have been judged to be a man. Paul's desire to be 'found in Christ' means the same: he wants whoever looks at him, to see him as a man in Christ; whatever his experiences should turn out to be, he wants to face them as a man in Christ. Jesus is his permanent address. Paul may be in Rome, Philippi, Jerusalem; he may be healthy, sick, worried, free of care – but he will always be *in him*.

## 2. Satisfied to be blessed by him

In this 'permanent address', 'in Christ', there was one particular treasure: *righteousness*. In Christ, Paul describes himself as *not having a righteousness of my own, based on law, but that which is through faith in Christ, the righteousness from God that depends on faith.* There is a righteousness which does not satisfy (*not . . . a righteousness of my own*); there is a righteousness which meets the requirements (*the righteousness from God*); and there is a way by which this desired righteousness can be obtained (*that which is through faith in Christ, the righteousness from God that depends on faith*).

*Righteousness* means being 'in the right with God'. Paul believes that in Christ, by faith, it is possible to stand under divine scrutiny and to secure the verdict: 'Paul is in the right'; 'Paul is all that I require him to be'; 'Paul is righteous'.

### a. The righteousness which he abandons

Being 'found in him', Paul has no wish for *a righteousness of my own, based on law.* This is a 'do-it-yourself' righteousness; it has arisen through self-effort or personal good works. These good works have been patterned on a legal code, and hence it is a righteousness *based on law.* Paul had once been able to boast of such a righteousness when it was his claim that he was 'as to the law a Pharisee . . . as to righteousness under the law blameless' (verse 6). His own intense, demanding and sacrificial labours had produced conformity to a legal code of behaviour.

Of what worth was this conformist righteousness? Just that and nothing more, a 'certificate of good behaviour'! It was a righteousness *based on law,* literally 'out from the law', such a righteousness as proceeds from conforming to a standard. Now, such a righteousness does not give security. It does not make us confident that God will judge us favourably, and that for two reasons. First, even if we ever did attain such an unbroken record, we have still to maintain it until the judgment day, and one slip is enough to make the law pronounce an adverse verdict and make our 'righteousness' evaporate into nothing. But, more important, secondly, such a righteousness is self-conferred. We have weighed our own merits, examined our own right to the verdict. We have been both defendant and judge. We could never be certain that our verdict would command God's respect, or that our prejudiced and partial self-knowledge was as penetrating as his holy scrutiny. In particular we might award ourselves a high pass-mark by excusing or overlooking our inner defections from the path of obedience – just as Paul found himself beaten by the law when he faced its condemnation of covetousness.[1] A certificate of good behaviour which we have awarded to ourselves is not enough to give us confidence as we face the judgment of God.

[1]Rom. 7:7.

## b. The righteousness which he desires

There is, however, the possibility of a certificate of righteousness which God awards, and in this case we can indeed be confident. For if God pronounces us right with him, then we are indeed secure for ever. This is what Christ means to Paul, and it is this which sheds lustre on his satisfaction at being *found in him*. He tells us of its origin, the condition on which it is offered, and the way in which it is personally appropriated.

As to its origin, it is *the righteousness from God,* and here again the word means 'out from'. This righteousness proceeds out from God; it is his award. The importance of this cannot be overstressed. There can be no salvation unless God is satisfied. Christ might die (may we say it reverently) a thousand deaths; sin might be cleansed away a thousand times; but if God is not satisfied with what has been done, then it is all a waste of time, effort and suffering. If God will not have us back, then every effort to bring us back is misconceived and pointless. But here is a salvation for sinners with which God is satisfied. It is a righteousness which 'proceeds *out from God*'. Therefore it is certain from the start.

Secondly, it is offered on condition of *faith*, 'the righteousness from God that depends on *faith*'. Here is the simplicity and freeness of this salvation. Gone are the exertions of law-keeping, gone the disciplines and asceticisms of legalism, gone the anxiety that having done everything we might not have done enough. We reach the goal not by the stairs but by the lift. *Faith* means that we abandon works and efforts, and God pledges his promised righteousness to those who will stop trying to save themselves.

But this is not any old faith! There is a 'faith' (so-called) which is nothing more or less than credulity. Faith is valuable only when it is reposed in a trustworthy object. Of supreme value, then, is the righteousness which is ours *through faith in Christ*. How utterly and completely marvellous! We rely upon the very Son of God himself to bring us home acceptably to God. The Son of God is the Mediator of the righteousness of God to those who place their faith in him.

What framework of knowledge did the Philippians possess, to enable them to understand these deep truths which Paul has expressed so briefly in verse 9? We must ask the same question for our own benefit: have we a framework of knowledge within which these references to righteousness, law and faith make sense?

Three keywords go far to providing the necessary setting. The first is *substitution*. Our Lord Jesus Christ is the full expression of the righteousness of God: his words and teaching, his inner character and outer deeds, the works he accomplished, his relationships, his attitude to himself and his obedience to God, the absolute completeness of all he was, taught and did – in a word, everything that could ever be seen in him, said of him or sought from him is absolutely what the righteous God requires. It is not just that (so to speak), as far as he went, he matched what God required. It is rather that the Lord Jesus is the sum total of all that (even) God could ever ask. He *is* the righteousness of God. Now, in biblical thinking, it is this which fits him (and him alone) to be our substitute, to stand in our place, accept our condemnation and receive the penalty due to us. 'Your lamb shall be without blemish.'[2] 'He made him to be sin who knew no sin.'[3]

Move on now from substitution to *accountancy*. There is another side to the substitutionary work of Christ, for just as he became totally identified with us in our sin, so, in him, we become totally identified with his righteousness.

> Behold him there! the risen Lamb!
> My perfect, spotless Righteousness.[4]

He was 'made sin for our sake . . . so that in him we might become the righteousness of God'; 'your life' is 'in Christ Jesus, whom God made . . . our righteousness'; 'by one man's obedience many will be made righteous'.[5]

It is this total package – our sins laid on Jesus and his righteousness accounted to us – that we accept by simple faith. He has done it all; God promises all to us; we rest in faith on the divine promises and enter into the stated benefits. It is *not . . . a righteousness of my own . . . but that which is through faith in Christ, the righteousness from God that depends on faith.*

[2]Ex. 12:5.    [3]2 Cor. 5:21.
[4]C. L. Bancroft, 'Before the throne of God above'.
[5]2 Cor. 5:21; 1 Cor. 1:30; Rom. 5:19.

The third keyword is *clothing*. 'You . . . have put on the new nature', Paul says.[6] That is to say, God's gift of righteousness is more than an act of accountancy; it is a new creation,[7] a new heart and life within matching the perfect righteousness of Christ, ready and waiting to express itself outwardly in practical righteousness as we obey God as Jesus did – as we 'put on' the Lord Jesus Christ in our daily lives.[8] To this thought Paul now leads us in Philippians 3:10.

### 3. Satisfied to be made like him

So free is this salvation, so completely independent of any efforts or merits of ours, that it is even open to the charge of making a virtue of sin. Paul faced this when he repeated the question some had levelled at him: 'Why not do evil that good may come?'[9] For surely, if while we were sinners God showed this astonishing mercy to us, ought we not to continue in sin and thus provoke yet more and greater mercy? If, apart from our works and merits, God has blessed us with his gift of righteousness, ought we not to remain without works and merits and look for additional benefits?

The very fact that Paul's gospel is open to this charge is proof that he preached and believed in an absolutely, totally free salvation. If he had allowed the least room for us to contribute to our salvation his teaching could not have been slandered in this way. Salvation is indeed as free as that.

But we who have been saved have been given the gift of God's *righteousness*, and this implies a consequent 'right living'. For this reason Paul moves from verse 9, where he has taught free salvation, to verse 10, in which he shows that the Christian is brought by salvation into the sphere of strict moral enterprise and endurance. Paul, characteristically, calls it becoming like Christ. And does it not stand to reason that if we are satisfied with Christ for salvation, we will not rest until we are like the One who satisfied us so?

The topic of becoming like Christ is introduced with the words *that I may know him*. In scriptural terms, our definition

[6]Col. 3:10.    [7]2 Cor. 5:17.    [8]Rom. 13:14; Col. 3:12.
[9]Rom. 3:8.

of 'knowledge' as truth held in the mind offers only a third of the total. The Bible would add, first, a practical dimension. Nothing is truly known until it becomes part of daily conduct: 'To depart from evil is understanding.'[10] Secondly, the Bible would add a personal dimension. In personal relationships, to 'know' is to enter into the deepest personal intimacy and union: 'Adam knew Eve his wife.'[11] The Bible speaks in this way, not through reticence on sexual matters, but because this is what marriage is and this is what knowledge between persons is – deep, intimate union. Consequently, having been saved wholly and solely by Christ, Paul wants to enter into the deepest possible union with him. He wants to *know him.*

What does this involve? The career of Christ, as depicted in 2:5–11, was one of descent into death leading through into the glory of the ascension. To be made like Christ, to enter into intimate union with him, to know him, necessarily involves the same experiences, becoming *like him[12] in his death, that if possible I may attain the resurrection from the dead.* How surprised we often are when (as we say) life brings its trials to us! But what did we expect? Do we want to be made like Christ or not? Christlikeness must lead to Calvary. We must be ready for – and we cannot hope to avoid – the downward path of the Crucified. It was true of Paul: down to the dungeon and thence to the executioner's block. 'All who desire to live a godly life in Christ Jesus will be persecuted'; the servant must be made like his Lord; we must not 'be surprised at the fiery ordeal . . . as though something strange were happening . . . But rejoice in so far as you share Christ's sufferings'.[13] This is the way the Lord Jesus went, and it is the way of Christlikeness for us.

But in dwelling on 'becoming like him in his death' we have taken the verse out of order. We must now retrace our steps and see what encouragements Paul uses as brackets round this reality of the cross in the experience of the Christian. First let us ask why he speaks of the resurrection of Christ before he has

---

[10]Jb. 28:28.    [11]Gn. 4:1.

[12]The verb *symmorphizomai,* only here in New Testament. It contains as one component *morphē,* 'form' (*cf.* on 2:6 above). Thus an identity of nature and (therefore) of life style with Jesus is implied. *Cf.* the adjective *symmorphos,* Rom. 8:29; Phil. 3:21.

[13]2 Tim. 3:12; Jn. 15:20; 1 Pet. 4:12f.

mentioned his death. Surely he has reversed the events of our Lord's experience? Indeed he has, but with a deliberate purpose. For Christ, death preceded resurrection, but for the Christian who sets out to follow the Lord along this path the power of the risen Christ is the first fact of experience. Thus, as we walk the path of Christlikeness in an apostolic determination to 'be made like him', even to the extent of sharing his sufferings, his risen power is made available to strengthen, keep and lead us through.

More than that, however, is available. For again, before he spoke of 'becoming like him in his death' Paul referred to 'sharing', or 'fellowship' in, his sufferings. Why does he thus make a double reference to the cross of Christ? It is for this reason: he wants us to see that in desiring to follow him as faithful cross-bearers we are not left alone; he keeps fellowship with us; we are not copying a dead Model but walking in fellowship with a living Saviour.

These emphases on power and companionship encourage us on the way. But the goal also encourages us: we aim at *the resurrection from the dead* (verse 11). We could be misled by *if possible*, which seems to suggest that, after all, Paul was not sure of final salvation. If the verse meant this, it would not only be discordant with verse 9, but would flatly contradict 1:23, and many other passages in Paul's writings.[14] Yet this verse does express uncertainty, not of the goal but of the way. The resurrection is certain; the intervening events are uncertain. We neither know how many days we have left on earth nor what those days will contain, but we do know that, be they many or few, smooth or rough, at the end of them there is the glory, *the resurrection from the dead*. Paul, therefore, encourages himself and us along the path of Christlikeness by sharing openly his determination, as though he said, 'so that by whatever route God in his providence shall ordain – and what it will be I do not know – empowered by the risen Christ and accompanied by Christ himself I will follow him, bearing my cross, descending with him into death, and then for all eternity, still with him, enjoy the glory of the resurrection'.

[14]*E.g.* 2 Cor. 5:1; Rom. 8:38f.

## 4. Satisfied to satisfy him

We come at the end of our study to a 'stock-taking' verse. Paul has expressed his readiness to 'go all the way' with Christ, so complete is his satisfaction in him. Now he pauses to assess the past (*Not that I have already obtained*), the present (*I press on*), and the future (*to make it my own*; cf. RV).

Three truths are stated here. First, *the new perceptions* which conversion brings. We observed above that if we presume to be both defendant and judge in our own trial, we may not in fact arrive at a correct estimate of ourselves. We now see that that is indeed the case. Once upon a time Paul thought that he had 'arrived', for he judged himself 'as to righteousness under the law blameless' (verse 6). But hear his estimate now: *Not that I have already obtained this or am already perfect.* Sinless perfection is not the experience even of an apostle this side of glory. He sees himself with new eyes; he has received a spiritual understanding. Furthermore, knowing that he has not yet 'arrived', he sees something else: that he is personally responsible to *press on*. The same Paul who, in verse 9, reminded us that we cannot by our efforts obtain the righteousness which is from God, is now determined to make every effort to live the righteous life. He says, *I press on*. The word is vigorous – 'I pursue', 'I persecute' – as vigorous as the action with which once he persecuted the church (verse 6).

Secondly, we learn what is the *inner story of conversion*: *Christ Jesus has made me his own.* We treasure the memory of our conversion, when we reached out the empty hand of faith to Jesus. But, behind this, making it possible, giving it reality, was the act of God who chose and took hold of us. Did Paul choose Christ? Indeed he did, but only because Christ first chose Paul. Christ's was the real choice; anything we did was derived from what God in Christ had already decided. We responded to, and were indeed enabled by, his prior choice. Thus Jesus himself said: 'You did not choose me, but I chose you.'[15] It is this that gives us security and confidence: we are 'in Christ' because of his changeless, loving will that it should be so.

Finally, we find here *the sole objective* of those who are truly

[15]Jn. 15:16.

converted: *to make it my own.* The Revised Version is quite explicit: 'that I may apprehend (*i.e.* grasp, accomplish) that for which I was apprehended by Christ Jesus'. What did he have in mind when he took hold of me? In one sense there are as many purposes as there are individuals because, for each, God has already decided upon the good works by which we should serve him.[16] But at the same time, for every converted person there is an identical goal: to be satisfied with Jesus and to grow into his likeness.

[16]Eph. 2:10.

# 3:13–16
# 18. On to maturity

*Brethren, I do not consider that I have made it my own; but one thing I do, forgetting what lies behind and straining forward to what lies ahead,* [14]*I press on toward the goal for the prize of the upward call of God in Christ Jesus.* [15]*Let those of us who are mature be thus minded; and if in anything you are otherwise minded, God will reveal that also to you.* [16]*Only let us hold true to what we have attained.*

A bird's-eye view of verses 13–21 reveals that they are held together by two repeated ideas. According to verses 15 and 17 Christians are called to model themselves deliberately on the pattern set by Paul, and according to verses 14 and 20 this apostolic pattern of life is to be lived out by keeping our gaze steadfastly upon the future. The 'calls' issued by verses 15 and 17 are not substantially different from each other, but the future on which we are to look is variously expressed by the other two verses. According to verse 14, we have a goal to be attained, and according to verse 20 we have a Saviour to be awaited. Thus, there are two aspects to the life modelled on the apostolic pattern. On the one hand it is a life of personal commitment, effort and determination (verses 13–14); on the other hand, it is a life resting upon great certainties, in particular the abiding truths of the cross (verses 18–19) and the coming (verses 20–21) of the Lord Jesus. It is a life, therefore, of consecration and conviction.

Turning now particularly to verses 13–16, they fall into two sections. We find Paul's example in verses 13–14, as he continues the personal testimony which started in verse 4. Here he shares with us his determinations for the remainder of his life on earth. Verses 15–16 turn to the task of exhortation, for Paul has not spoken of himself out of a spirit of display but to provide a guide to the church and a standard of Christian living to which he does not hesitate to call other Christians. It is instructive to see here in Paul's experience a harmony often lacking in ours: the confidence of the leader and the companionship of the brother. Paul does not hesitate to put himself 'out front'. It is part of his calling as an apostle to give a lead to the church and he has a sturdy confidence that the life he has been enabled to live is not only exemplary but normative. Yet at the same time he speaks as a brother to *brethren* (verse 13) and with gentle grace allows the *I* of verses 13–14 to become the *us* of verse 15. We could not have a better illustration of the companionate leadership which we discussed in chapter 2 (on 1:1).

Paul is ever the attractive man, but even if his engaging revelation of himself in these verses failed to capture our attention, surely the subject he discusses must do so. For his topic is the Christian's energetic progress, heavenly goal and present maturity. Furthermore, he is confident that here is a scheme of things which God himself will teach to those who might at any point think differently.

## 1. Paul's example

*Brethren, I do not consider that I have made it my own; but one thing I do, forgetting what lies behind and straining forward to what lies ahead, I press on toward the goal for the prize of the upward call of God in Christ Jesus.*

Paul's formula for Christian growth, spelt out in terms of his own example, has four elements in it.

### a. A correct self-estimate

*Brethren,* he says, *I do not consider that I have made it my own* (verse 13).

In the matter of progress towards perfection Paul is a brother among *brethren*. Christian leadership is a very demanding thing, costly in time and energy, imposing severe demands on mind and body, requiring much to ensure the present and future welfare of the church of God and the care of others. These things are absorbing as well as demanding and they come with the force of inescapable priorities in the leader's programme. It is easy, therefore, to be a leader and to forget to be a Christian, allowing personal targets of spiritual growth to become misted over; to encourage others to prayer and Bible-reading and to let one's own attention to these means of grace become perfunctory or even negligible – always with the excuse of the next duty, the coming meeting, the pressing appointment.

Paul did not say, 'I would love to pursue personal growth in holiness but sadly I must be otherwise occupied.' Neither will he allow anyone else to say, 'Such pursuit of holiness is only for apostles, not for ordinary folk like me.' It is for the *brethren*, the whole range of believers.[1]

Paul's correct self-esteem, then, first puts him in company with all Christians, imposing alike on each one, himself included, the obligation to pursue perfection. But, secondly, he recognizes that he has not yet attained to all that God purposes for him, nor yet made it his own. The wording *made it my own* (verse 13) derives from the identical words in verse 12. In that verse Paul defines what he is determined to 'make his own', namely to be 'perfect'. This word, in turn, summarizes the theme of verses 9–10. To be 'perfect' means to become increasingly like our Lord Jesus Christ, with his righteousness, not only as an inward, spiritual gift but as an outward way of life. His pattern of life is reproduced as we suffer even unto death which alone issues in a resurrection like his. In all this Paul has not yet 'arrived' but was still on his way. Truly, knowing Christ has brought Paul to a very different self-estimate from that which his Pharisaic upbringing had inculcated (verse 6) – and a more realistic and sobering one at that. He did not 'think

[1] We must not impute to Paul the nuance which our ears, sensitized by much talk of 'sexist' terminology, find in the masculine form of address. The apostle, believing as he did that in Christ 'there is neither male nor female' (Gal. 3:28), can only have used the masculine generically of all believers.

of himself more highly than he ought to think'[2] and this lowly self-estimate was a springboard to progress.

## b. A single-minded zeal

There is an impressive *activity* about Christian progress. It has, as a matter of fact, been a point of considerable stress in Paul's letter to Philippi: recall his exhortations to 'stand firm', 'work', 'run' and 'labour',[3] the bond-service of 2:22 and the 'nearly died' of 2:30. There is no room for indolence in the Christian life. And here, when Paul is dwelling on his own personal growth as a Christian, his 'sanctification', he reveals himself as one shouldering a responsibility and getting on with a job. Sanctification does not permit spiritual abdication.

Equally impressive is the emphasis on *concentration*. The Greek (of verse 13) says literally, 'One thing! Forgetting what lies behind . . .'. Needless to say we are not to imagine Paul forgetting God's past mercies – for he has, indeed, been dwelling most pointedly upon them since verse 7. Nor would he forget the valuable lessons of the past – these too have been his recent theme (verses 2–6). What, then, is this forgetting of the past which he urges with such emphasis? It is the sort of dwelling on the past that hinders our present effort and our future progress. We do well gently to remind ourselves that a bereavement can sometimes make Christians live in the past; similarly we easily harbour a persistent bitterness about past wrongs (real or supposed). There are few things that have such power to lock us into the past. Again, there is despair over past sins which, in its severest form, can make believers doubt if they will ever be forgiven or which, in less tragic forms, gives rise to defeatism and backward-looking. There are many similar things that make us like the man in Zechariah 2:1–4 who wanted to measure the ruins of Jerusalem, allowing bygone glories and past failures to decide the dimensions of the future. By contrast the progressing Christian must cultivate a concentrated forward look to where the goal lies.

This requires *determination: straining forward . . . I press on.* Here is the runner in the games, 'extended' in every fibre of

[2]Rom. 12:3.    [3]Phil. 1:27; 2:12, 16.

his being – 'the eye outstrips and draws on the hand, and the hand the foot'[4] – everything is at a stretch to breast the tape. The metaphor changes with *I press on*, literally 'I pursue, I persecute'. No obsessive hatred ever dogged the heels of its adversary with more tenacity than the apostle held to the target of Christian perfection. This is a far cry from the teaching on sanctification which calls believers to 'let go and let God'. There was not much 'letting go' about Paul, but rather an example of the truth that the regenerate believer must appropriate the sanctifying grace of God by actively obeying him.

### c. An absorbing desire

What is it that holds Paul's gaze as he turns from the past and preoccupies himself with the future? It is *the goal . . . the prize* (verse 14).

Sometimes a thing is all the more impressive for being left undescribed. Paul tells us neither what the goal is nor what the prize will be. Yet suddenly the earthly scene with all its strivings, sufferings and sacrifices is suffused with heavenly glory. One scriptural picture after another fills and elevates the mind: the Lord's own 'Well done!';[5] 'the crown of righteousness, which the Lord, the righteous judge, will award to me on that Day';[6] 'the unfading crown of glory', gift of the chief Shepherd;[7] the privilege (above all) that his servants should worship him, see his face and have his name written on their foreheads;[8] the blood-cleansed robes[9] and the unending presence of the Lord.[10] All this and, in addition, 'What no eye has seen, nor ear heard, nor the heart of man conceived, what God has prepared for those who love him'.[11] That is the goal and the prize!

### d. A sure foundation

All this activity is not 'whistling in the dark'; it is not the panic of someone trying by every means to make certain of some-

[4]J. A. Bengel, *Gnomon of the New Testament, ad loc.*
[5]Lk. 19:17.     [6]2 Tim. 4:8.     [7]1 Pet. 5:4.
[8]Rev. 22:3–4.     [9]Rev. 7:14.     [10]1 Thes. 4:17.
[11]1 Cor. 2:9.

thing about which he feels basically insecure. In this active doctrine of sanctification which Paul is preaching by his example, he is not abandoning justification by faith; he is not denying that salvation is free. It is in fact because both our salvation and our sanctification have been perfectly and fully accomplished for us by Christ[12] that we can be saved by responding in faith without works, and sanctified by responding in faithful obedience.

Paul ends his delineation of his example on this note of security and certainty. The prize towards which he is drawn in disciplined and concentrated activity is described as belonging to ('of') *the upward call* (or 'high calling') *of God in Christ Jesus.* A study of the idea of 'calling' in the Epistles of Paul will reveal that its meaning is not 'invitation' into gospel privileges but the power of God over the wills of his people. It is not God's invitation to be saved; it is God's determination to save. The prize is part of, and is guaranteed by, God's saving purposes at work in Paul, and in all his called children.[13] It is for this reason that, in the other passage where he mentions a 'prize', Paul depicts himself fighting 'not as aimlessly' or 'uncertainly'.[14] His final salvation, with all the glories of its rewards, was secured for him by and with God's calling of him in Christ.

## 2. Paul's exhortation

*Let those of us who are mature be thus minded; and if in anything you are otherwise minded, God will reveal that also to you. Only let us hold true to what we have attained.*

As always in the Bible, we learn not only what is true but also how to respond to the truth. In the present passage Paul turns to make clear what bearing his example is to have on Christian living. He underlines two points: that the apostolic example he has set is normative for Christians (verse 15) and that Christians are to grow by honouring and responding to the truth as they at present grasp it (verse 16).

Paul was confident that he held a key place in relation to

---

[12]As in Phil. 2:12–13; *cf.* Heb. 10:10–14.     [13]*Cf.* Rom. 8:29–39.
[14]1 Cor. 9:26.

other Christians. In other passages in his letters he asserted his authority as an apostle in matters of doctrine,[15] requiring the churches to receive what he taught as the commandment of God. But here his claim touches on his manner of life: he sets the pattern which every Christian is to follow.

His confidence comes out in two ways. First, he believes that every mature Christian will want to adopt the apostolic lifestyle (*be thus minded*, verse 15). The word *mature* in verse 15 is the adjective which corresponds to the verb 'am perfect' in verse 12.[16] Bengel helpfully suggests that both are drawn from the vocabulary of athletics: 'Am perfect' means 'crowned as victor', 'having attained the prize'. 'Mature' means 'fit', 'in training', 'ready for the contest'. Such a Christian, Paul believes, will fully approve and adopt the apostolic principles and pattern of life.

Secondly, we see Paul's confidence in his own example in his assertion that God will set the seal of his approval on it. If anyone should diverge from the apostolic way of looking at life, God will even 'reveal this' – Paul's principles and practices – to that person. The mind of God and the mind of the apostle are at one.[17]

[15]E.g. 1 Cor. 2:10–13; 14:37; 1 Thes. 2:13.

[16]The adjective *teleiōs* moves between the two meanings of '(fully) perfect' (*e.g.* Mt. 5:48; Rom. 12:2; 1 Cor. 13:10; Eph. 4:13) and 'adult', 'mature' (*e.g.* 1 Cor. 2:6; 14:20, where it stands in contrast to what is childish or infantile; Heb. 5:14, where it contrasts with what is inexperienced and infantile).

[17]The very general terms in which verse 15b is expressed are not altogether easy to pin down, but the above understanding seems the most satisfactory. Two observations are fundamental: first, the word *otherwise* (*heterōs*) is too broad to make it refer to any specific point of Paul's teaching and it is best, therefore, to understand *in anything* (*ti*, accusative of reference) rather as increasing the vagueness ('at all otherwise') than as pinning it down to a difference 'on some isolated point' (Kent). Secondly, the verb *minded* (*phronein*) does not signify thinking about this or that item of belief or practice but 'the general disposition of mind ... dispositions which underlie the spiritual life' (Vincent). It is the verb used of the 'mind' of Christ in 2:5ff. – his way of looking at life, the principles which animated his lifestyle. Paul is therefore alluding to such attitudes as his lowly self-estimate (as contrasted, for example, with any ideas of 'sinless perfection'), his positive and sacrificial pursuit of holiness (as contrasted with any idea of instantaneous holiness, or holiness imposed by divine action on a pass-

This claim is both enormous in itself and also of great practical importance. The New Testament teaches the uniqueness of the apostolic band. Since the days of Paul and his fellow apostles, no-one has been able to say, 'Am I not an apostle? Have I not seen Jesus our Lord?' No-one has been able to say, 'The gospel which was preached by me ... came through a revelation of Jesus Christ.' No-one has been able to say, 'Be imitators of me, as I am of Christ.'[19] The apostolic band had the unique, unrepeatable position of church-founders.[20] They were organs of revelation, infallible teachers. But they were also – as here in the case of Paul – divinely-given examples of the way to live the life of Christ in the world. The church today is apostolic, not by virtue of any man or order of men claiming to be apostolic, but by virtue of its adherence to apostolic doctrine and its imitation of apostolic life as enshrined in and taught by the Scriptures. Doctrine and demonstration go hand in hand. There is a knowledge of the truth which accords with godliness and there is a manner of life which adorns the doctrine.[21] Since we today live at a time of (unprecedented?) challenge to apostolicity on both counts, we must be very watchful indeed. Paul anathematizes those who would alter the terms of the gospel of Christ;[22] his words 'God gave them up' refers to those who, by exchanging the truth of God for a lie, committed themselves to the dishonouring of their bodies, to lesbian and homosexual practices and to the subversion of all moral norms.[23]

Even though Paul knew that he possessed this authority in the church, however, the spirit in which he writes to the Philippians is very far from authoritarian. Bishop Moule wrote at one point in the margin of his Greek New Testament, 'Apostolus, non papa!' – 'An apostle, not a pope!' Paul exercised authority, not dictatorship. He addresses himself to those who, not in name only but also in reality, were his *brethren*

---

ive subject), his certainty of the heavenly reward (as contrasted with that sort of uncertainty about heaven which suggests a lack of understanding of the finished work of Christ and which deprives present life of the confidence it ought to display).

[18]1 Cor. 9:1; Gal. 1:11–12; 1 Cor. 11:1.     [9]Rev. 21:14.
[20]Tit. 1:1; 2:10.
[21]Gal. 1:6–10.     [22]Rom. 1:24ff.

(verses 13, 17). He modulates the *I* of verse 14 to the *us* of verse 15. Apostle thought he is, yet he is a believer among believers, needing their fellowship,[23] taking a common stand with them in the pursuit of holiness. When, therefore, he faces the fact that not all will at once concur with his teaching (verse 15), his word to such is not one of intolerance: 'Look out! I am the final arbiter in such things.' Rather he commits all to what God will reveal (verse 15b) and enunciates a rule of life for each individual (verse 16): *Only* – that is to say, 'understand all I have said in the light of this' – since we have each attained to some standing in Christ and some understanding of his truth, *let us hold true to what we have attained.* This is the way forward. The exercise of private judgment is essential if the individual is to grow in Christ.

In thus calling the individual to make responsible decisions, Paul is not countenancing the arbitrary or the whimsical: he is calling for a disciplined pattern of life in the light of truth already possessed in Christ. He addresses those who *have attained* and commands them to hold true. Each of the verbs he uses is important. First, the idea of attainment shows that he is not saying that in religious matters any individual's opinion is as good and valid as that of any other. That which has been attained can be only some awareness of the objective truth revealed in and by Christ. Paul, therefore, is not envisaging a situation where people stubbornly maintain their personal whims or intuitions or opinions against every argument to the contrary, but rather a situation where each Christian must be faithful to what he knows of Christ.

Secondly, the verb translated *hold true* indicates that he has in mind a thought-out and maintained lifestyle, based on and displaying the truth of Christ as the individual knows it.[24] In other words, putting the matter in our own context, the individual believer is free to work out a rule of thought and behaviour in the light of the Word of God. This is the way of Christian progress, for we will constantly develop in both our beliefs and our conduct as God allows more and yet more light to break forth out of his Word.

[23]Phil. 1:19.
[24]This verb is *stoicheō*, 'to walk according to rule', 'to practise a rule of life'; *e.g.* Acts 21:24; Rom. 4:12; Gal. 6:16.

Three remarks must be added, briefly, in conclusion of this study. First, what Paul proposes here is a true educational procedure. Education, growth to maturity, involves risk, for it has to make room for a process of trial and error. A child guarded by over-fond parents from every knock of life and every adverse result of its own behaviour will never emerge from childhood. Thus God 'takes the risk' of giving us his Word. The totalitarianism of an all-provident ecclesiastical authority, complete with all the answers, shouldering all the responsibilities, cushioning from every adversity, sounds safer. But such safety can be purchased only at the expense of fixation in spiritual infancy. We need the 'trial and error' of living by Scripture in order to grow: to discover what the Bible teaches, put it to the test, find where we were mistaken, return and try again. This is truly 'scientific'.

Secondly, since each biblical truth must be held in the context of all biblical truth, this call to exercise 'private judgment' does not put a premium on isolated 'individualism'. We live in the fellowship of the church, heirs to all that the past has garnered in understanding the Scriptures, enriched by the light which we contribute to each other in the mutuality of church life. It is as James says regarding progress to maturity: 'the harvest of righteousness is sown in peace by those who make peace.'[25]

And finally, the risk is not all that great! For Paul does not expect us to achieve everything on our own. There is a God who is over all, whose irresistible purpose is to make us like his Son. As we obey the truth he has already given us, he will himself take charge of the process, and where we are still in error, deficient or weak, he *will reveal that also.*

[25]Jas. 3:18.

## 3:17–19
## 19. Enemies of the cross

*Brethren, join in imitating me, and mark those who so live as you have an example in us.* [18]*For many, of whom I have often told you and now tell you even with tears, live as enemies of the cross of Christ.* [19]*Their end is destruction, their god is the belly, and they glory in their shame, with minds set on earthly things.*

For the second time within a few verses Paul calls us to follow his example. The summons in verse 15 (to share his determination to 'press on') follows naturally from his extended testimony in verses 4–14. Because he is an apostle of Christ, the way he lives sets the standards and enunciates the principles of true Christian living – his growing delight in the Lord Jesus, reliance on him alone for salvation, determination to be like him and to do his will, single-minded pursuit of the prize (verses 8–14). The summons in verse 17 is significantly different: we are to esteem the truth as he did, marry the truth to love, and balance individualism with pastoral care.

The truth occupied a primary place in apostolic living. When he commands us to follow his example (verse 17) he adds an explanation: *For . . .* (verse 18). The link between the verses is as follows: Imitate me because by doing so you will live a life which accords with the truth about the *cross* (verse 18) and the *coming* (verse 20) of the Lord Jesus Christ. In other words, when the truths about the cross and the coming are grasped, a certain way of life naturally follows. This integration between what we believe and what we do lies close to the centre of Paul's thinking. He expressed it beautifully in writing to Titus: some 'profess to know God, but they deny him by their deeds'; Christians must 'adorn the doctrine of God our Saviour' by the way they live.[1]

The truth – rather, we ought to say, the knowledge of the truth – must be married to love. Paul was a great weeper. He wept over those whom he taught and over those whom he rebuked.[2] Here he weeps for those against whom he must warn. In him there was a sincere union of truth and love. Paul engaged in controversy, but he was no hard-faced controversialist; he taught the truth but he was not a detached, disinterested teacher; he warned about error and wept over those who held it. This is part of his example to us.

There is also a third new feature in Paul's example. He has previously shown himself as a zealous individualist, all out for his own spiritual growth. The prize-winner dare not pause to help others over the hurdles. But see here another side of the apostle, when he weeps with care for people, and when he takes pains to lead the Philippians in the way of Christ. Individual care for one's own spiritual progress must keep in touch with pastoral responsibility for the souls and welfare of others. The Christian has no right to expect anything else but that he must bear his own load.[3] Yet he must be ready at all times to bear the other's burden.[4] There is of course a due priority to be observed, for Paul depicted himself as the zealous runner before he turned to be the zealous pastor,[5] and it must always be so. 'Take heed to yourselves and to all the flock'; 'Take heed to yourself and to your teaching.'[6] We can never help keep someone else's vineyard if we neglect our own, but the apostolic example says to us, 'This you should have done, and not have left the other undone.' Both activities are equally obligatory.

## 1. Contrast

Having observed these incidental aspects of Paul's example, we turn to the main line of his teaching. He has already outlined his

---

[1]Tit. 1:16; 2:10.    [2]Acts 20:19, 31; 2 Cor. 2:4.    [3]Gal. 6:5.
[4]Gal. 6:2.    [5]Phil. 3:13–14, 17–18.    [6]Acts 20:28; 1 Tim. 4:16.

manner of life and called for unanimity and imitation. Now, in order to sharpen our awareness of what he is asking of us, he gives us a negative example. He calls attention to the life he requires by contrasting it with the life he rejects. We shall more clearly see what to follow if we know what to avoid.

Whom precisely is he warning us against? Some say that these 'enemies of the cross' are the 'Judaizers', the 'Christ-plus' people of verse 2. Some say that he is warning against anti-nomianism, the sin of those who abuse their liberty in Christ, making it an open licence to every sort of indulgence.[7] Or, equally, he could be warning against the pull of the world, the ever-open door to depart from the way of Christ.[8] In the long run it makes no odds whom he is decrying, and it is better not to attach the verses too firmly to any situation in the past. For the threat is still present to the Christian, as we shall see, and the description is perfectly clear even if names are absent.

First, Paul says that *their end is destruction*. He looks beyond this world to the next and finds no hope at all for them there, nothing but eternal loss. The same fate awaits them as awaits the opposing world and the 'beast' of Revelation – a fate described as 'the lake of fire' and 'the second death'.[9] Bible students differ as to how this is to be understood, and it would take us far off course to enter into details. It is enough to know that their ultimate end is an eternal and irreversible separation from God. But the 'end' for Paul, the goal and outcome of the apostolic life, is very different: 'the prize of the upward call of God in Christ Jesus'.[10]

Secondly, they worship themselves: *their god is the belly*. They recognize no need and no authority outside personal satisfaction. Their appetites dictate their lives. Again, this is not the apostolic way. Paul, who had 'no confidence in the flesh', testified to being far from perfect ('not that I have already obtained this or am already perfect') and very far from content with present attainments ('straining forward . . . I press on . . .').[11] Thus, again, two ways of life are in contrast.

Thirdly, they find cause to glory in things of which they ought to be ashamed. Their sense of values justifies as allowable

[7]*Cf*. Rom. 3:8; 6:1.    [8]*Cf*. Rom. 12:2a.
[9]Phil. 1:28; Rev. 17:11; 19:20; 20:14.
[10]Phil. 3:14; *cf*. 1:23.    [11]Phil. 3:3, 12–14.

things which it ought to condemn. Paul was wholly absorbed in 'glorying in Christ Jesus' (verses 3, 7–12) and in making every effort to attain what Christ had purposed for his life. The contrast here is between making the self and making Christ the moral authority for life.

Finally, there is a contrast of horizons. They are earthbound. Their minds are *set on earthly things*. Their whole attention, their point of view or way of looking at things, their general frame of mind, their customary objects of study – all these are earth-centred and bounded by the horizons of this world. But Paul's eyes are on heaven, and the prize of the heavenly calling (verse 14).

Why does Paul go out of his way to depict this contrasting life? Because he must warn against it. This is no external danger or far-off contingency. He sees his Philippians as faced daily by this contrary example: *mark those who so live* (verse 17). There are two ways of life constantly inviting the obedience of the Christian, and Paul had nothing else to offer but the constant pulling of the one against the other. There is no recipe for 'peace' (so-called) here. There is no promise of deliverance from struggle, tension and persistent temptation. Like Israel of old, the Christian of today stands between the blessing and the cursing, the way of life and the way of death,[12] and the whole Christian pathway is the battle to choose life. This is the meaning of the stark contrast between the life of the apostle and the life of those whom he calls *enemies of the cross*. Faithfully and in love to us Paul has raised the warning sign.

## 2. Diagnosis

Since we can never escape the pull of temptation till we are safe with Christ, we must dwell a little on Paul's diagnosis in order to see more precisely the character of those whose end is destruction. As they progress towards this end, there are three points of spiritual degeneration: *their god is the belly*, their *glory* is *in their shame*, and their *minds* are *set on earthly things*.

The first point at which they are spiritually degenerating is *their devotion to self-indulgence*. Their appetites and emotions

[12]*Cf.* Dt. 30:19.

have ceased to be subject to them and have been accorded the place of lordship and worship. They are governed by self-pleasing in bodily matters. Paul does not elaborate. He does not call them fornicators or drug-addicts or particularize their pet sensualities. If he did so we might stand aloof from the warning, if it did not happen to apply to us. The warning is not against particular sins, but against the underlying sin of pandering to self. In one Christian the temptation may be towards sexual sin, in another towards gossiping, in another towards lying in bed instead of being alone with God in the morning. Paul raises the warning. Here is the downward path and those who walk it are enemies of the cross of Christ. There must have been many mature believers in the church at Rome, for Paul was inspired to write to them his major doctrinal epistle. But he still thought it appropriate to call them away from revelling and drunkenness, debauchery and licentiousness.[13] The bodily sin is never far beneath the surface even of the most advanced saint, and the warning is always necessary.

Paul's second observation as he diagnoses spiritual degeneration is *their reversal of moral standards* : *they glory in their shame*. In other words, they exalt things and practices which they ought to be ashamed of but are not. Clearly this is the next stage downward. First they give themselves to indulgence; next they justify themselves in doing so and say that this is a proper and allowable way of life. Long ago the prophet Isaiah saw the very same thing in the life of his nation. He observed those who 'call evil good and good evil'. He noted two aspects of their reversal of moral standards: they 'put darkness for light and light for darkness' and they 'put bitter for sweet and sweet for bitter'.[14] Light and darkness are objective facts governing all alike. By this illustration he showed how they tried to make their topsy-turvy moral code a law of public behaviour. Bitter and sweet are matters of individual preference. By this illustration he showed that their public code was rooted in their life of self-pleasing. So it is with those whom Paul describes. But once more he does not particularize. There is no dwelling upon this or that reversal of moral values, but upon the thing itself. The warning has been given. Here is the downward path and those

[13]Rom. 13:13.    [14]Is. 5:20.

who walk it are enemies of the cross of Christ.

We are sometimes inclined to think that no period of history has ever been like ours in attempting to reverse moral standards. This is most unlikely to be true. Now, as always, the world is preaching its own standards and very, very often they are not the standards of God's Word. The Christian must remember that we are called not only to believe revealed doctrine but to obey revealed law, and the book of the law should not depart from our mouth, but we should meditate on it day and night in order to make our way, our public life and conduct, prosperous.[15]

In the final diagnosis the root of the trouble is discovered in *their cultivation of an earthly mind*: their *minds* are *set on earthly things*. At the very centre of their being, where their life finds its direction, where attitudes and tendencies are fashioned which subsequently influence decisions and govern likes and dislikes – at this vital centre the world and its ways are the whole object of attention. The mind is set upon earth.

Consider another passage in the Bible in which Paul reveals why the world is under the wrath of God. Men 'suppress the truth'; 'although they knew God they did not honour him as God'; they 'became futile in their thinking'; 'they exchanged the truth about God'; 'they did not see fit to acknowledge God'; 'God gave them up to a base mind'.[16] The point of spiritual collapse was where people know, grasp truth, reason, make up the mind. The rebellion of the mind from God is the fundamental state of the sinner.

Turn now to other passages in which Paul reveals the life of regeneration: 'be transformed by the renewal of your mind'; 'be renewed in the spirit of your minds'; 'set your minds on things that are above.'[17] What a vital part the mind plays in the experience of the Christian! Paul will soon say to the Philippians, 'Whatever is true, . . . honourable, . . . just, . . . pure, . . . lovely, . . . gracious, . . . think about these things' (4:8). The wise man advised, 'Keep your heart with all vigilance; for from it flow the springs of life.'[18] The mind astray from God is the most potent of all forces for spiritual disaster. Paul has raised

[15]Jos. 1:8.    [16]Rom. 1:18–32.
[17]Rom. 12:2; Eph. 4:23; Col. 3:2.
[18]Pr. 4:23.

his warning again. Here is the downward path, and those who walk on it are enemies of the cross of Christ.

## 3. Remedy

The fourfold description, touching on the destiny, emotions, conscience and mind of those over whom Paul weeps, is summed up in one statement: they are *enemies of the cross of Christ*. It is easy to see why destruction should be the destiny of an enemy of the cross, for no-one but Christ can bring us to God, and no name but his can save.[19] It is by his cross that he achieved these purposes, bringing us to new life in his kingdom.[20] But in what ways do self-pleasing, perverted standards and a worldly cast of mind class us as enemies of the cross?

The first answer to this question is the hardest to accept. We are by nature in a state of enmity against God and these conditions of the emotions, conscience and mind are at the heart of that hostile nature. When we think of ourselves in our pre-conversion days, or when we look around at our non-Christian friends, 'enmity' against God and Christ is not a word which would all that often spring to our minds. For the most part, we did not feel hostile. It was just that we did not really want to be bothered, or to have to face the demands of Jesus, or to think too much about that rather threatening business of giving our lives over to him. But we must remind ourselves that Jesus described as his 'enemies' those 'who did not want me to reign over them'.[21] We are no more the best judge of our condition than is the patient who, on hearing the doctor's diagnosis of cancer, replies, 'But I feel all right.' The divine Diagnostician notes that it was 'while we were enemies' that 'we were reconciled' by the death of Christ, and that 'the mind of the flesh is enmity against God'.[22]

Secondly, when we contemplate the cross – or rather, the One who died on the cross – we see embodied there values directly opposed to, inimical to, those against which Paul warns us in verse 19. In Gethsemane our Lord denied himself. On the cross he upheld and displayed the righteousness of God

[19]Jn. 14:6; Acts 4:12.
[20]Eph. 2:13–19; Rom. 5:8–9; Col. 1:13–14.
[21]Lk. 19:27.     [22]Rom. 5:10; 9:7, RV.

and his law,[23] took with the utmost seriousness (even as far as death) all the legal demands against us, and cancelled them, nailing them as receipted bills to his cross.[24] In all this he had the 'heavenly mind' we studied in 2:5–8: the determination to obey God and love sinners, whatever the cost to himself.

Thirdly, on the cross Christ identified himself with all our self-pleasings, reckoned as his own all our shady moral compromises and open moral lapses, and became in himself the sin which anchored us to earth and destined us for hell. By bearing our sin in his own body on the cross, he discharged our debt before God, wiped away our past and re-created us in his own image. To continue in sin as if he had never died, to value sinful practices as if he had not exposed and discredited them, to live within earthly horizons as if the Son of God had not opened before our eyes a vision of heaven, and to remain bound by the trammels of the old life when he has achieved new life for sinners – is not this to oppose all that the cross means? Is it not enmity?

But those who love his cross find it to be 'the power of God',[25] and find their union with the crucified but now living Christ to be the ground and means of transformed living. Bishop Handley Moule died in 1920. In January 1919 he wrote to a nephew: 'I have often prayed that daily, and to the end, I may live as in a tent pitched between the Cross and the Grave of our Lord – the *empty* Cross, symbol and seal of His finished work of sacrifice and redemption, the *empty* grave, likewise the evidence and pledge of His eternal victory for us over the last enemy, death, and of our life hid with Him in God. May your tent be ever there also'[26] – and there, we might say, not only because of the power of the cross and resurrection in the face of death, but also because of their power in the face of life:

> Safe sheltered from alarm and loss
>  I sit within my quiet tent;
> 'Twixt here a Grave and there a Cross
>  My days and nights in peace are spent.

[23]Rom. 3:25–31.     [24]Col. 2:14.     [25]1Cor. 1:18.
[26]*Letters and Poems of Bishop Moule*, ed. J. B. Harford (1921), p. 15.

Peace, grace and glory now he gives,
   Fair fruits of his unfathomed woes,
And with me in my tent he lives,
   The Lamb that died, the Life that rose.[27]

[27] *Ibid.*, p. 115.

## 20. Christ our hope

*But our commonwealth is in heaven, and from it we await a Saviour, the Lord Jesus Christ, [21]who will change our lowly body to be like his glorious body, by the power which enables him even to subject all things to himself.*

The Bible is a great book for insisting on living in the present: '*Now* is the day of salvation.'[1] But it never draws a foolish line between past, present and future. Successful life in the present takes account of the lessons and blessings of the past, and of the demands and prospects of the future. In this present passage, Paul has already shown that life lived in the apostolic mould rests upon the past event of Calvary. It is a proper relation to and love for the cross of Christ which rescues us from the danger of spiritual degeneration. But equally we must have that forward look which was such a characteristic of the New Testament. Did the apostles believe that Christ would come back in their lifetime? Of course they did, for no other attitude is permitted to the New Testament Christian – then or now.

This is a doctrine that has very largely been forgotten – where it is not denied altogether – by the church today. And very often in those sections of the church where it is still held and studied, the joy of the Lord's return is lost in controversies and speculations of a most forbidding nature. Paul has a word for all in these present verses. Those who have forgotten the

[1]2 Cor. 6:2.

Lord's coming again will find here a thrilling reminder of it. Those who have almost lost sight of the coming Saviour amid the complexities of theories about when and where and how, will be recalled to the bare and glorious essential, that he will come again. Those who dismiss such a doctrine – for whatever reason – must face here an apostolic reaffirmation of it in the most unequivocal terms.

## 1. A distinctive Christian belief

In the last study we saw how the life and prospects of the enemies of the cross of Christ contrasted, point by point, with the personal life and hopes of Paul. In verse 20, where he turns to speak of the hope that is common to all Christians, he naturally changes from the 'I' of testimony to the *'we'* of shared truth. But again, and as if deliberately, he points up the contrast between the 'enemies' and those with whom he identifies himself.

The 'enemies of the cross' are heading for destruction (verse 19), but we are waiting for *a Saviour* from heaven (verse 20). They are devoted to the body, worshipping and making a god of its appetites. But we, quite the reverse, look for its transformation, for we consider it to be *our lowly body*, literally 'the body of our humiliation' (verse 21). They have a perverted, topsy-turvy scale of values, glorying in shameful things, but we possess a true perception of value, having some appreciation even now of his glory (verse 21). And finally, they are earthbound, while *our commonwealth is in heaven* (verse 20).

Thus the contrast is complete, but the description – or the implied description – is unexpected. They are 'enemies of the cross of Christ'. We might have expected that when the apostle describes the opposite sort of people he would call them 'lovers, or friends, of the cross of Christ' – and such a description would be true, for Calvary is the source of all that makes us different from Christ's 'enemies'. But he does not do so. He describes us as 'watchers for the return' – *we await a Saviour.*

This parity of the cross and the return is noteworthy. Is it not true to say that we think of the cross as a cardinal Christian doctrine to a degree that we do not usually accord to the second coming? But Paul makes the two events equally the basis of present Christian living. Indeed the more one studies these verses the more it becomes apparent that Paul could equally well have described the 'enemies' as hostile to the Lord's return and Christians as living on the basis of his past work of salvation on the cross.

The return of Christ, then, is a distinctive Christian doctrine and cannot be jettisoned from our statement of faith if we are to return to the New Testament. We must learn, in fact, to think in God's way. We have been taught already that 'he who began a good work in you' is continually completing it with a view to 'the day of Jesus Christ'.[2] The second coming is the designed end of all God's saving work. Again we have been taught that the death of Christ has been the subject of deliberate divine appraisal and response; that God has responded to the cross in the supreme exaltation of Jesus above every conceivable authority,[3] and that the intended outcome of this is universal submission to Jesus Christ who is Lord. In God's estimation Calvary requires the return as its only just and adequate acknowledgment. Nothing else will suffice to express what God thinks of the obedience of his Son. To deny the return is to fail to appreciate the cross; to forget the return is to lose hold of the excellence of the cross.

## 2. The Christian's personal longing

Because he has this awareness of the return of Christ as a central Christian belief, alongside the cross, Paul expects that all Christians will be one with him in looking for it expectantly. He speaks, therefore, of *we*. What is this expectation?

First, we note a longing for the blessings which the returning Christ will bring with him. Very practically Paul puts his finger on the point of our present need, *our lowly body* (verse 21). It is no wonder that he had to warn us so strongly of the power of the example of those whose 'god is the belly' (verse 19). For Christians are very aware of the downward pull of their bodies. Here is an area where Christians constantly fall short and fail: we fail to control our lust, manage our tongue, overcome the laziness which keeps us out of bed too late at night and in bed

[2]Phil. 1:6.    [3]Phil. 2:8–11.

too late in the morning, and subdue the 'unwilling flesh' which clogs the ambitions of the 'willing spirit'.[4] This is not to mention the gradual failing of bodily strength with the passing years, so that our mental powers wane and understanding diminishes, or the debilitating and often humiliating aspects of illness, or failing sight, or any of the other numerous ways in which the body holds us back and keeps us down – truly *our lowly body*.

But we hope for One who will change our lowly body *to be like his glorious body*. Paul elsewhere described this refashioning as the continuation of personal identity in the midst of remarkable alteration: the seed growing into its own characteristic flower.[5] A seed is a humble thing, unprepossessing and to all outward appearance unpromising. Yet this seed becomes that flower in a continuous process of wonderful transformation. So it will be for our loved ones who are already with the Lord. We shall know them when we see them, for there is continuity within the glory; so it will be for us who love his cross and his coming.

When Paul says that our destiny is *to be like his glorious body*, we must be cautious in what we understand it to mean. The (literally) 'body of his glory' is the vehicle of outward action and expression which perfectly matches and responds to his inner, perfect nature. But what do words like 'outward' and 'inner' mean in relation to the heavenly state? We are in no position at present to say. The Bible – indeed Jesus himself – permits us to use the familiar language of space and time in relation to heaven, while giving us reason to believe that it all transcends our present powers of thought and description.[6] We have a clue to Paul's meaning here in the fact that *like* in verse 21 translates the same word as *like* in verse 10.[7] There it obviously refers to experiences like his, not to an appearance like his. In the present verse surely the balance must be the same: when the Lord Jesus comes again it will be to bring us into full possession of the total salvation he obtained on the cross. In particular,

---

[4]*Cf.* Mk. 14:38; Rom. 7:18–24.    [5]1 Cor. 15:35–49.

[6]Jesus spoke of 'where' and 'there' in relation to heaven, *e.g.* Jn. 14:1–3; 17:24. We have no other vocabulary at our disposal, yet we must keep what we say within the context of 1 Cor. 2:9.

[7]Here *symmorphon*; in verse 10, *symmorphizomenos*.

according to the present verses, in place of a body which is so often at odds with spiritual aspirations, so often a drag on our spiritual endeavours, there will be a body matching his in being the perfect means of living the full, whole life of Christ. Yet, at the same time, can we exclude the thought that in appearance, too, we shall each reflect something of the likeness of our Saviour? After all, it is into his image that we are being transformed, and the glory of the day of his coming will in part be that we shall find ourselves like the One we shall then see.[8]

The blessings which the returning Lord brings are thus very great, yet they are not the primary object of our longing expectations. The first longing is for the Lord himself: *we await a Saviour, the Lord Jesus Christ.* The verb (*apek-dechomai*) expresses concentrated eagerness and persistence of expectation. It suggests an eye detached from every other object to watch only for him when he comes in the fullness of his office as *Saviour* (here again is the link between the coming and the cross) and in the fullness of his divine-human Person, *the Lord Jesus Christ.* We can catch something of Paul's own longing in that he omits nothing here from the full title of his Saviour – *the Lord Jesus Christ.* It is he himself who is the supreme attraction in the Christian hope. We may well look forward to many things: deliverance at last from even the presence of sin and temptation; meeting the great ones of old – Abraham, Isaiah, Paul himself; reunion with loved ones we knew on earth; the glory of the heavenly places. Yes, indeed, all these things, but beyond them all that one feature which gives coherence and meaning and focus to heaven, that one Person through whom alone this great company is gathered and for whom alone is the glory, 'the Lamb standing, as though it had been slain', 'the Lamb in the midst of the throne',[9] the *Saviour, the Lord Jesus Christ.* 'So shall we always be *with the Lord*', wrote Paul in another place.[10] 'His servants shall worship him; they shall see his face', promised John.[11]

---

[8]Eph. 4:24; 1 Jn. 3:2.    [9]Rev. 5:6; 7:17.    [10]1 Thes. 4:17.
[11]Rev. 22:3–4.

## 3. A guaranteed certainty

No argument against the possibility of the second coming can survive the teaching of these verses. Here indeed is something that deserves the description 'hope', for in the New Testament there is no uncertainty in hope, but the assurance that what we hope for will happen at an unspecified time. Paul offers no dates for the return of Christ. It is an imminent possibility for which the Christian must be in constant readiness and it is capable of tarrying for a thousand years.[12] But nothing can stop it happening at the moment which God the Father has fore-ordained for it.[13]

The guarantee is expressed here in the words *by the power which enables him even to subject all things to himself* (verse 21). The ability of the Lord is stated in three ways here. First, it is available power, the power resident in his divine nature. This is expressed by the verb *enables*. This Greek word (*dynamai*) has contributed the word 'dynamite' to the English language, and that is not a bad pointer to its force. But, secondly, that is not all. Many people possess great powers, even great resources, but lack the opportunity, or the right, or the wisdom, or the ability to make them effective. Not so our Lord! His power is also effective power. We have already met the verb corresponding to the noun here translated *power* (2:13). Its significance is 'power in exercise', a 'working' which comes right in on target and cannot be deflected from its aim.

Thirdly, it is the invincible power enabling him *even to subject all things to himself* – the 'forces' of nature, the ordered universe, the unbelieving hearts of men, spiritual wickedness in heavenly places, the prince of the power of the air: mention any opponent of the return of Christ and Scripture will nullify its opposition by the power that subdues all things. The power of Christ is thus inherent, applied and invincible, and it is this power which underwrites the promise of his coming again.

## 4. Present implications

We do not gaze into the future in order to satisfy the

[12]Phil. 4:5–6; 2 Pet. 3:3–10.    [13]Mk. 13:32; Acts 1:7.

'horoscope' mentality. The promise of his coming is given without date so that we may live daily preparing to meet our Lord.[14] Life in the present is motivated by awareness of the future. Indeed, Paul opens his discussion of the future coming with a present tense: *Our commonwealth is in heaven.* The word is really 'citizenship' (as RV), the noun corresponding to the verb discussed at 1:27. Christians are, even now, citizens of the commonwealth of heaven, and this is our status as we await our Saviour. We belong to a far-off homeland and wait for the King of that land to come and fetch us. Our names are on the citizenship rolls there and our place is secure, but while we wait here we must live as if we were there.

All this would have appealed to the Philippians, for they were already living as citizens of the far-off Rome and they knew the sort of life citizenship involved. In our heavenly homeland, the primary feature is the constant presence of the King. Very well, then, as citizens, that is the present privilege of our lives; in the heavenly homeland, all are conformed to his likeness: let us occupy ourselves till he come in becoming 'like him in his death, that if possible I may attain the resurrection of the dead'.[15] In heaven, all things obey his will: we must give ourselves to the primary duty of obedience. And in heaven the reality of his almighty power is evident and experienced: this is the power at work in us[16] and available to us to live out our lives in the apostolic pattern and in accordance with the truth of Christ.

[14]Lk. 12:35–48.     [15]Phil. 3:10–11.     [16]Phil. 2:13; Eph. 3:20.

# 4:1-3

# 21. Meanwhile

*Therefore, my brethren, whom I love and long for, my joy and crown, stand firm thus in the Lord, my beloved.*
*²I entreat Euodia and I entreat Syntyche to agree in the Lord.*
*³And I ask you also, true yokefellow, help these women, for they have laboured side by side with me in the gospel together with Clement and the rest of my fellow workers, whose names are in the book of life.*

Paul does not need our help to draw conclusions. We ended the preceding study by suggesting some of the implications of the idea of citizenship. Such thoughts are correct in their place, but they must not distract us from the fact that, by the *Therefore* of 4:1, Paul proceeds to draw some conclusions of his own. He will now tell us how to live in the 'meanwhile' between Calvary and the coming.

First, he sees the Philippians' need to *stand firm* (verse 1). They are in the midst of enemies, especially the 'enemies of the cross of Christ' (3:18). There is a real danger that they will be drawn away by this present threat and a consequent need for a resolute *stand*. Alongside this, there was, secondly, the practical need for unity in the local church (verses 2–3), for Christians cannot stand fast from a position of division and disharmony.

Two otherwise unknown believers are mentioned by name: *Euodia* and *Syntyche*. Paul calls on them to settle their differences. The call is all the more impressive in that the cause of disagreement is not mentioned. Was it doctrinal, ethical, ecclesiastical, personal? What was it? We do not know. The thing that grieves Paul and rouses him to exhortation is not that they had fallen out over some particular issue, but simply that they had fallen out and brought division into the fellowship.

In the first place, such divisions are *contrary to the apostle's mind.* His attitude towards other Christians is expressed in verse 1: *my brethren, whom I love and long for, my joy and crown . . . my beloved.* If this is the way Christians should view each other, then division is scandal indeed, for we must remember that apostolic attitudes are Christian ideals.[1] Christians belong in a family unity: to Paul, they are *my brethren.* It was a triumph of grace that this should have been so. Paul had been a proud Pharisee, intensely aware both of his own privileged status and of Gentiles as outsiders: 'separated from Christ, alienated from the commonwealth of Israel, and strangers to the covenants of promise, having no hope and without God in the world'.[2] Paul wrote these words full of missionary enthusiasm and love and longing for the lost. Imagine, instead, that he was simply describing – even being satisfied with – the status of the Gentiles, and we have some idea of the gulf between Jew and non-Jew in the ancient world. But now, in Christ, they are brothers; all are in one family;[3] they have a Father, and a Saviour, and a Comforter in common. The division of Christians is the sin of fratricide.

Tender affection is the next element in the apostle's attitude towards his fellow-Christians: *whom I love and long for . . . my beloved.* The repetition underlines the emotion. He really loves them. 'This is my beloved Son', said God,[4] and Paul uses the same word of his feeling towards his fellow-believers. (*Cf.* the repeated 'beloved' in RV.) But he adds to it a word of very great intensity, *long for.* He used it previously of his longing for the Philippians in 1:8, and gave it a characteristic setting in the case of Epaphroditus[5] who, he says, was 'longing for them all', or 'was homesick'. We need not develop the idea any further. To put it just like that rebukes our lukewarm affection for our fellow-Christians. We have a long way to go before we are

---

[1]*Cf.* Phil. 3:15, 17; 4:9.    [2]Eph. 2:12.    [3]*Cf.* Eph. 2:18ff.
[4]Mt 3:17.    [5]Phil. 2:26.

feeling the emotions of Christ towards each other as Paul was[6] –
we who so easily dismiss from our reckoning those whom God
has accepted and reconciled, and who so lightly offend those
for whom Christ died.[7] If we felt for each other as Paul did, we
should soon recognize the scandal of division.

But he went one step further. Other Christians were to him
the objects of pastoral concern, *my joy and crown*. When Paul
thus uses these words he has his mind fixed on the day of Christ
and our gathering together to him.[8] It is part of Paul's love for
his Christian friends that he longs for them to be ready and
acceptable to Christ on the day of his return. The *crown* can be
equally that 'of victor or of holiday-maker' (Lightfoot). To
Paul it is a victory to see them accepted before the throne, and
at the same time the proper garland of one who is banqueting
with the King of kings and his chosen guests. Thus, in part, his
zealous and affectionate concern for them is explained. He sees
them in the light of Calvary, where they were purchased, and of
the coming by which they will be gathered into glory.

On all these counts, therefore, division scandalized Paul. It
was the very reverse of his apostolic mind. But also, a divided
church is *contrary to the nature of the church*. Incidentally to
verse 3, in which Paul summons certain other Christians to the
aid of the quarrelling women, we see what the church would be
like were it true to its nature. Of three truths about the church
found here, the first is that it possesses a *single task*: *they have
laboured side by side with me in the gospel*, or 'they and I were
co-workers in the gospel'. Where there is agreement as to what
the gospel is and what ought to be done with it, there is no
room for personal disagreement. The one ought to exclude the
other. Very often, of course, as at Philippi, it does not; but it
ought to. To agree on the gospel is the most fundamental form
of unity: it involves a unity of mind and heart as to the doctrine
and personal experience of salvation. To agree on what the
gospel demands in its proclamation to the world is to cement
unity by common action. The singleness of the task ought to be
reflected in the singleness of the workers.

Furthermore, the church should be marked by *mutual*

[6]*Cf.* Phil. 1:8.    [7]*Cf.* Rom. 14:3, 15–20.
[8]On his 'joy', *cf.* Phil. 2:16–18, and on 'joy and crown', *cf.* 1 Thes.
2:19.

*helpfulness*: *help these women*. No Christian, we might say, is at liberty to stand aloof from the needs of any other Christian. The very existence of the need is of itself a call to come to the rescue. Paul does not say to Euodia and Syntyche that they should ask the 'true yokefellow' for his help. The command is to him to make the first move (uninvited, save by Paul). We do not know who this person was. Some have suggested that the translation should be 'Synzygos, well-named' – a man who by name and nature was a 'yokefellow'. But may be Paul is summoning Christians in general to the rescue of the troubled women: 'If any of you would live up to your place and duty as Christians, take this yoke on you and help the women out of their tangled life.' Maybe so, we cannot say; but we can say that Paul assumed that this element of mutual assistance was an essential part of inter-Christian relationships.

Finally, Paul displays the church as a place of *fundamental oneness*: *whose names are in the book of life*. There is a heavenly reality about the church, and there are no divisions in heaven. All who are there are 'one in Christ Jesus', for the only people to enter that kingdom are those who 'have washed their robes and made them white in the blood of the Lamb', and their security of tenure depends on their names being in 'the Lamb's book of life'.[9] Divisions contradict this fundamental 'fact of life'. The church on earth is called to be a replica of the ideal or heavenly. This is involved in the possession of heavenly 'citizenship': to live here and now in the privileges and duties of the far-off homeland. Thus it is against the nature of the church, the community of the redeemed,[10] to confess unity in heaven and practise disunity on earth.

In this incidental polemic against disunity and division, Paul reminds us, thirdly, of the practical point, that division among Christians is *a serious flaw in the church's armour against the world*. For the second time Paul is allowing his thoughts to travel along the same line. In 1:27–28 he called the church to 'stand firm in one spirit', for he discerned that there were 'opponents' whose opposition could easily 'stampede' the Christians in terror. Here, in 4:1, he calls us to *stand firm . . . in the Lord*, for Paul has descried enemies of the cross whose

[9]Rev. 7:14; 20:12–14; 21:27.     [10]Acts 20:28.

pernicious example could entice Christians from apostolic ways into paths of spiritual danger. He developed his exhortation in chapter 1 by showing that only a united church could present a united front, resolutely facing opposition and not giving ground. Therefore in 2:2 he required them to be 'of the same mind'. In the same way, in 4:2 the requirement of unity is made: *agree in the Lord*. The parallelism of thought is striking. Twice over Paul takes the same line, that only a united church can hope to face its foes and stand firm. Where there is disharmony inside there is bound to be defeat outside. Where Christians cannot bear the sight of each other, they will not be able to look the world in the face either. They cannot win on the main 'front' of their contact with the world if they are secretly carrying on warfare on a 'second front' of their own devising.

In summary, then, this is why Paul sees disunity as such a solemn and disastrous thing: it is contrary to the apostolic mind; it is a denial of the nature of the church; and it is a flaw in the church's armour against the world. In the light of all this, how noteworthy that Paul (who apparently knew all about the differences between the two women in question) neither specifies the problem nor tries to act as mediator. He does not sum up their rival claims; he does not say to the one or the other, 'You are wrong; you must apologize.' He does not sit on the fence with 'There are two sides to every story; you are both partly right and partly wrong. So kiss and make up.' It is not a matter of who is right and who is wrong or what rightness and wrongness exists on each side. The plea *I entreat* is made to each contestant alike. No doubt each said, 'I am right, she is wrong'; but to Paul each was under the same obligation to make the first move.

Relationships can become atrociously tangled, and Christian relationships are no exception. Starting, however, where things are fairly simple, there is the situation where one believer has wronged another. Maybe it was this for Euodia and Syntyche. Neither is to wait for the other. The one is not to say, 'I am perfectly ready to accept an apology when it is made', nor the other, 'I am perfectly ready to make an apology when I have a hint that it will be accepted.' Each must make the first move.

More difficult is the case where each believes the other to be in the wrong and where no amount of 'talking the thing through' can make sense of it. Yet even here there is no need to allow a breakdown of Christian love and communication. 'Conditional' apologies are in order: 'I do not see where I have wronged you, but it is plain that you feel I have hurt you, so please forgive me' – and all the realities of grace and power, forbearance and gentleness available *in the Lord* can be brought to our aid; the place of prayer is open, and even though the past cannot be resolved it need no longer be an open sore.

Worst of all are cases where a breakdown in trust is involved: perhaps one Christian has betrayed a confidence and the other, the betrayed, has to say, 'How can I ever trust him again?' And, sadly, the answer sometimes has to be that the old trust cannot be recovered, that from now on all serious communication must be with a third party present to vouch, if necessary, for what was said, and that where there was once frankness, now there must be wariness. It is sad when things are so, but fellowship is not foolishness and we need to be as aware of each other's weaknesses as we are admiring of each other's strengths. Nevertheless, *in the Lord* we can find strength to eradicate bitterness of heart, and even though we cannot speak of the past again, never mind mend it, we can understand one another, express practical concern and pray for each other.

While we may thank God that the first and easiest of our three examples is more common than the others, it is in itself no matter for thanksgiving but rather for action. The matter of dispute between Euodia and Syntyche is not described and we may each fill in our own details. Likewise, the *true yokefellow* is left anonymous: here also we may put our own names, ever alert to discern and then to heal the cancer of disunity in the fellowship of the church.

**4:4–9**

# 22. The peace of God and the God of peace

*Rejoice in the Lord always; again I will say, Rejoice. ⁵Let all men know your forbearance. The Lord is at hand. ⁶Have no anxiety about anything, but in everything by prayer and supplication with thanksgiving let your requests be made known to God. ⁷And the peace of God, which passes all understanding, will keep your hearts and your minds in Christ Jesus.*

*⁸Finally, brethren, whatever is true, whatever is honourable, whatever is just, whatever is pure, whatever is lovely, whatever is gracious, if there is any excellence, if there is anything worthy of praise, think about these things. ⁹What you have learned and received and heard and seen in me, do; and the God of peace will be with you.*

Public problems require private solutions. We have already traced the parallel between Paul's teaching from 1:27 to 2:2 and his teaching from 3:18 to 4:2. In each case he was insistent that only a united church can face the world without retreating. But the parallel between the two sections goes one step further. In 2:2–4, when tackling the problem of a divided church, he focused his teaching upon the individual Christian, 'each of you' (verse 4). In the last analysis therefore the public success of the church along the front where it faces the world depends upon the measure of sanctification of each individual Christian.

The teaching is the same, though differently expressed and developed, in the later passage which now lies before us. In calling for unity and unanimity within the local church fellowship, Paul starts with the quarrelling individuals Euodia and Syntyche (verse 2), but then he proceeds with a general exhortation to all individuals. He uses plural verbs, *'Rejoice'*, *etc.*, but the command is common rather than corporate, for his point of conclusion is 'your hearts and your minds' (verse 7) – the inward state of the individual church members. We shall study his teaching under three headings: the needs, the promises and the conditions.

## 1. The needs

At the risk of being tedious, let us see again the structure of this passage. It presents the same pattern which we found in 1:27 – 2:4. Again we have an inverted triangle with the long side uppermost and the point at the bottom. The long side represents the frontier where church and world face each other: the 'enmity' of 3:18. The point on which the church is supported for the conflict is the individual believer – the 'hearts and minds' of 4:7. The needs of this believer in the parallel passage in 1:27 – 2:4 were the characteristics of glad self-submission and obedience to the will of God which were exemplified in Christ (2:5–8). But as Paul analyses the individual's needs here, he speaks not of virtues to be practised but of blessings to be enjoyed: *the peace of God . . . will keep your hearts and your minds* (verse 7) and *the God of peace will be with you* (verse 9).

First, there is the need of a garrison (for this is the meaning of the word *guard*) around *hearts and minds*. We have already referred to passages of Scripture which will enable us to understand why Paul sees this as a real Christian need. *Hearts and minds* point to source and outflow. The source is the *heart*, that comprehensive term which the Bible uses to include functions which we would distribute between mind, will, emotions and conscience. It is the inner side of the personality, and in particular the inner source from which all outer life springs. The *mind* is the outflow from this source in terms of definite plans which we entertain, imaginations which captivate us, and so forth. Now, the *heart* in this sense has much the same meaning as 'mind' in 3:19, the inner source and spring of life, and as we saw there it is the mind astray from God which is the cause of man's downfall and the primary object of God's wrath.[1] It is the mind renewed in Christ which is the growing-point of the new life of the child of God.[2] Since, therefore, the outward impact of the church upon the world depends upon its own inward unity, member to member, and since this in turn depends upon sanctified individuals, the first and most crying need is for a transformation and keeping of *hearts and minds in Christ Jesus*, lest they go the way of the enemies of the cross of Christ and individual degeneration jeopardize the cause of the gospel.

Hard on the heels of this need Paul mentions another: the need for the conscious presence of God: *the God of peace will be with you* (verse 9). Why does Paul feel it necessary to affirm this promise? It may be that he is seeking to correct a wrong conclusion regarding his teaching about the return of Christ. One of the marks of this age of the church is, after all, that the Lord is not here; he has gone away. Nevertheless, the position of the believer is not simply one of waiting for an absent Lord to return; it is also one of enjoying the reality of a Lord who is always present.

Yet, even here, there is an element of danger. The presence of God can become a credal formula rather than a living reality. Theoretically we know that he is with us; experimentally we forget him and, lacking a vivid sense of his presence, we fall into sin and slackness which would surely not mar our lives if we were sharply conscious of the Lord alongside. Hence we have a real need to know that *the God of peace* is *with us*.

## 2. The promises

Against this background, Paul paints in three promises expressed in the words *which passes all understanding, the peace of God . . . will keep,* and *the God of peace will be with you.*

The first promise is that our lives will be touched with a mark of the supernatural, something that *passes all understanding* (verse 7). The meaning here is not of something mysterious and incomprehensible in its own right, but of something which man cannot explain or explain away; something which runs

---

[1]*Cf.* Rom. 1:18ff.    [2]*Cf.* Rom. 12:2; *etc.*

beyond the range of human comprehension.

Much of our difficulty in standing firm for Christ is that people do not see why we want (as they say) to be different. The world puts our attempts to live by different standards down to personal whim – like the lady whose obituary notice remarked that 'her chief hobby was religion'. What we need today – as at every period of history – is the touch of the supernatural, something that cannot be explained except by saying, 'This is the finger of God.'[3] This is what is now promised, a peace *which passes all understanding* standing guard over our hearts.

The second promise is that God's peace will guard us and God himself will be our companion: *the peace of God . . . will keep . . . the God of peace will be with you.* This is a picture of a besieged citadel. It is the castle of the mind of the Christian. If the castle can be held, progress in sanctification and renewal goes forward; if it can be captured, then backsliding and spiritual decadence begin. But it is garrisoned strongly. Its walls are constantly patrolled. Its sentries never sleep at their posts. The troops are the Household Guards of the King of kings and they march behind the standard of the peace of God. Meanwhile, inside the citadel, hearts and thoughts alike are kept in quietness, for their Companion is the King himself, *the God of peace* who is with them. Whether or not Paul had such a picture in mind, this is the upshot of his words: the presence of God in power and in experience.

The third promise is peace, *the peace of God . . . the God of peace . . .* Detached from its New Testament content, the word 'peace' is a sort of spiritual marshmallow, full of softness and sweetness but without much actual substance. But if we study the scriptures which associate 'peace' and 'God' it is surprisingly full of strength and vigour. The 'God of peace' is the God who makes peace between himself and sinners. Thus peace is linked with God's work of salvation. For example, when the risen Christ visited his disciples in the locked upper room on the first Easter evening, his word to them was, 'Peace be with you.' This was no conventional greeting, for he repeated it almost at once, 'Peace be with you', as if to underline a

[3]Ex. 8:19.

surprising and splendid reality.[4] John does well to link the word of 'peace' with Christ's showing of his hands and side,[5] for peace is the first-fruit of Calvary. The God of peace is the God of salvation who does away with sin by the cross of his Son.

The God of peace is also the God of power, for it is 'the God of peace who brought again from the dead our Lord Jesus', and the resurrection is, in the New Testament, the great demonstration of divine power.[6] Another passage says that 'the God of peace will soon crush Satan under your feet'.[7] The God of peace is thus the God of victory. In the light of all this the promise of peace is very comprehensive indeed – salvation, power and victory all in one.

Each of us is placed in a position of great responsibility: the onward march and the resolute stand of the church in the world depends, in the final human analysis, on the state of my heart, the quality of my holiness. In this situation, God is the mighty Indweller (2:13) and the God who sets a supernatural mark on our lives. He is our Guard and Companion. He gives us his peace. The task is great; the power is equal to it.

We must be careful, in stressing the inner effectiveness of this guardian peace, not to limit it to the realm of peaceful feelings – a 'sense' of being at peace. The New Testament idea of 'peace' takes its origin in the Old Testament where 'peace' (shālôm) possesses the root meaning of 'wholeness'. It is, to be sure, the inner wholeness of the fulfilled person, but it is also a relational word including (upward) 'peace with God' and (outward) peaceful integration within the society of God's people. It would, therefore, be an unnatural constriction of Paul's thinking to understand him as offering, say to Euodia and Syntyche, a peace powerful enough to master anxiety but impotent to mend their broken relationship, or to imagine him inviting them to lay hold of God's strong peace only as an interior fortress and not also as an antidote to their ill-feeling towards each other. Surely it is also in these outward areas of demonstrable effectiveness that

[4] Jn. 20:19, 21.  [5] Jn. 20:20.  [6] Heb. 13:20; Eph. 1:19–20.
[7] Rom. 16:20.

the peace of God is to become apparent as the mark of the supernatural on our lives.

## 3. The conditions

So far we have been reading verses 7 and 9, so as to dwell on the promises they make. In doing this, we have hitherto left out of account a most important word which they have in common: the word *and*. Verse 7 does not say, *The peace of God . . . will keep your hearts*; it says, *And the peace of God . . .* Similarly verse 9 says, *And the God of peace will be with you*. In other words, the promises are consequent upon something else which has been stated previously. In each case, the 'something else' is a series of commands. The Word of God is saying to us that, if we want to enjoy the promises, then we must obey the commands. We shall spell out these commands as four laws.

First, there is *a law for our relationships*, the centrality of the Lord Jesus Christ: *Rejoice in the Lord always . . . Let all men know your forbearance. The Lord is at hand* (verses 4–5). Glorying in Christ Jesus was the central feature of the religion of the covenant people of God (3:3), and this was but another way of saying 'Rejoice in the Lord' (3:1). The essence of the matter is so to value Jesus Christ, and so to long for the smile of his approval, that nothing else matters. He is all our joy. And naturally, in the present context, we cannot hope to enjoy the peace of God if we give less than the first place to him who is our peace.[8] But this is not in fact the main thrust of Paul's command. When he says here that we are to 'rejoice in the Lord', he continues by urging us to imitate him in our behaviour as we wait for his coming: *Let all men know your* (gentle) *forbearance. The Lord is at hand.* Paul must be looking back to the example of Christ which so occupied him when earlier he was exhorting the individual to sanctified relationships (2:5–8). He sums up the Lord's attitude towards others in the lovely word which we have translated as 'gentle forbearance' (*epieikēs*), the uncomplaining readiness to accept others as they are and to submit oneself to their demands. Such was Christ, and such must be those who claim to rejoice in him: all

[8]Eph. 2:14.

the more so in that he is near, his coming is at hand. How he will rejoice in us if he finds us so rejoicing in him that we are content to be like him!

Secondly, there is *a law for our circumstances*, the antidote of prayer: *Have no anxiety about anything, but in everything by prayer and supplication with thanksgiving let your requests be made known to God* (verse 6). Paul offers here a timeless and universal remedy for anxiety: *Have no anxiety ... but in everything ...* The antidote to anxiety, and the prelude to the enjoyment of peace, are to be found in the linked exercise of prayer and thanksgiving. In prayer, anxiety is resolved by *trust* in God. That which causes the anxiety is brought to the One who is totally competent and in whose hands the matter may be left. In thanksgiving, anxiety is resolved by the deliberate *acceptance* of the worrying circumstance as something which an all-wise, all-loving and all-sovereign God has appointed. Prayer takes up the anxiety-provoking question 'How?' – How shall I cope? – and answers by pointing away to him, to his resources and promises. Thanksgiving addresses itself to the worrying question 'Why?' – Why has this happened to me? – and answers by pointing to the great Doer of all who never acts purposelessly and whose purposes never fail.

The richness of the vocabulary which Paul uses underscores the importance which he attaches to this recipe for peaceful living. The word *prayer (proseuchē)* is general: its inner thought is that of addressing a request to God. In a time of anxiety it is easiest to retreat into a corner complaining to ourselves, but it is when we bring the matter to God that we find release. Our gaze should be so constantly upward that all of life is at once reflected, as by a mirror, to the throne. *Supplication (deēsis)* points to our lowly status as suppliants and to the bringing of our *needs* to the Lord. *Requests (aitēma)* respond to his kindly question 'What do you want me to do for you?'[9] Paul writes to us in a simple, practical way: here is the high-road to peace. He uses imperatives, for he is writing about things we should do and practise as believers. He gives us a *law* for our circumstances.

Thirdly, there is *a law for our thoughts*, discipline for our

[9]Mk. 10:51.

minds: *whatever is true . . . think about these things* (verse 8).
The translation *Finally* has the unfortunate consequence of
making a separation between the law for our thoughts and the
earlier laws; but the reference to *the God of peace* (verse 9)
reminds us of *the peace of God* (verse 7) and makes a break
between verses 7 and 8 unlikely. Besides, Paul's Greek does not
require it.[10] The passage would be better served by 'next': our
prayers are to be bolstered by our thoughts as we seek to know
his peace.

The verb *think about* (*logizomai*) means to ponder, to give
proper weight and value to, and to allow the resultant appraisal
to influence the way life is to be lived.

An old subject is thus brought before us again: the cardinal
place occupied by the Christian's mind, for good as well as for ill.
Just as a carnal mind is the surest passport to the downward path,
so a mind drilled in the things of which God approves is the
steadiest way into practical holiness. If, in a difficult relationship,
we allow our minds and judgment to be clouded by half-truth, or
if we allow frivolous and damaging thoughts about the other
person to simmer in our minds, we are hardly being like Christ.
We should rather determine to think only the truth about the
other person, to value what is attractive and praiseworthy about
him. This will prove to be the way of peace.

We are to meditate on, to prize as valuable, and to be
influenced by all that is *true*, all that merits serious thought and
encourages serious-mindedness,[11] all that accords with justice
and moral purity, all that is fragrant and *lovely*, all that brings
with it a good word, that speaks well,[12] whatever has genuine
worth of any sort and merits *praise*. It is the will of God that by
giving attention to things of which he approves we should
shape our minds to be like his: to those who do so, he pledges
his guardian peace and his own presence as the God of peace.

[10]RSV 'finally' translates *to loipon*: see on 3:1.

[11]RSV 'honourable' translates *semnos*, which in the New Testament would
seem to be better served by 'serious-minded' (not lacking a sense of
humour and afraid to laugh, but dreading superficiality and flippancy):
*e.g.* 1 Tim. 3:8, 11; Tit. 2:2.

[12]RSV 'gracious' translates *euphēma* (its only occurrence in the New Testament). The noun *euphēmia* in 2 Cor. 6:8 means 'the circulating of a good
opinion' about Paul, a 'well-speaking'. The adjective therefore describes
that which 'speaks well' of a person or thing, that which 'commends'.

Fourthly, we find here *a law for our behaviour*, the authority of the Word of God: *What you have learned and received and heard and seen in me, do* (verse 9). If we are to know the presence of the God of peace, then, for certain, we must seek the life of which he approves. 'God will reveal that also to you', said Paul, referring to his own apostolic example (3:15). Paul practised what he preached (*heard and seen*); he had apostolic authority to require his readers to accept what he taught (*received*). For us, who no longer have Paul, nor any apostle, the commandment requires us to submit to the apostolic word, the continuing apostolate of Holy Scripture in the Christian church.

These, then, are the laws, or preconditions, for enjoying the promises of God. If we are, as a church, to stand fast in the face of the world, then we must attend first and foremost to our personal sanctification, the state of our own heart and thoughts. If, however, we are to enjoy the power of God at work in our inner being, then we must give attention to these outward laws which God imposes upon us. We must model our relationships on Christ, surround our circumstances by prayer, drill our minds in godly thinking, and subject our life to the Word of God. Do this, '*and* the peace of God, which passes all understanding, will keep your hearts and your minds in Christ Jesus . . . *and* the God of peace will be with you'. If we ignore the laws we must be prepared to forgo the blessings.

## 23. The contented Christian

*I rejoice in the Lord greatly that now at length you have revived your concern for me; you were indeed concerned for me, but you had no opportunity.* <sup>11</sup>*Not that I complain of want; for I have learned, in whatever state I am, to be content.* <sup>12</sup>*I know how to be abased, and I know how to abound; in any and all circumstances I have learned the secret of facing plenty and hunger, abundance and want.* <sup>13</sup>*I can do all things in him who strengthens me.*

<sup>14</sup>*Yet it was kind of you to share my trouble.* <sup>15</sup>*And you Philippians yourselves know that in the beginning of the gospel, when I left Macedonia, no church entered into partnership with me in giving and receiving except you only;* <sup>16</sup>*for even in Thessalonica you sent me help once and again.* <sup>17</sup>*Not that I seek the gift; but I seek the fruit which increases to your credit.* <sup>18</sup>*I have received full payment, and more; I am filled, having received from Epaphroditus the gifts you sent, a fragrant offering, a sacrifice acceptable and pleasing to God.* <sup>19</sup>*And my God will supply every need of yours according to his riches in glory in Christ Jesus.* <sup>20</sup>*To our God and Father be glory for ever and ever. Amen.*

It is easier to be a Christian at some times than at others. Ask a preacher whether he is more zealous for the Lord on Saturdays, when he is aware of his responsibility for Sunday's preaching, or on Monday morning when 'the fight is o'er'! Circumstances sometimes press us closer to the Lord and sometimes conspire to edge us away from him. For all of us, at some time or another, in varying degrees we hear our Lord warn that 'when tribulation or persecution arises on account of the word, immediately they fall away'.[1]

None of these things moved Paul. As he turns to autobiography in these closing verses of the epistle, he is a man of unshakeable contentment. Do his circumstances vary from one extreme to the other ? Then *in any and all circumstances I have learned the secret of facing plenty and hunger, abundance and want* (verse 12). Has he received a helpful gift from the Philippian church? Then whatever they sent contents him, *I have received full payment, and more; I am filled* (verse 18). Does he face an uncertain future? Then *I can do all things in him who strengthens me* (verse 13).

Here indeed is Christian contentment. As Paul testifies to his contentedness, he shows that three factors helped him to master his variable circumstances.

## 1. Christian generosity

Paul had enough because other Christians contributed to his need, and he was glad to acknowledge his indebtedness. He thus enunciates a principle: *one Christian has enough because another Christian is generous.* Or, since 'every good endowment and every perfect gift is from above',[2] *the Lord uses generous Christians to help needy Christians.*[3]

The Philippians' generosity to Paul was *an ever-present sentiment: you were indeed concerned for me* (literally, 'keep on being concerned'), *but you had no opportunity* (verse 10). It would appear that it was not always easy for the Philippian church to communicate with Paul or to cater for him as they would have desired, but they maintained their concern even when they could not act on it. As soon as an opportunity opened up they were swift to grasp it. A spirit of generosity, a truly Christian spirit, prevailed among them.[4] We may take it that this is written for our learning.

As Paul saw it, such a generous sentiment was inseparable

[1]Mk. 4:17.  [2]Jas. 1:17.
[3]*Cf.* 2 Cor. 8:1–15, esp. verses 13–15.
[4]*Cf.* Rom. 12:13; 2 Cor. 9:1, 6–7; 1 Pet. 4:8–9.

from Christian relationships. It was, in fact, *a means of Christian fellowship*, and he commends and approves of it as such. *It was kind of you*, he says, *to share my trouble* (verse 14). His need was not a remote thing to them. They felt it themselves. It touched them at the point of fellowship and they responded, and in Paul's estimation (literally) 'did beautifully' in so acting. It was an 'admirable' thing to do. One member was suffering and all took note of it.[5]

Thirdly, this generosity *lays up treasure in heaven* (see verse 17). Paul was always sensitive about receiving monetary help from the churches which he founded, in case anyone should say that he was motivated by self-advantage. Consequently here, though he needed the help which the Philippians sent, and made no bones about his joy and comfort in receiving it – indeed (verse 15), he noticed when churches failed to respond to the claims of gratitude towards him – yet he did not covet what they sent. He is even prepared to risk seeming brusque in order to emphasize the real value of the gift. His words in verse 17 have the air of a disclaimer, *Not that I seek the gift*. What a response to an act of sensitive Christian fellowship! But this was not the apostle's intention. It was just that he was so contented to abide by whatever circumstances the Lord appointed for him that he genuinely did not covet their loving gifts. But he did covet something for them – *the fruit which increases to your credit* (verse 17). And he seems to suggest that this is a proper motive for Christians to cultivate: they should seek out opportunities to expend their generosity upon the needy, because by selling what they have and giving alms they would make for themselves 'purses that do not grow old . . . a treasure in the heavens that does not fail'.[6] For God would not be unrighteous and forget their work and the love which they showed him when they ministered to the saints.[7]

It is on this note that Paul ends his incidental teaching on Christian generosity. It is *a work acceptable to God: a fragrant offering, a sacrifice acceptable and pleasing to God* (verse 18). There are many references to 'a fragrant offering' in the Bible, but the first sets the scene for the rest. After the Flood, Noah

---

[5]*Cf.* 1 Cor. 12:26f.; Jas. 2:14–16; 1 Jn. 3: 16–18.   [6]Lk. 12:33.
[7]Heb. 6:10.

offered a burnt offering to God, and we read, 'when the LORD smelled the pleasing odour, the LORD said in his heart, "I will never again curse the ground because of man . . ." '[8] The picture is homely, the teaching plain. The burnt offering expresses obedient consecration to God, and God delights in his people dedicated to himself. Paul teaches here that when Christians take note of Christian needs and generously sacrifice to meet them, it is, for God, the burnt offering all over again, and he delights to accept it.

## 2. Christian discipline

The first factor, then, which makes for Christian contentment is the generosity of others, as the Lord uses the resources of one to meet the necessities of somebody else. But the second factor in producing contentment is a Christian's own attitude towards circumstances. As Christians we may start complaining when times are hard; or we may discipline ourselves to be content, reckoning that we have enough, no matter what. Paul is speaking personally in these verses, and he testifies that 'enough' and 'contentment' are relative terms – relative to what we feel ourselves to need. There is a discipline of self whereby one does not need more than one has.

First of all we must *decide not to covet*. We have already noted how jealously Paul preserved his financial detachment from the rewards of gospel preaching,[9] and how he even endangered the sincerity of his expressions of thanks to the Philippians for their generous gift. *Not that I complain of want* (verse 11); *Not that I seek the gift* (verse 17). But in reality he is not giving backhanded or grudging thanks; he is safeguarding the great Christian opposite of covetousness, that is, contentment. It had been used by the Stoic philosophers to describe the man of emotionless, wooden impassivity, the man whom nothing could touch because in himself he had found a completely satisfying world. Paul rescued the word and made it mean the 'restful contentment' of the Christian, the opposite of the desire for more. Because he had freed himself from the covetous spirit, he was able to 'ride' every sort of circumstance

[8]Gn. 8:21.    [9]See also 1 Cor. 9:18.

(verses 11–12). David of old, great man though he was, fell before the temptations of hardship and of prosperity alike.[10] Joseph, earlier on, had triumphed in each arena.[11] Paul was in the line of Joseph. Circumstances no longer had power to touch him, for he was content.

This contentment was *something which he learned*. The expression *I have learned* (verse 11) stresses the personal pronoun, as though Paul was also enquiring whether the Philippians and we ourselves shared his experience; '*I* have learned (have you?).' When did he learn it, and how? We could understand the verb to speak of a decisive and memorable past event, possibly on the Damascus road, or, if 3:7 refers to some other occasion than that, some experience of Christ which once and for all drove the desire for worldly prosperity right out of his mind. But it is more likely that he uses this decisive verbal form in order to show what a fixed and unchangeable feature of his character this is. He will never be different. For in the second half of verse 12 he uses another verb, *I have learned the secret*, which was used in the Greek mystery religions to describe people who had worked their way up through the various lower 'degrees' and had finally been admitted into full possession of 'the mystery' itself. Paul say, 'I have made my way up through the degrees of progressive detachment from the things of the world, its comforts and its discomforts alike, and finally I have reached maturity on this point. I know the secret; circumstances can never again touch me.' Thus contentment is the mark of a mature believer, and an objective to be cultivated by all believers who want to grow in Christ, who had 'nowhere to lay his head'.[12]

It is interesting to compare this with the account of events at Massah, when Israel was journeying from Egypt. In Exodus 17:7 we read that 'he called the name of the place Massah and Meribah, because of the faultfinding of the children of Israel, and because they put the LORD to the proof by saying, "Is the LORD among us or not?" ' But in Psalm 81:7 it says, 'I tested you at the waters of Meribah.' Massah and Meribah were not accidents on the way, but purposeful

---

[10]1 Sa. 27:1; 2 Sa. 11:1ff.    [11]Gn. 39:9; 40:8.    [12]Lk. 9:58.

acts of God to 'test' the faith of his people,[13] trying the quality of their devotion to him. But the people met the test in a spirit of faithlessness. They tried to force God's hand. 'If God were really with us this would never have happened. Let him deliver us and we will trust him.' Thus they 'tested' God. How different was their reaction from the purpose of God! If they had trusted, how trustworthy they would have found him!

Paul had learned the lesson. Bit by bit, test by test, circumstance by circumstance, he persevered through the lower 'degrees' until he finally 'graduated' and the 'secret' was his. Contentment did not come easily. He purchased it at the price of exacting discipline. But as we shall now see, he found God's grace in it, for his heart, weaned away from 'things', was wholly and solely God's.

## 3. Christian trustfulness

Paul, the contented Christian, gives the sole glory to God. Verse 20 expresses such familiar ideas that we might easily fail to see the wonder of it. What is he giving glory to God about? The times when the Philippians could not help him (verse 10), the times of hunger and of plenty (verse 12), the churches who neglected him and those who remembered him (verse 15) – he accepted all his circumstances as from God, and glorified God in them all. Paul was contented because God was trustworthy and to be glorified even when (by worldly standards) he seemed not to be! The apostle had learned to be content because he had learned to trust.

He expresses this in two ways. First, in terms of personal experience: *I can do all things in him who strengthens me* (verse 13). No circumstance could ever arise which would be too much for Paul's God, and therefore no circumstance could ever beat Paul. Here is vigorous faith. The verse refers to two sorts of power. On the one hand there is the power which Paul experiences in concrete situations of life, 'I am able for all things.' Here is the power which goes out to meet specific circumstances and subdue them. It is the power of victory over the demands of every day. But it arises from another sort of

[13]*Cf.* Dt. 8:2.

power, not inherent in Paul but derivative from elsewhere. Paul has this daily strength for daily needs because of One who (as we might paraphrase) 'endues me with dynamite'. God secretly infuses power (*dynamis*) into his apostle, and when the need arises it is ready for use.

But the keyword is *in*. Paul is able only when he is *in him who strengthens me*. What does this mean? When Israel in Egypt took shelter on Passover night in the houses where the blood of the lamb marked the door, they were, we might say, 'in the lamb', because they were in vital, personal contact with the advantages accruing to them from its death. They sheltered beneath its blood and they fed upon its flesh. So Paul was 'in Christ' – and so are we – by living daily under his sheltering blood and feeding daily and momently upon his flesh,[14] that is to say, by preserving a living relationship with the Lamb himself, our once crucified and now risen Lord, and by living in the good of the benefits which he has purchased for us. This relationship of being 'in Christ', however, is something which we enjoy by consciously attending to it. Thus the psalmist wrote, 'Under his wings you will find refuge.'[15] He is someone else who is 'in' God. Just as a chick runs to the mother hen for protection, so he runs to God. In the same way Paul, and we ourselves, are 'in Christ' by fleeing to him, and pressing close to him, covering ourselves in him, hiding in him, by seeing the danger and taking shelter in him.

Paul's experience of the trustworthiness of God can therefore be ours. We too can find ability to do all things (meet all circumstances with contentment) 'in' him who infuses us with dynamic power – if we attend to the preposition 'in'. Power arises by constantly and restfully enjoying the benefits of the atonement, constantly and deliberately taking refuge in his proffered security. This sort of trust produces that sort of victory.

Lest, however, we should feel that what Paul expresses in terms of personal experience must be peculiar to him and cannot be our experience as well, he also states the trustworthiness of God as a Christian doctrine: *my God will supply every need of yours according to his riches in glory in Christ Jesus*

[14]*Cf.* Jn. 6:51–56.     [15]Ps. 91:4.

(verse 19). The *all things* of personal experience (verse 13) is matched by the *every need* which might come upon the Philippians or us. Nothing will prove beyond the capacity of this God whom Paul knows well enough to call *my God*. And he will not be mean in giving to them. He *will supply . . . according to his riches in glory*. He will meet your need to the full. In so doing, his supply will not be limited to the size of your need, but rather *according to* (that is, in a manner which befits) *his riches*.

And as if this were not reassurance enough to carry with us into the future, Paul adds the words *in glory*. It is hard to know precisely what they mean. They may supplement the verb 'supply': 'He will supply . . . in glory', that is 'in glorious measure'. They may describe the riches: 'He will supply in a measure appropriate to his glorious riches'. They may mean 'in the glory (-land)' – all the resources of heaven laid at the disposal of the Christian on earth. Such is the wealth of his supply.

But the key to it all is *in Christ Jesus*. He mediates to us all the benefits and blessings of God. More than that, he is himself the sum of all the blessings, for the preposition is not 'through' but 'in'. He is not a channel along which they flow, but a place in which they are deposited. It is finally because of Christ that Paul is contented, and it is Christ whom he offers to us as the means and guarantee of our contentment. For Paul, the person who possesses Christ possesses all.

4:21–23

# 24. The grace of the Lord Jesus Christ

*Greet every saint in Christ Jesus. The brethren who are with me greet you. ²²All the saints greet you, especially those of Caesar's household.*
*²³The grace of the Lord Jesus Christ be with your spirit.*

Paul began his letter to the Philippians by addressing the saints and commending them to the grace of the Lord Jesus Christ (1:1–2), and he ends his letter in the same way by greeting the saints and commending them to the Lord's grace. From one point of view this is unremarkable, for these are more or less Paul's conventional ways of opening and closing his correspondence. But in another way, surely it is most remarkable. In the course of four chapters many things have come to light about the Philippians – how they are placed, their needs, the duties and dangers before them, the love they should share and the divisions that are marring the church. Paul has also given us a rich revelation of the Lord Jesus – who he is, what he has done, what can be expected of him. At the end it is to the same grace and the same Lord that Paul commits the saints. His grace is enough for them! It is the remedy for every human need. Jesus' grace reveals all his glories – his power, his helpfulness, his riches – and makes them available to his people. Grace is an all-sufficient supply; grace is Jesus being gracious.

The verses with which Paul ends Philippians are, therefore, worth thinking about. They reveal in turn the people who have received the grace of the Lord Jesus (verses 21–22) and the Lord from whom the grace flows (verse 23).

## 1. The world-wide fellowship

On the surface, the world Paul lived in seems very different from ours. But really the similarities outnumber the changes. The racial, national, social and religious divisions with which we are familiar are nothing new. It was exactly the same in Paul's world, where Greek despised barbarian, Jew scorned Gentile, and the benefits of Roman civilization were conferred along with the crosses on which national freedom fighters choked their lives to an end.

But Paul knew of a new humanity which had come to birth, a new people which superseded and transcended man's cherished jingoisms, a truly 'third world' bestriding the cultural boundaries of Greek and barbarian, the religious boundaries of Jew and Gentile and the political boundaries of imperial Rome and its rebellious subjects. As he pens his final words he could well think of the Philippians as they noted those who arrived, as Paul himself once had done, from the dockside at Neapolis. Here and there they would find members of the new humanity, and he urges them to reach across the old barriers which used to divide and to *greet every saint in Christ Jesus.* In the same spirit, Paul looks around his immediate company in Rome and associates them with the Philippians as fellow-members of one family: *The brethren who are with me greet you.* Then his thoughts range more widely. He recalls the full membership list of the church at Rome – and doubtless the world-embracing list of those whom he knows in all the churches. There is not one who would not consent to send greetings to Philippi: *All the saints greet you.* And there are those, too, whose natural affection had been given new intensity and new dimensions through a shared experience of Christ. Many at Philippi were veterans of Roman wars who had been settled into new homes as part payment for service to their nation. These would still have links with the continuing members of the imperial entourage: *especially those of Caesar's household.* They are a separate, distinct people on earth, *the saints*; they have a mutual affinity, *greet every saint*

*. . . all the saints greet you*; they are effectually related to each other in family bonds as *brethren*.

This is the people we belong to as Christians; yet we know so little of the reality, excitement or practical implications of it. We have allowed the church to lose its distinctiveness as the new humanity; we have identified it with nationalistic causes; we think nothing of it when Christians take up weapons of war, prepared in principle to kill their brothers and sisters in Christ; we have lost our love in denominations which blandly unchurch those who own the same Saviour and owe their eternal security to the same precious blood. There is a shame and a pity here that go beyond words to express. Is it any wonder that, as we look around at the poor, fragmented, inadequate thing that passes for the church of Christ, we find it powerless against worldly assault and doctrinal error?[1] We have lost the unity without which a resolute stand is impossible. To be sure, Paul did not have in mind as he wrote the mountainous problems of our denominational divisions, but how he would have wept if he had foreseen them! Where is the people of God, the saints of the Most High? And what is the solution to our monumental disunity?

The fair vision in verse 21 should spur us to repent of all that needlessly holds us apart, to pledge ourselves to whatever detachment from worldly loyalties may be necessary in order to honour our superior loyalty to the new humanity, to mourn for what might have been and to cry to God that it might yet come to pass. A quarter of a century's experience suggests that it is doubtful if denominational commissions will rediscover the larger and glorious unity which Paul intended. Adjusting the position of frontier posts is not enough, nor even deciding to man joint frontier posts against all the rest! We need a new work of God, acting through the medium of circumstances, acting by the direct quickening of his Spirit, to sweep away the barriers of the years. It is good, then, that we can follow Paul as he moves on to set before us a God of all grace who is himself all we need, our Lord Jesus Christ.

[1]Phil. 1:27–2:4; 3:17–4:3.

## 2. The Lord Jesus Christ

Suppose that only Philippians remained to us of all the Scriptures. How then would we understand verse 23? Who is the Jesus of whom it speaks? What is the grace for which it asks?

### a. Jesus is God

Four strands in the letter weave together to support the claim that our Lord Jesus Christ is fully divine. First, there is the title, *Lord*, which is given to him. In the Old Testament, God revealed to his people that his personal name is I AM. This name is found in the Hebrew Scriptures as 'Yahweh' from Genesis 4:26 onwards, and was explained to the people through the ministry of Moses.[2] It sometimes appears in English translations as Jehovah. From motives of mistaken reverence, however, the use of this name was considered to be too holy. People retreated from their God-given privilege of calling him by his name and substituted for Yahweh a Hebrew word (*'dōnāy*) meaning 'Lord' or 'Sovereign'. This came into the New Testament (in the Greek word *kyrios*) as the distinctive title of Jesus. By being *Lord* he is God, Yahweh, the God of Israel, the one and only God. This is 'the name which is above every name' which 2:9 says was conferred on Jesus in consequence of his obedience to the point of death. Every tongue will confess that 'Jesus Christ is Lord' (2:11), not in the sense that now for the first time he is truly God, but that now for the first time his deity is known, proclaimed and confessed. Behind this New Testament passage lies Isaiah 45:23, 'To me every knee shall bow, every tongue shall swear.' The words are those of Yahweh; Paul takes them and applies them to Jesus.

Secondly, Jesus is said to be God in his own right and nature. This is the evidence of 2:6, that he was 'in the form of God'. The NIV offers the correct interpretation: 'in the very nature of God'. Thirdly, and matching this, there is the Father's estimate of Jesus, expressed in the fact that he so exalted him that every tongue in heaven acknowledges him

[2]Ex. 3:14–15.

225

and every knee bows, where God alone must be worshipped.

Furthermore, fourthly, Jesus is God in the experience of people. Paul describes himself and Timothy as 'servants of Christ Jesus' (1:1). He thus sets himself alongside those whom the Old Testament calls 'my servants the prophets'.[3] As the prophets drew their authority from the Lord who called them, so Paul looks to the Lord Jesus, 'a sure token of his awareness of the Lord's divine nature.'[4]

### b. Jesus and salvation

The Lord Jesus Christ is called 'Saviour' in 3:20, but the word which Philippians uses to sum up the saving work of Christ is 'righteousness'. The answer to our need to be right with God is a gift of righteousness which God gives (3:9). The gift is inseparable from Christ: Paul did not possess it before he possessed Christ (3:4–7), but, being 'found in him', righteousness – a righteousness which God accepts – became his by faith in Christ. The Lord Jesus is thus the central figure in salvation: the gift comes when we possess him; it is ours by faith in him. And, in addition, this saving faith, a personal leaning upon Christ, is no credit to us, for it 'has been granted' (1:29) to us by him 'who began a good work' (1:6) in us. Salvation is all of God and all in Christ.

Both our status before God and our ongoing relationship with him are, therefore, solely due to Christ. We constantly need grace and it comes to us through Christ (1:2; 4:23). Only in him are there sufficient strength and heavenly riches to meet our needs (4:13, 19). It is 'the help of the Spirit of Jesus Christ' (1:19) that will carry us through to final salvation, and at every point of our pilgrim way our 'hearts and minds' are 'garrisoned' in Christ Jesus (4:7).

### c. Jesus, Lord of life and service

The life which begins with God's gift of righteousness in Christ aims to produce 'fruits of righteousness'. On the one

---

[3] Zc. 1:6.    [4] Martin, on Phil. 1:1.

hand, these come about 'through Jesus Christ'. He, the one who saves us, is also the one who brings about holy fruitfulness in us. But, on the other hand, it is up to us to set ourselves to produce these fruits (1:10–11).

Behind this thought of the gift of righteousness producing a life of righteousness lies the central idea in the biblical doctrine of sanctification: we are to become (in conduct) what we are (by virtue of our new nature). Philippians expresses this thought in another way also: a heavenly citizenship has been granted (1:27; 3:20) with a whole new set of privileges to be enjoyed, powers to be used and duties to be fulfilled.

At the centre of our citizenship, just as at the centre of our righteousness, stands the figure of our Lord Jesus Christ. Living the new life, demanding though it is – like standing firm under attack (1:27) or pressing on in a race (3:14) – is not a feat of stoical endurance but a response of love and devotion. One of Paul's most famous sayings comes in Philippians: 'to me to live is Christ' (1:21). The thought it expresses finds different wording in the command to 'rejoice in the Lord' (3:1). Paul speaks with heartfelt warmth of glorying in Christ (3:3), of growing in knowledge and appreciation of him (3:7–8) and of making it our personal target for the future to show a life-size enlargement of him, whether 'by life or by death' (1:20). The model for the new life of righteousness, the heavenly citizenship, is Christ Jesus (2:5–8) and our commitment to him is such that we must set out to conform ourselves to his death and resurrection (3:10). We must love his cross and wait expectantly for his coming (3:17, 20).

In our personal experience, obedience to Christ is the key factor in working out the salvation he has given us (2:12), and it is as we obediently serve him that we come to possess our possessions. Jesus is Lord of our service. He decides where and how we serve him. For Paul this meant imprisonment for Christ (1:13), and any hope he entertained of release was carefully subjected to the Lord's will (2:24). We are his bondservants (1:1), but he, on his side, is not an aloof, far-off master. He ministers power for service (1:14), it is in him that his church stands firm (4:1) and it is his Spirit who is supplied to keep us on course for final salvation (1:19).

Our characteristic service to the world is to preach Christ

(1:15, 17–18). He is our topic, as well as our Lord and our power; our characteristic in Christian relationships is to display his mind (2:5); our characteristic in personal ambition is to make 'our own' all that he had in mind when he made us his own (3:12).

### d. Jesus our Hope

Paul's delight was to know Jesus now, daily to know him better and in the end to know him fully.

Death is transformed in Christ: to die is gain (1:21). This is the heart of the 'gain', that we depart and are with Christ, which is far better (1:23). But we may not die. Our earthly life may be terminated by the coming of a Saviour from heaven (3:20). The Lord Jesus Christ fills our vision of the age to come. Philippians has much to say about this coming. It is guaranteed by the Father's declared purpose that every knee shall bow to his Son and every tongue confess him as Lord (2:9–11). To this end, the Father is momently at work, perfecting every saint for the great day (1:6) – and the day will come, for Christ himself is of power to subdue everything to his will and to transform us into his glorious likeness (3:21).

One of the greatest incentives to holiness in the New Testament is that we might be ready for him when he returns. Philippians does not lack this emphasis. We must work out our own salvation in the light of the coming day (2:12, 16); we must strive to be pure and blameless, filled with the fruits of righteousness ready for his return (1:10–11).

In all this Paul himself affords us a superb example. When he looked up he saw the reigning Lord Jesus Christ, enthroned at the pinnacle of heaven (2:9–11). When he looked back he saw the Christ of Calvary, the bearer of our curse (2:8), the author of righteousness (3:9). When he looked forward he saw the returning Saviour (3:20). When he looked into his own heart he found perfect satisfaction in the Lord Jesus Christ (3:7–12). But when he looked at Christ himself, he saw riches stored up which he had only begun to possess in experience – more of Christ to know and gain, more of his fellowship to enjoy, more of his likeness to display, more of his will to learn and do.

There is, then, no more fitting conclusion to Philippians that the simplicity of the final prayer. For us, as for himself, Paul wanted nothing but a daily and deepening experience of Jesus, satisfying and unsearchable:

*The grace of the Lord Jesus Christ be with your spirit.*

# Appendix:
# Where Paul wrote Philippians

One certain thing about Paul's letter to the Philippians is that he wrote it from prison.[1] This narrows the possibilities regarding the city from which he wrote. Of the four known imprisonments which he suffered, the one in Philippi itself[2] may be ruled out; and the Jerusalem imprisonment[3] was too short to allow for the range of activities implied in the letter. This leaves Caesarea[4] and Rome[5] as possible points of origin. In addition, many students assume an imprisonment at Ephesus in the period covered by Acts 19.

There are six further facts stated in or plainly deducible from the letter to the Philippians which help to narrow down the possibilities.

1. When he wrote to the Philippians Paul envisaged an imminent solution of his case: either release or death.[6] His opinion was that the former was the more likely. If, as it appears, he is referring to the death penalty, then he must be in Rome. Being a Roman citizen, were he elsewhere he could always have secured a stay of execution by appealing to the emperor. In the light of his conviction that the welfare of the church required his continued ministry,[7] it is inconceivable that he would have submitted – at Ephesus or elsewhere – to

---

[1]Phil. 1:13.    [2]Acts 16.    [3]Acts 22 – 23.
[4]Acts 23:31 – 26:32.    [5]Acts 28:30–31.
[6]Phil. 1:19-26.    [7]Phil. 1:24f.

execution rather than ensure an extension of earthly life by making the appeal.

2. During his imprisonment there were many comings and goings between Paul and Philippi. The Philippians had received news of Paul's circumstances and this had revived their concern; Epaphroditus came with their gift; news of Epaphroditus's illness reached Philippi; word came to Paul of the Philippians' distress over Epaphroditus; Epaphroditus is about to carry the letter to Philippi; and Timothy will soon visit them so as to bring back to Paul news of their situation.[8] What sort of proximity to Philippi does all this require? This is the only really strong argument for an imprisonment in Ephesus, but it is not conclusive. It is by no means an insuperable obstacle for the Roman and Caesarean theories of origin. According to Acts, Paul is in Philippi at Passover time and sees it as possible to be in Jerusalem for Pentecost, i.e. seven weeks later. Even though it took him five days to reach Troas he is at sufficient ease about his schedule to spend seven days there.[9] In the view of J. A. T. Robinson[10] this timetable is consonant with the Caesarean origin of the letter (for which he argues). It cannot therefore be an objection to the shorter journey to Rome.

3. Paul looked out from his prison on a vigorous church life.[11] It is sometimes urged that this favours Rome rather than Ephesus or Caesarea as the place of origin, but there is no reason why this should be so. The comment by D. Guthrie that 'Caesarea does not easily fit this requirement'[12] is unsupported by argument. Indeed, the impression of Caesarea or of Ephesus created in Acts[13] provides a satisfactory background to Philippians 1:13ff. – as does also the epistle to the Romans for a Roman origin. In fact Paul neither says nor suggests anything about the size of the church he sees through his

---

[8]Phil. 4:10, 18; 2:26, 25, 19.        [9]Acts 20:6, 16.
[10]J. A. T. Robinson, *Redating the New Testament* (SCM Press, 1976), p. 78.
[11]Phil. 1:13–18.
[12]D. Guthrie, *New Testament Introduction* (IVP, 1970), p. 527.
[13]Acts 21:8–16; 19:1–19.

window; he speaks only of its vigour. We know that it is just as easy to find largeness and lethargy together in the same church as to find a small company vibrant with life.

4. Among the other purposes it fulfilled, the letter to Philippi was a 'thank you' for gifts received[14] after a period of non-contribution. Paul graciously glosses over this intervening period. But is it possible that he is speaking of the ten years between the early gifts[15] and his Roman imprisonment? If he had received no gifts during this period there would be substance in this argument. But how then could Paul speak of a fellowship unbroken between the first day and 'now'?[16] This aspect of Philippian giving might lend weight to the thought that Paul wrote the letter in Ephesus, and suggests an almost negligible gap between the presents of 4:10 and 16. But this possibility is at once nullified by the absence of any reference in the Philippian letter to the great collection for the 'poor saints' in which the Macedonian churches were so much to the fore.[17] Robinson notes that

> on the contrary, stress is laid upon the Philippians' collection for Paul's personal needs . . . which he is specially sensitive to dissociate from the other collection (II Cor. 8.16–24; 12.13–18; Acts 20.33–35). It looks then as if Philippians must come from a period well before or well after the project that occupied so much of Paul's time and thought.[18]

5. Ephesian and Caesarean origins are supposed to be more suited by the element of Jewish controversy which obtrudes in Philippians 3:2ff. In both places Paul was in the thick of this particular problem, whereas Acts 28 reveals a most courteous attitude on the part of Jewish leaders in Rome. But Paul does not say in Philippians 3 that he is engaged in this controversy, but that he has good reason to believe that it is for the safety of the Philippian church that he should repeat what he had already

---

[14]Phil. 4:10.     [15]Phil. 4:16.     [16]Phil. 1:5.
[17]2 Cor. 8:1–5; 9:1–4; Rom. 15:26ff.
[18]J. A. T. Robinson, *op. cit.*, p. 59.

told them. It is to their situation, not his, that the passage points.

6. Are the references to the 'praetorian guard' and 'Caesar's household'[19] helpful in determining the place of origin? Plainly they suit a Roman imprisonment where, as an imperial prisoner, Paul would doubtless be guarded by the Praetorians and would be in contact with slaves and others of the household. But the reference could be to Herod's praetorium.[20] It is also known that praetorians were quartered at Ephesus, and, according to Guthrie, 'there appears to have been a House of Caesar at Ephesus from the time of Augustus'.[21]

In the light of all this, it is a very moderate comment to say that the evidence is nicely balanced! Can we achieve further or greater clarity by approaching the question negatively?

## Ephesus

A serious difficulty in the Ephesian hypothesis is that there is no reference in Acts or elsewhere to an Ephesian imprisonment. Only the most unequivocal circumstantial evidence could overcome this lack, and it is difficult to see that there is any. On the contrary, Paul's alternatives of death or release tell heavily against Ephesus, as does his exclusive praise of Timothy[22] when we remember that Timothy went from Ephesus accompanied by Erastus[23] and these two men were apparently selected from a wider circle of Paul's associates. With Aquila and Priscilla on the team, would Paul have been able to write that 'they all look after their own interests, not those of Jesus Christ'?[24]

## Caesarea

The major difficulty in the Caesarean hypothesis is that Paul expected either death, or release and return to Philippi. It is

[19]Phil. 1:13; 4:22.    [20]Acts 23:35.
[21]D. Guthrie, *op. cit.*, p. 535.
[12]Phil. 2:20–21.    [23]Acts 19:22.    [24]Acts 18:26; Phil. 2:21.

true that Paul does not *say* that his death will come through the legal penalty. If there were no other factors in the situation we could go along with Robinson in his reference to the determination of the Jews, during Paul's Caesarean period, to bring about his death by means of a murder squad.[25] But there is one factor which makes this interpretation untenable: Paul sees release and continued ministry as the alternative to his death. As Acts 25:3 shows, imprisonment in Caesarea protected Paul from the murder squads to the extent that the Jews had to scheme to have Paul's case transferred to Jerusalem so that they could take the opportunity of the journey to make their assassination bid. If Paul, then, were thinking of death at the hands of the Jews, far from this being an alternative to release, his release would be the very way to commit himself, unprotected, to his murderers.

## Rome

The traditional origin of the letter to the Philippians in Paul's Roman imprisonment is the only one which explains the strict alternatives of death or release, and, while it can hardly be taken as proved, it is the most free from problems. Its only major hazard is the possibility of so many journeys to and fro between Paul and Philippi, but, as we noted above, this is by no means out of the question. The Roman imprisonment is still most widely held to be the place of origin of this letter, which would thus be dated at whatever length of time after AD 59 (the commencement of the imprisonment referred to in Acts 28:30) allowed for the various communications between Paul and Philippi to take place.[26]

[25] J. A. T. Robinson, *op. cit.*, p.60; Acts 25:3.
[26] The dating of Philippians and its place of origin are well discussed in all the commentaries and introductions to the New Testament. D. Guthrie gives a very full and fair survey in *New Testament Introduction*, pp. 526–536. A notably succinct account is provided by H. A. Kent, in F. A. Gaebelein (ed.), *The Expositor's Bible*, vol. 11 (Pickering and Inglis, 1978), pp. 97f. The masterly examination of the question by J. A. T. Robinson, *Redating the New Testament*, pp. 57–79, must not be missed.